THE ELUSIVE QUEST

SOCIAL PROBLEMS AND SOCIAL ISSUES
An Aldine de Gruyter Series of Texts and Monographs
SERIES EDITOR
Joel Best, *Southern Illinois University at Carbondale*

Joel Best (ed.), **Images of Issues: Typifying Contemporary Social Problems** (Second Edition)

Joel Best (ed.), **Troubling Children: Studies of Children and Social Problems**

James J. Chriss (ed.), **Counseling and the Therapeutic State**

Donatella della Porta and Alberto Vanucci, **Corrupt Exchanges: Actors, Resources, and Mechanisms of Crime, Deviance, and Control**

Jeff Ferrell and Neil Websdale (eds.), **Making Trouble: Cultural Constructions of Crime**

Ann E. Figert, **Women and the Ownership of PMS: The Structuring of a Psychiatric Disorder**

Mark Fishman and Gray Cavender (eds.), **Entertaining Crime: Television Reality Programs**

James A. Holstein, **Court-Ordered Insanity: Interpretive Practice and Involuntary Commitment**

James A. Holstein and Gale Miller (eds.), **Reconsidering Social Constructionism: Debates in Social Problems Theory**

Philip Jenkins, **Intimate Enemies: Moral Panics in Contemporary Great Britain**

Philip Jenkins, **Using Murder: The Social Construction of Serial Homicide**

Valerie Jenness, **Making It Work: The Prostitutes' Rights Movement in Perspective**

Valerie Jenness and Kendal Broad, **Hate Crimes: New Social Movements and the Politics of Violence**

Stuart A. Kirk and Herb Kutchins, **The Selling of *DSM:* The Rhetoric of Science in Psychiatry**

John Lofland, **Social Movement Organizations: Guide to Research on Insurgent Realities**

Donileen R. Loseke, **Thinking About Social Problems: An Introduction to Constructionist Perspectives**

Leslie Margolin, **Goodness Personified: The Emergence of Gifted Children**

Donna Maurer and Jeffrey Sobal (eds.), **Eating Agendas: Food and Nutrition as Social Problems**

Gale Miller, **Becoming Miracle Workers: Language and Meaning in Brief Therapy**

Gale Miller and James A. Holstein (eds.), **Constructionist Controversies: Issues in Social Problems Theory**

Bernard Paillard, **Notes on the Plague Years: AIDS in Marseilles**

Dorothy Pawluch, **The New Pediatrics: A Profession in Transition**

Erdwin H. Pfuhl and Stuart Henry, **The Deviance Process** (Third Edition)

William B. Sanders, **Gangbangs and Drivebys: Grounded Culture and Juvenile Gang Violence**

Theodore Sasson, **Crime Talk: How Citizens Construct a Social Problem**

Wilbur J. Scott, **The Politics of Readjustment: Vietnam Veterans since the War**

Wilbur J. Scott and Sandra Carson Stanley (eds.), **Gays and Lesbians in the Military: Issues, Concerns, and Contrasts**

Jeffrey Sobal and Donna Maurer (eds.), **Weighty Issues: Fatness and Thinness as Social Problems**

Jeffrey Sobal and Donna Maurer (eds.), **Interpreting Weight: The Social Management of Fatness and Thinness**

Robert A. Stallings, **Promoting Health Risk: Constructing the Earthquake Threat**

Frank J. Weed, **Certainty of Justice: Reform in the Crime Victim Movement**

Carolyn L. Wiener, **The Elusive Quest: Accountability in Hospitals**

Rhys Williams (eds.), **Cultural Wars in American Politics: Critical Reviews of a Popular Myth**

THE ELUSIVE QUEST
Accountability in Hospitals

Carolyn L. Wiener

ALDINE DE GRUYTER

New York

About the Author

Carolyn L. Wiener is professor of sociology in the Department of Physiological Nursing and the Department of Social and Behavioral Sciences, School of Nursing, University of California, San Francisco. She has published extensively on topics related to sociological and organizational behavior in the health care arena.

ALDINE DE GRUYTER
A division of Walter de Gruyter, Inc.
200 Saw Mill River Road
Hawthorne, New York 10532

This publication is printed on acid free paper ∞

Library of Congress Cataloging-in-Publication Data
Wiener, Carolyn L. 1930–
   The elusive quest : accountability in hospitals / Carolyn L. Wiener.
     p. cm. — (Social problems and social issues)
   Includes bibliographical references and index.
   ISBN 0-202-30630-5 (cloth : alk. paper) — ISBN 0-202-30631-3 (pbk. : alk. paper)
    1. Hospital care—Quality control.   2. Hospital care—Evaluation.   3. Responsibility.
I. Title. II. Series.

   RA972.W534 2000
   362.1'1'0973—dc21   99-059684

Manufactured in the United States of America
10 9 8 7 6 5 4 3 2 1

To Anselm Strauss, my mentor and friend,
who taught me to see with a sociological eye, and
whose encouragement I sense always,
despite his physical absence.
And to Stanley Wiener, my husband,
whose estimation of my abilities has always surpassed my own.

CONTENTS

PREFACE

In recent years, American politicians and social commentators have embraced the word "accountability" with a vengeance. Practically daily, one institution or another—in government, the military, education, health care—is being told by critics that some part of its work suffers from a lack of accountability. Through overuse, the term is rapidly losing its respectable meaning: being answerable for our actions. Accountability has become an umbrella concept to signal not only the perfecting of performance but the ability to track improvement and demonstrate it through statistical "outcome measures." Frequently, however, the finer distinctions of a job well done do not lend themselves to quantitative measurement. Furthermore, the criteria required to convince others that one is indeed accountable can lead to all sorts of folly. Too often, with typical American optimism and belief in progress, we impose one mechanism upon another to better the situation, little heeding how we may be skewing priorities in the process. In our zeal to hold our institutions accountable, we must decide if we are measuring what is important or expending dollars and energy making important what we can measure.

This book provides an opportunity to look at what has happened to one institution—the American hospital—that has been caught up in the accountability endeavor. The quest referred to in the title is the search for the best means to hold hospitals accountable for: (1) the resources they use; (2) finding a way to improve clinical care; and (3) measuring improvement so that it can be demonstrable to oversight agencies and the public. Despite the nobility of this goal, multitudinous factors intervene to make its achievement elusive.

Sociologists have long been interested in the unintended consequences of well-intentioned social interventions. They are hardly alone in their interest: "A nearly universal fascination with the topic is manifested by an array of technical and popular terms—counterproductivity, negative results, backlash, boomerang effect, perverse incentive, Pyrrhic victory, Promethean fallacy, two-edged sword, and going to sea in a sieve" (Sieber 1981, 3). Calling these consequences "regressive outcomes," Sieber notes that failure to achieve a desired goal—or worse still, causing a deterioration instead of alleviation of the situation—is demoralizing because it assaults "the very foundations of our faith in the amelioration of social

problems, the efficacy of rational planning, and the good intentions of public agencies and political representatives" (Ibid., 18). Furthermore, although
by definition one cannot hope to anticipate the unanticipated, this is not
true of the unintended (Deutscher 1983). As the call for accountability
increases, policy planners and politicians would do well to look at the experiences of enterprises already deeply enmeshed in such efforts to see if
they can anticipate the unintended. The analysis in this book is offered in
that spirit.

Despite all of the effort in the quest for accountability, there remains a
restless tension between measurement of quality improvement and the desire to make changes in the delivery of hospital care; between achieving
perfect quantitative data sets that reflect quality of care and examining
qualitatively what happens in the daily patient/provider encounter; between social interest and the profit-driven industry that has grown around
the issue of quality improvement. There is tension as well as we trim and
tinker with incremental reform. For example, in late 1999, UnitedHealth
Group, the nation's second largest managed-care company, announced
that it would no longer interfere with doctors' decisions about patient care
by requiring them to obtain authorization when choosing a course of treatment. Within twenty-four hours, commentators were warning that this
simply meant a change in strategy—a way to reduce patient complaints,
lower administrative costs, and head off a federal Patients Bill of Rights.
By retaining the option of profiling physicians and dropping those who
were deemed to be "overusing," the company still held sway over medical
decisions.

As this book goes to press, a report released by the Institute of Medicine
(IOM) has created a stir. It deals with the subject of medical error, discussed
in Chapter Six. Pinpointing medical mistakes as the leading cause of preventable death in the United States, the report advocates setting up a government sponsored mechanism for reporting these occurrences and using
this database as a source of education and prevention (Kohn et al., 1999).
Sound advice has been given by the committee, which recommends that
health care look to the aviation industry for guidance. That high risk industry found that for optimum effect the reporting agency must remain
separate from the regulatory agency, that avoiding a punitive stance was
obligatory so that people would report near misses as well as problems,
and that confidentiality must be assured. Yet, tension arises between setting up a system to rationalize error correction and the drive to cut costs
by expecting hospitals to function with less manpower. Sociologist Charles
Bosk, while supportive of the IOM's surfacing of medical error, asked appropriate questions in a televised discussion: How is this work going to be
piggybacked on to already overworked workers? Just how efficient can we
expect an error-ridden, difficult, cognitively complex, manually compli-

cated, interdependent system like health care to be? What are we willing to pay to reduce error?

The technology of medical miracles expands daily. But further tension exists between this capability and serious weaknesses in the delivery of health care. In California alone, nearly 7 million people, one-quarter of residents under age 65, are uninsured. Early retirement, not so long ago envisioned as an opportunity for travel and new experiences, has been revealed more realistically by a study that found that 46 percent of those ages 45 to 70 who retired before age 50 did so because of health problems and that those who retire early are more than twice as likely to live in poverty as those who retire after age 50 (California Work and Health Survey 1999). It should no longer be a surprise to learn that people who are poor delay treatment, their attention and dollars eclipsed by competing demands for food and shelter, making them sicker than need be when they finally reach out for health care. Thus, these demographics spell increased problems in the coming years. Meanwhile, those who are fortunate enough to have health care coverage are bewildered by frequent changes made by their managed care companies regarding authorized physicians and authorized treatment—and by the fact that availing themselves of the ever-growing fund of medical miracles is not the clear-cut proposition they envisioned.

Twenty years of research in the field have left me with respect and admiration for health care providers who, with few exceptions, entered what they viewed as service, not commercial, professions out of a desire to help others. They live with daily reminders of the tragedy of illness and how little the cost of care matters when one is sick. The sources of their tension rise as nurses translate understaffing as an indication of their perceived lack of worth, doctors express their discontent by giving deceptive documentation to insurance companies in order to get authorization for treatment of life-threatening conditions, and quality improvement coordinators spend more and more time on paper exercises that they feel do not adequately reflect the real work of improving the quality of care. Add to the mix the tension between an American population that wants the best care but is not willing to pay for it and politicians who know reform is necessary but want to get re-elected by promising budget cuts.

That some tensions will continue to plague us is without question—built in to the nature of human activity. But there is much to be learned from close scrutiny of the unintended consequences experienced within the hospital accountability movement. Ideally, by examining what has been effective and where action has been misguided, we will be in a better position to place a more realistic definition on "accountability."

ACKNOWLEDGMENTS

When Sanford Feldman, retired surgeon and dear friend, first suggested that I talk to a staff person he had encountered who knew more about the workings of the hospital than most doctors, little did I know that a research project was aborning. That first interview with the director of what was then called Quality Assurance piqued my interest to pursue the topic. I am grateful to Dr. Feldman for the insight he has provided along the way, stemming from his vast knowledge and his lifelong interest in improving the quality of health care. I am also grateful to my colleague, Jeanie Kayser-Jones, who told me to "go for it" when I explored with her the idea of applying for a research grant. The support I received from both the Academic Senate and the School of Nursing Alumni and Friends Fund, University of California, San Francisco (UCSF), was invaluable as a reflection of their confidence in the worth of this project.

Many professionals within the arena contributed to this research. Their cordiality, forthrightness, and accessibility made data collection, though at times overwhelming, possible. I am indebted to all of the nurses and physicians who allowed me to sit in on their meetings and answered my questions frankly and to the administrators who allowed me to do field work in their hospitals. Special thanks to Ruth Higgins, Carol Walovich, Nancy Christman, Carmella Roy, Carol Ann Lemmon, Judy Scott, Lisa Miller, and Denise Burke for their availability when perplexing questions arose.

I thank the members of the Patient Care Assessment Council of Northern California, comprised of professionals who do the work of quality improvement, for welcoming me to their meetings and candidly discussing the issues that concern them in my presence.

Reading a book in manuscript form is not an easy task. For their careful reading and critiques, I am beholden to Barbara Suczek, Stephanie Hettel, Sanford Feldman, Ruth Higgins, Nancy Christman, Carmella Roy, and Taun Relihan. Deep appreciation is extended to Emily Fang, an extraordinary librarian at UCSF, who took an interest in my research and not only skillfully guided me through literature hurdles but showed such joy in my progress. My thanks also to Phyllis Tsujihara who, with her usual grace, eased me through all administrative tasks. Having started my career when "cut and paste" was literally the way one wrote a manuscript, I have enormous respect for the wonders of word processing. But these wonders occasionally disappoint. For rescuing me at these times, I thank my nephew, Ron Licht, who did so calmly and with good humor. Appreciation is also extended to Peter Smith who attended to the copyediting of this book with sensitivity and respect for its intention.

Most significantly, as my dedication indicates, I have been fortunate to have had the intellectual support of the late Anselm Strauss, who first encouraged me to enter the Sociology Program at UCSF, then included me in stimulating research projects, and always managed to make scholarly exchange challenging but comfortable. He and his wife Fran became cherished friends who have enriched my life. Lastly, unending gratitude is extended to my husband, Stanley Wiener, for his persistent faith in me through the highs and lows of the sociological pursuit. In his confidence that data collection was doable despite the scope of the project, analysis would yield pearls, and this book would eventually be completed, he was the source of strength he has been throughout our marriage.

To all of these people and to the reader without whom there would be no point in writing, I say thank you.

Introduction

Until little more than a decade ago, public faith in the competence and responsibility of health-care professionals in the United States seemed unshakable. Since then, an elaborate enterprise costing millions of dollars has been constructed to monitor the quality of American health care. Its purpose is to "improve performance," in the current language, and make physicians, health plans, and hospitals more accountable. This massive endeavor continues to grow, engaging the services of a wide range of experts bent on finding how best to enhance quality of care and measure the results, called "outcomes." A voluminous literature addresses the subject. Although some critics have questioned the methods of this endeavor, it has taken on a momentum that appears unstoppable, if only because many people now have career stakes in "the quality business."

Meanwhile, prompted by the drive to stem costs, hospitals are looking to industrial corporations to guide them in redesigning their organizational structure, resulting in extensive changes in work roles and the division of labor. Other economy measures include strict restriction by payers of length of hospital stay (called "utilization review") and increased efforts to provide clinical procedures on an outpatient basis. Accordingly, patients considered sick enough to be hospitalized are much sicker than they used to be—at a time when nursing staff and support services such as pharmacy, radiology, and respiratory therapy have been cut to save money. Enthusiasts argue that the information revolution can and should transform the delivery of health care (Millenson 1997; Brook et al. 1996). Yet, there is a growing discrepancy between outcomes as measured by the experts and how people-as-patients assess their experiences as recipients of health care.

Sincere and serious people are searching for the best means to improve the quality of hospital care. They know that errors and near misses occur, that some patients are dissatisfied with their care, that coordination could be better. Some are assiduously seeking models of improvement. Others are no less energetically trying to devise the means by which hospitals will be held accountable for improved quality. As the machinery for hospital accountability becomes more and more elaborate, it is increasingly urgent to look at what is being done, what is missing, and where emphasis should be placed.

1

That has been the focus of the research I have done for the past five years on the evolution of the accountability enterprise in U.S. hospitals. This book examines how care in hospitals is monitored, assessed, guided toward improvement, and how improvement is measured. Examination of this complex, elusive accountability endeavor has prompted a nagging question: Is all this effort geared toward making hospitals better or toward making them only *look* better?

The 1990s have become a decade of enormous change in how the United States finances and delivers health care, heightening anxiety among its citizens as they struggle to understand the impact of this rapid transformation. Hardly a "system" in the sense of rational planning, U.S. health care is a web of extraordinarily complicated relationships, where progress in one area can lead to setbacks in another, and where unintended consequences abound. For example, a computer game called SimHealth lets one construct a national health care strategy and try it out on a simulated U.S. economy. Players select goals based on the principles of liberty, equality, efficiency, and community.

> Throughout the game you can check out conditions at the hospital and back on Main Street. If you rely too heavily on medical technology, the buildings on Main Street will begin to shrink because the health care system is drawing too much money from other programs. If you cut doctors' salaries too much and their numbers decline, then the hospital waiting room overflows with people. If your health care plan inflates the federal deficit, the government buildings along Main Street begin to decay. (Siegmann et al. 1993)

Would that this enormous health care apparatus were only a game!

Since hidden costs are obviously hard to pinpoint, concern over the cost of health care has led to a focus on the most obvious targets: older, sicker adults; premature, low-weight infants; medical greed; medical malpractice; overcharging by hospitals; etc. The research on which this book is based was designed to look at *only one* of the hidden costs of health care: how the quality of care in hospitals is monitored and assessed, and by what means improvement is sought. This book examines what happens when all interested parties—hospitals, insurers, health care professionals, employers, government, and the public—grapple with their often conflicting opinions on what constitutes quality care.

Accurate measurement of health care performance has become an international concern, shown by the existence of the International Society for Quality in Health Care (ISQua) which has grown, in a few short years, to a membership of professionals in nearly sixty countries. In addition to publishing the *International Journal for Quality in Health Care*, the society organizes meetings where members explore quality issues and the need to balance them with those of cost and access. In the United States, as in all countries, health care is embedded in national values—the symbols, ideas, objects, or states of being that a society holds to be worthy of pursuit. Values, however, often conflict. For example, Americans are presumably committed to good health and want comparable services to be available anywhere. But we also defend the right to choose our own doctors and that of health workers to choose where they will work. We say we want better planning, but when decisions are handed down by fiat we balk and engage in all the maneuvering available in a free society. We drifted into managed care and then revolted when we discovered that we had sacrificed choice and access to medical services for a reduced insurance premium.

Economic and political factors have also affected the evolution of health care policy: an estimated 44.3 million Americans lacked health insurance in 1998 (Campbell 1999). As Rothman's analysis (1979) makes abundantly clear, because the United States waited so long to discuss national health insurance, the issue surfaced just as medical costs were skyrocketing. This made the two goals—improving access to care and reducing expenditures—at best in conflict and, at worst, incompatible. Rothman explains, "Governments in Germany, England, and Canada certainly had to estimate costs and, after implementation, find ways to control expenditures. But for them, other noneconomic values could assume greater prominence on the national agenda, including judgments about what services a government owed its citizens and what citizens owed each other." Furthermore, inconsistencies exist among the states regarding not only access but also the regulations, discretion, and responsibility governing health care. Calls for a "major national program of outcomes management" (Ellwood 1988), meaning a system linking medical management decisions to systematic information about outcomes, minimize the value placed on states' rights, to say nothing of individual rights.

Important historical forces have emerged in the twentieth century to exert a dramatic impact on health care. First is the *technological imperative,* the sinew of contemporary medical work. Medicine's primary aim is to solve perplexing problems by acting with all available resources, even in the face of scant hope of success. Physicians absorb this technological imperative with their medical education. Physicians have always taken pride in the noneconomic nature of their work, attempting to allay the fears of the patient and control the uncertainty of disease. Furthermore, peer pressure among physicians is a sometimes subtle but nonetheless serious influence, for the sin of omission contains the inherent risk of provoking accusations of malpractice and of professional censure. In the last several decades, innovations such as renal dialysis, hip and knee replacement, heart bypass surgery, and new diagnostic techniques using electronic imagery, have become available to aid the physician's pursuit.

Steady advances in biomedical technology have led to a remarkable increase in the average American's lifespan. This produces a second driving force, the *chronic illness imperative,* since unfortunately longer life also increases the possibility of suffering from one or more of the chronic illnesses—cancer, diabetes, arthritis, and cardiac, pulmonary and renal disease—diseases that are now "chronic" because modern technology sustains them. Fewer people die of the first heart attack; chemotherapy and radiation increase the chances of averting death from the first onset of cancer, and, thanks to new drug combinations, AIDS has also become a chronic illness. A significant change in the demographics of chronic illness has occurred: "Although older persons constitute the majority of the population with serious chronic care needs, and the risk of disability increases with age and reaches its apex among the very old, chronic conditions are not the exclusive province of older persons. Significant numbers of people requiring chronic care services are under age 65" (Benjamin 1996, 75). Not only has medical science strikingly increased the prospects for survival of people disabled by chronic diseases, but the technological imperative has created a population at the other end of the age scale whose life is attributable to the skill of intensive-care nurses and doctors, and the technology they use. Infants whose lives have been saved by heroic measures, however, often leave the hospital with lifelong disabilities.

Chronic illnesses are characterized by acute phases that are often costly, since stabilizing each episode usually requires hospital treatment. Researchers have found that chronic ailments afflict 100 million Americans—more than a third of the population—and account for nearly three-quarters of U.S. health spending (Hoffman et al. 1996). In the 1980s, policy analysts became alarmed at the annual rate of increase in hospital costs, which were rising faster than inflation due to increased demand and to the fact that hospitals are labor-intensive. Americans were assessed to be "victims of their own success," as characterized by William Schwartz (McNeil Lehrer 1984), enjoying the fruits of the research undertaken over the last thirty years. Thus, dominating the last half of the century has been a third force, the *cost-containment imperative,* the attempt to stem health-care spending by attacking it at all levels, from examining hospital costs to curtailing open reimbursement by enticing people into managed care plans, where cost control is the credo.

Under these three imperatives, hospitals have been called upon to do more and more with less and less, leading to the growth of a fourth force, the *accountability imperative.* As concern mounted over whether hospitals were sacrificing quality to contain costs, a quality-assurance movement emerged. Since it quickly became evident that quality could not be "assured," the drive for accountability has evoked a variety of labels. A leader in the field, addressing an international conference in late 1997, educed knowing smiles from the audience when he looked back on the struggle-over-terms that marks this arena. *Review* and *assessment*, he said, fail to convey either continuity or the need to improve; *monitoring* smacks of snooping; *control* is too coercive; *assurance* too presumptuous; *management* too manipulative. (Donabedian, 1997, 53). Names aside, the sense of the movement has remained the same: to establish rational tools and regulatory mechanisms that will assure hospital accountability.

The four imperatives in health care—ever-expanding technological capability, the drive for cost containment, increased chronic illness, and the quest for accountability—will continue to interact to create complicated new problems. Harking back to the ancient Egyptians, who measured the quantity of their agricultural output in order to achieve what today's planners call "performance improvement," statistical evaluation (in business, education, and now health care) has become an accepted strategy for assessing quality. Thus, on the one hand there exists a growing army of people who are earnestly trying to measure the health care patients receive, supported by an information industry happily building the computerized system that is supposed to enlighten this effort. On the other hand, every day, as reform either grinds its wheels or attempted reforms create new problems, many people who encounter health care "delivery" experience dissatisfaction, frustration, and a feeling of powerlessness. If they are assertive they can do better than some but their assertiveness is just as likely to lead to more frustration. All parties seek quality of care. The question remains: Is the current accountability enterprise the best way to achieve this end?

THEORETICAL STANCE

Sociologists, some more self-consciously than others, come to research with a point of view, a "theoretical stance" or "frame of reference" regarding how the world works. The author was steeped in the sociological tradition of the late Anselm Strauss, having learned as a student how to "do" sociology under his tutelage, and then benefitting from collaboration with him on a number of research projects. Thus, the stance of this book stems from the interrelationship of three Straussian frameworks: action, negotiation, and social arenas.

Action

Strauss assumes that we confront a universe marked by tremendous fluidity, one that will not and cannot stand still. It is a universe where nothing is strictly determined, "a world that is complex, often ambiguous, evincing constant change as well as periods of permanence; where action itself although routine today may be problematic tomorrow; where

answers become questionable and questions produce ultimately questioned answers" (1993, 19). Derived from the tradition of symbolic inter-
actionism, this sociological stance is based on the perspective of George
Herbert Mead as developed by the Chicago school of sociology (Strauss
1956; Fisher and Strauss 1978), and asserts that people select and interpret
meanings from their environment, forming many "definitions of the situation." The individual acquires a commonality of perspective with others
as they learn and develop together the symbols by which aspects of the
world are identified. In other words, there is a *social construction of reality*.
The commonly accepted way of doing things is transmitted from generation to generation, resulting in a totality that Berger and Luckmann call the
"symbolic universe," which "hardens and thickens" gradually to assume
the appearance of objective reality (Berger and Luckmann 1968). This is not
to say that the world is not real, but rather to indicate *the manner in which
it is real*. As expressed by Kleinman et al., "According to interactionists, individuals live in worlds of meaning; they construct yet are constrained by
these meanings. Neither fieldworkers nor interviewers assume that they
know what actions or events mean to participants, but instead find ways
to understand how those they study experience their situations" (1944, 45).

Thus, within any hospital, one can expect to find multiple definitions of
situations. Although a common culture has developed based on broadened
and crystallized "reality," hospital actors each bring with them their personal and work biographies, affecting their perspectives on any situation,
issue, or experience. There is constant movement between policy and its
application as programs devised by policy makers play out differently in
different settings and as hospital personnel question how policy *affects
them* in a continually changing and emerging fashion.

Negotiation

While certainly not evident to the average patient, negotiation is the
essence of hospital work (Strauss et al. 1997). Hospitals, like all organizations, contain diverse groups of individuals with diverse and sometimes
divergent perspectives, purposes, goals, and power. The hospital's "social
order" is maintained through the processes of negotiation: bargaining, per-
suading, maneuvering, compromising, trading off, coercing, and restraining. Policies are questioned, examined, debated, and interpreted by those
called upon to implement them. Policies may be accepted, resisted, ignored, rejected, even sabotaged—overtly or subtly. The legitimation of
policies may cover the spectrum from wholehearted to grudging acceptance. When conflict arises over implementation, hospital personnel *negotiate* the *meaning* of these policies.[1]

In their landmark study of mental hospitals, Strauss and his colleagues

(1964) demonstrated how the rules that guide the actions of various professionals in the hospital are not extensive, clearly stated, or clearly binding. Geist & Hardesty, applying the negotiation perspective in their study, explain:

> For example, physicians have considerable leeway in the areas of medical decision making. Other personnel, oftentimes, break and stretch the rules. In order to 'get things done,' hospital workers must not only violate certain rules periodically, but also must cooperate when no rules exist. This leads to constant communication to negotiate which rules are to be followed and which roles persons are expected to take. In addition, the 'product' of the organization, a healthy patient, is subject to differing perceptions, dispute, and negotiation among members of the health care team. There are preferences among medical staff for certain treatment modes, such as a preference for surgical rather than pharmacological intervention, that may not be shared by other team members. Disparate treatment philosophies can lead to disputes among medical specialists or between physicians and nurses about what procedures to follow. (1992)[2]

The hospital accountability endeavor has simply added more layers to the importance of negotiation in getting hospital work done.

Social Arenas

The third framework, that of social arenas, is not meant to evoke the image of a circumscribed amphitheater but rather to convey the abstract concept of a sphere of action where debate and negotiation take place. (Strauss 1978; Wiener 1981; Hilgartner and Bosk 1988; Wiener 1991). An arena brings together people with a common concern but different aspirations and perspectives. Arenas comprise the social worlds through which individuals act, most visibly through the organizations that form within these social worlds. Examples are opera, baseball, surfing, stamp collecting, country music, etc. All of these worlds vary—some small, some large; some international, some local; some inseparable from given spaces, others less spatially identifiable; some highly public and publicized, others barely visible; some barely emergent, others well established and organized; some very hierarchical, some less so or scarcely at all.

The accountability arena brings together representatives of the worlds of medicine, nursing, business, government, hospitals, insurance, etc. With amorphous and permeable boundaries, arenas are the "social space" where policy is played out by these representatives. Sociologically, this concept is a vehicle for identifying which groups and interests are involved in a specific policy debate and the nature of their interaction. It provides a way to study and understand collective action in contemporary society: society's "complexities, diversities, boundary permeabilities, intersecting group-ings, and its speedy changes" (Strauss 1993, 212). While sociologists with a more positivistic bent find the lack of definitive boundaries disconcert-ing, it is precisely *because* of the fluid borders that this concept retains its usefulness.

The interests and dominance of specific groups wax and wane in all are-nas. For example, in the accountability arena, when representatives of the business world have formed coalitions in order to manage the cost of care, medical organizations have lost a good deal of their long-held power. Some arenas have periods of growth followed by constriction. For now, the ac-countability arena continues to expand as the quest for accountability be-comes more intense, taking on a momentum marked by growing career opportunities and ever-greater marketplace potential. The countless sem-inars, conferences, consultants, oversight organizations, articles, books, computer software, and legislation devoted to accountability issues demon-strate this expansion.

Structural Conditions

All three of the Straussian components complement each other while drawing upon their roots in symbolic interaction. Accompanying this phi-losophy is the understanding that the behavior and orientations of actors are inseparable from the structural conditions that impinge upon them, and vice versa. One part of society cannot be understood in isolation from other parts. People go about constructing their social reality, making their worlds, but not exactly as they might please. There is a reciprocal, ongoing relationship between the acts of individuals and historic, economic, and sociological conditions—or organizational, religious, and cultural condi-tions. The challenge of this type of research is to tease out the relevant con-ditions and map out the reciprocal relationships.

In sum, the theoretical stance that informs this book, by integrating an action, negotiation, and social arena frame of reference, focuses on the com-plexities, ambiguities, and uncertainties of the accountability enterprise and how these evolve. In one of Strauss' last contributions, an introduction to the 1997 edition of *Mirrors and Masks*, written forty years after its first publication, he looked back at his "view of society" and characterized it as involving "an explicit argument against explanations of social order that overstress rules and regulations while ignoring *how* they are promulgated, maintained, manipulated, escaped, altered, and even totally destroyed and superseded. All this can only happen if one has a view of humans as shap-ing their worlds to some extent—but in the face of inevitable structural constraints."

THE RESEARCH PROJECT

I started this project in 1993 by interviewing what were then called Quality Assurance, Assessment, or Management directors (or coordinators) in a variety of hospitals. What I found was a relatively new career path, in California mainly comprising nurses who had been conscripted from other jobs in the hospital and who were desperately trying to keep up, not only with ever-changing regulations and standards, but with inconsistency among the agencies doing external oversight. I soon realized that I was observing an evolving arena, one where an emerging identity can be tracked by looking at the meanings that have been placed on the names successively used by hospital quality departments. The most commonly used labels for quality when I started the research—assurance and assessment—have now been replaced essentially by "improvement," called by many arena participants QA/I, which I shall use when an acronym is appropriate. The important point is that these terms symbolize the ever-evolving emphasis of the Joint Commission on Accreditation of Healthcare Organizations, the private organization responsible for verifying that hospitals have met approved standards. In true symbolic interactional fashion, these meanings are being imposed on a structure, the hospital organization, that has established its own social reality. Interviews were "open-ended," conducted in a conversational style, in a sequence that flows from the respondent's perspective of the situation. Detailed narratives and personal anecdotes from professionals about their QA/I work provided a contextual richness on how these experiences are understood and acted upon by different people.

The project enlarged when I obtained an entrée into two hospitals in order to do participant observation. One, with 344 beds, is located in a large metropolitan area and serves a lower-economic population of diverse cultural backgrounds. The other is a 438-bed hospital in a suburban community, serving a largely middle-class population. Participant observation, also called "ethnography," integrates observation in the field with key informant interviews, enabling the researcher to study people in their own time and space (Buraway 1991). This research technique relies on natural interaction rather than instruments as a source of data Reinharz 1979) and is intentionally unstructured, so as to maximize discovery and description rather than systematic theory testing. Participant observation allows the researcher to compare observational data with interview data, that is, compare what people say they do with what they actually do. It also provides an opportunity to follow up preliminary data with a more intensive examination of significant behavior and events. Within the two hospital sites, field work consisted of observation at meetings devoted to QA/I review, preparation for accreditation visits, nursing issues, administrative matters, the use of QA/I techniques, and redesign planning and troubleshooting. Field work also included observation at seminars, workshops, and conferences devoted to QA/I topics. This aspect of research, however, consists of much more than observation at meetings. For instance, contacts made during a meeting (sometimes through something as subtle as glances exchanged during a controversial interaction) often lead to significant data. A dialogue is created between participant and observer and meaningful data often are obtained in the hallway or elevator both preceding and following a meeting or may lead to an in-depth interview. Frequently, as trust is established, key informants seek the researcher out, suggesting a coffee break to discuss troublesome issues or to enlarge on comments made in initial interviews.[3]

Participant observation requires flexibility, a suspension of expectations, and an openness to discovery that defy strict scheduling of data collection. A valuable source of data came about in the combination of accident and sagacity that marks unstructured research. Pasteur captured the sense of this marriage of the unanticipated with the strategic in his oft-quoted aphorism: "Chance favors the prepared mind." At an early stage in the research, while attending a conference sponsored by the Patient Care Assessment Council, an organization of QA/I professionals, I was invited to attend future meetings. I was welcomed as an observer since, as is so often the case in this type of research, those on the front lines felt that their concerns were not being heard. Discussions at these meetings turned out to be an invaluable source of data. The members of this organization remained key informants throughout the analysis and writing of this book.

Up-close observation and interviews were further informed by a continuing review of the literature. During my twenty years of research in health care, I have witnessed vast changes in attention to this topic—from when writing about the social/psychological implications of living with chronic illness was whistling in the dark, to a time when health care has become a paramount issue for the public and for politicians. The health care literature reflects this intensified interest. Accordingly, concern about quality of care figures prominently in publications such as the *New England Journal of Medicine* and the *Journal of the American Medical Association*, to say nothing of the increased number of journals, articles, books, and web sites devoted exclusively to the subject. When I decided to place the accountability enterprise in its historical context, I turned to the literature increasingly to flesh out the sociological, economic, and organizational conditions that have affected the burgeoning accountability arena.

An additional source of data fortuitously came my way as this book was being written. Advised of the existence of an online network where quality professionals discuss common problems and seek assistance from their peers, I became a subscriber. The daily twenty-five to fifty messages served to verify the universality of the issues and dilemmas discussed in this book and added insight into the way regulations and policy were being negotiated in hospital settings throughout the country.

RESEARCH METHOD

If self-understanding and clear statement of one's theoretical stance are crucial for a sociologist, so too is the enunciation of the sociological method used to collect and analyze the data. The method used in this research is called *grounded theory* (Glaser and Strauss 1967; Glaser 1978; Strauss 1979; Strauss and Corbin 1998). Two simple points must be made regarding the name of this qualitative research method. First, the connotation surrounding the word "theory," by evoking an image of the physical sciences, is more formidable than it need be. The term simply means identifying the interrelationship between and among concepts in order to present a systematic view of the phenomena being examined, in order to explain "what is going on." Second, the term "grounded," meaning grounded in data, is often misunderstood. Obviously, anyone claiming to be a scientist would be seeking empirical grounding, at least in his or her own estimation. The term is meant to challenge the conventional approach by which existent theory is regarded as the *beginning* of research activity and imposed on the data. "Grounded" signifies that theory was systematically generated from the data *as part of the ongoing research process*.

It is not uncommon for qualitative sociologists to find their work belittled as "anecdotal," implying that sociological findings are only "facts" if they can be counted. Since qualitative work is still poorly understood in some quarters, there is a temptation to be pulled into quantitative or natural science standards and to try to apply these inappropriately. But every mode of discovery develops its own standards, and canons and procedures for achieving verifiable results. Thus, *grounded theory* sets forth basic procedures that should be followed. Interviews were recorded by audiotape and transcribed. Field notes were recorded by word processor immediately upon completion of each day's participant observation. All data were coded and analyzed concurrently. In this method, initial coding of data and their relationships is subject to verification and development as more data are collected and examined, a process that continues throughout data collection by using a system of "constant comparison." One respondent's answer is compared to another's in order to discover similarities and variation. Equally fruitful is the comparison of one social arena to another. In this research, comparison to the education arena—where emphasis is placed on "academic indicators," "teaching to the test," and rating schools on "report cards"—put similar hospital accountability practices into sharper focus. Dingwall et al., in a discussion of the contribution of *grounded theory* to health services research in Britain, give a straightforward description of the basic components—observe, infer, generalize—that comprise the constant comparison process:

> Begin with two observations. Ask whether they are the same or different and in what respects. When a generalization has been formulated which covers both, take a third case. Does this fit or do the generalizations need to be further reformulated to cover it? . . . If the case does not fit, it is necessary to perform a 'deviant case analysis' using the same logic to discover why it does not fit and how the emerging statements would need to be modified to accommodate it. After a while the examination of new cases no longer throws up anomalies. There is a generalization or a set of statements about regularities which explain every case that has been collected. (1998, 171)

Since the researcher is jointly collecting, coding, and analyzing the data, a question often posed is: how does one decide what data to collect next and where to find them? Unlike a project designed to test or verify a hypothesis, which requires strict adherence to a research design, with *grounded theory* data collection cannot be planned in advance (beyond initial forays into the field). The procedure followed by grounded theorists is called "theoretical sampling." The emerging theory points to the next steps—the sociologist does not know what they will be until guided by emerging gaps and/or research questions suggested by previous answers. Or, as described by Dingwall et al, "Suppose that the process of constant comparison has produced certain generalizations. These can now be tested by looking for circumstances under which they might not hold." (ibid.)

Discovery rests on finding patterns of behavior, rendering respondents' quotes important only insofar as they represent a patterned concept. The goal is to discover the basic social processes that account for *most* of the variation in behavior within the social life under investigation—processes meaning phenomena that show continuous change. The method therefore goes beyond answering the typical "what" question (the relationship between variables) to answering the "how" question (the processes that connect those variables) (Hall 1976). Further, there is a built-in expectation that contingencies will arise during a course of action. As expressed by Strauss, "Contingencies . . . can bring about change in its duration, pace, and even intent, which may alter the structure and process of interaction" (Strauss 1993, 36).

An important step for those who use *grounded theory* is to trace connections among the observed interaction and the conditions affecting it, as well as the consequences that flow from this interplay. Furthermore, acts themselves have consequences, many unanticipated, which then become conditions that affect subsequent acts. Far from being deterministic, this is a complicated view of social history in which conditions influence and nudge interactions and vice versa, in a continual emergence. Some interactions regarding accountability, for instance, are related to broad conditions (American values and our form of government as described at the beginning of this chapter). Others are traceable to narrower conditions (the status of the QA/I department within the hospital hierarchy). But these conditions are important to the extent that they affect action in the arena and the consequences of that action. For this reason, historical materials were examined as prime elements in my analysis. Discovering these paths of conditions and consequences, establishing the linkages, and weaving them into an explanatory account has been the challenge of this research.[4]

Finally, from sage observers, some important comments. The first regards the necessary acknowledgment of the process of selectivity in relating history. History has been jokingly referred to as "all the stuff that happens at the same time." Still, filtering out the least important "stuff" remains a formidable enterprise. Citing two venerable sociologists (Parsons and Shils 1954, 167), Carr calls history a "selective system" not only of cognitive but of causal orientations to reality. "Just as from the infinite ocean of facts the historian selects those which are significant for his purpose, so from the multiplicity of sequences of cause and effect he extracts those, and only those, which are historically significant; and the standard of historical significance is his ability to fit them into his pattern of rational explanation and interpretation" (1964, 138). Since, as newscasters are so fond of telling us, "this is *some* of what's happening" (meaning *only some*) it remains for the reader to assess whether the interrelationship of action, conditions and consequences described in this book fits into a pattern of rational explanation and interpretation.

The second observation concerns the role of intuition and creativity in research—readily recognized in the physical sciences (Bohm 1987; Watson 1980; Crick 1988; Hawking 1988), but often acknowledged only defensively in qualitative social science. May (1994) argues that expert knowledge in qualitative research consists of an exquisitely tuned capacity to know where to look and the ability to ferret out similarities and differences, based on experience. Although entering the field with as open a mind as possible has advantages—most notably the license to ask naive questions—in an undertaking this large, experience in the health care arena was an undeniable asset. For, as May puts it, "expert analysts are virtually always informed by extant knowledge and use this knowledge as if it were another informant." May sees the magic of creativity and intuition as an expression of methodologic expertise:

Moving from intuition to insight, from an interesting but quirky question to an important revelation—these processes are not governed by chance. Rather they may be governed by a readiness to see the possibilities when they are "there" and to bring them to the surface when they are not. (1994, 20)

OVERVIEW

Americans are notoriously ahistorical, perhaps a throwback to our pioneer, frontier origins, perhaps related to contemporary society's instant-gratification mentality. As one trend after another has engulfed the health care arena, there is always the sense that "this is going to be it." No less so in regard to the accountability enterprise. But Carr has stated with accuracy that history is a dialogue between events of the past and progressively emerging future ends where "the belief that we have come from somewhere is closely linked with the belief that we are going somewhere" (176). If quality of care is to be improved, we must examine how we got where we are and where the present approach seems to be going.

Chapters One and Two provide the background to where we are. Chapter One maps the unique historical course of America's hospitals, its medical profession, and health insurance system. Also examined are the growth of the federal research budget, and the effect of this investment on enhanced technological capability, increased chronic illness, and rising costs. The growth of the medical-industrial complex and the impact of this progression on the nursing profession are described, culminating in a discussion of where this leaves hospitals at the beginning of the twenty-first century. Chapter Two deals with attempts to rationalize health care delivery, from Health Systems Agencies to Diagnosis Related Groups to Managed Care. Also covered in this chapter is the effort to impose regulations and standards on hospitals, and then to re-engineer them so that they will adhere more closely to the tenets of an efficient and productive industry.

Chapters Three, Four, and Five set forth the *grounded theory* of my research, which deals with the processes that constitute building an arena in quest of hospital accountability. Chapter Three, "Formalizing the Accountability Endeavor," describes the subprocesses of *mastering the techniques* of quality management; *reorganizing the hospital* around efficiency; *experimenting with performance measurement* by quantifying outcomes; and *enlarging the arena*. In Chapter Four, "Implementing the Accountability Endeavor," the first subprocess discussed is *examining the assumptions* that support the state of the art in the hospital-accountability arena. It includes discussion of a major condition impeding smooth implementation of performance measurement: the complexity of health care delivery. The second subprocess is *examining the barriers* obstructing implementation of externally imposed regulations. This chapter concludes with a third subprocess, *working within the limitations.* Chapter Five, "Demonstrating the Accountability Endeavor," analyzes preparation for Joint Commission oversight surveys and a description of the surveys themselves, as observed in three hospitals. Since this process takes the form of an elaborately constructed presentation, I have used a theatrical metaphor. The subprocess *setting the scene* describes the backstage preparation that is orchestrated well in advance of the survey, such as getting tips on the most recent "hot issues" being scrutinized by Joint Commission surveyors and sprucing up the required documentation. *Rehearsing the cast* consists of coaching the leadership and the staff regarding appropriate answers to expected questions on policies and procedures, committee structure, and the hospital's mission statement. The chapter describes bringing hospital employees up to date on regulations and getting them involved in the necessary preparation, strategies for focusing their attention, and the preparation of visual aids to reinforce the opening presentation of the survey in order to make the hospital "look good." *Presenting the main performance* delves into the culmination of all of the anxiety and frenzy that permeates preparation—the survey itself, its successes and pitfalls, and its effect on staff morale. *Reconceptualizing the plot* consists of an analysis of three problems associated with the oversight process as currently practiced: the variability of surveyors, structural flaws in the survey mechanism, and the tendency of staff to engage in "defensive work"—self-protective and institution-protective strategies.

Chapter Six ties together the threads from the previous chapters and presents an analysis of how hospitals differ from the corporate industries with which they are usually compared. Analyzed also are five weaknesses in the accountability equation: (1) underestimating the unique qualities of contemporary health care; (2) overstating and overselling accountability proposals; (3) ignoring the irrational element inherent in rationalization ventures; (4) emphasizing the superiority of market forces to the neglect of other values; and (5) downplaying the issue of medical accident and error. Included in this chapter is a look at the most recent turn in the accountability enterprise: the multidisciplinary, root-cause analysis and external review of "sentinel events," now mandated by the Joint Commission. By requiring examination of "unexpected occurrences involving death or serious physical or psychological injury or the risk thereof," the sentinel-events standards manifest yet one more incidence of ferment and growth within the arena (more expert consultants, more "how-to" literature, and more debate and negotiation over definitions and parameters).

Although employing the academic style that requires meticulous citing of sources, this book is not addressed solely to policy makers. Of course, all sociologists dream of making an impact, in this case on health care reform. But ultimately, reform cannot happen in a democratic society without public support. In that regard, the movie "As Good As It Gets," released in late 1997, was heartening. When Helen Hunt, playing the mother of a chronically ill child, suddenly exploded at the injustice of the care that is now supposedly "managed," the audience at my viewing spontaneously burst into applause—a reaction that the press reported was repeated throughout the country. If, as seems to be happening, people are questioning the quality of their health care, it is important that they understand how we got to this point and what options exist for changing the course. Thus, in my attempt to write for a general audience—perhaps even to engage people in creating solutions—I have tried to keep specialized language to a minimum, while maintaining the scholarly rigor that will engender respect for the concepts and conclusions presented. As it has been throughout my research career, the quality of health care remains my overriding concern, for sooner or later we will all be patients and as Sir William Osler so wisely said, "The secret of caring for the patient is caring for the patient." In keeping with that spirit, this book is dedicated to the potential patient in all of us.

NOTES

1. For a more detailed discussion of negotiation as a sociological framework, see Strauss (1978); Hall and Spencer-Hall (1982); and Maines (1982).
2. To support their position, Geist and Hardesty cite Knafl and Burkett (1975).
3. Three fine resources for this type of research are Schatzman and Strauss (1973); Lofland and Lofland (1984); and Denzin and Lincoln (1994).
4. Strauss and Corbin call this aspect of analysis establishing "conditional paths." They have developed a methodological procedure they call "conditional matrix" for conceptualizing, diagramming, and keeping track of the conditions that bear on the phenomenon under study and its associated interactions. For a description, see Strauss (1993), Corbin and Strauss (1996), and Strauss and Corbin (1998).

1

Antecedents to the Accountability Movement

The Era of Growth

No social study that does not come back to the problems of biography, of history and of their intersections within a society has completed its intellectual journey.

—C. Wright Mills

This chapter and the next map the unique course U.S. hospitals have taken, which ultimately has led to the quest for accountability. Underlying this chapter is the understanding that: (1) social interaction, the conditions that affect it, and the consequences flowing from it are linked; and (2) consequences of interactions often become important conditions that affect subsequent social interactions. "History matters," Robert Putnam writes, because "social developments are 'path dependent.'" Moreover, "What comes first (even if it was in some sense 'accidental') conditions what comes later. Individuals may 'choose' their institutions, but they do not choose them under circumstances of their own making, and their choices in turn influence the rules within which their successors choose" (1993, 8). Identifying the path—the explicit linkages between social interaction, conditions and consequences—is, however, a complex analytic enterprise. "To arrive at explanations of phenomena, choices inevitably must be made from innumerable potential conditions and consequences that confront the researcher. These choices amount to the process of ordering that constitutes explanation, or analysis" (Corbin and Strauss 1996, 140).

This chapter examines the importance of the unique relationship between physicians and U.S. hospitals and of the decision to link health insurance with employment; the inflationary consequences of this interplay; the collapse of a national health care plan and the consequent expansion

17

of medical research; the effect of enhanced technology on the cost of care; the consequences of this interplay on malpractice claims; the hospital building boom; the consequences of the foregoing on the expansion of the medical-industrial complex; the effect of this growth on the nursing profession; and, finally, where this evolution leaves hospitals at the beginning of the twenty-first century—a state of affairs characterized by mergers, acquisitions, and joint ventures, where the traditional distinction between profit and nonprofit hospitals is blurred, and where corporate interests and marketplace values predominate.

INTERDEPENDENCY OF HOSPITALS AND PHYSICIANS

Hospitals in the United States originated, as in all pre-industrial societies, as humanistic, religious and philanthropic institutions.[1] Primarily places to die, hospitals were avoided by patients who could afford private physicians. Not until the late part of the nineteenth century did they become central to medical education and medical practice. "From refuges mainly for the homeless poor and insane, they evolved into doctors' workshops for all types and classes and patients. From charities, dependent on voluntary gifts, they developed into market institutions, financed increasingly out of payments from patients" (Starr 1982, 146). The modern hospital did not develop until the 1880s, with the emergence of round-the-clock skilled nurses and the ability to undertake major surgery (Stevens 1997). Between 1880 and 1914, medical science was transformed by the professionalization of physicians and the discovery and acceptance of the germ theory, "giving medicine the confidence that its major justification as a profession was its scientific base" (ibid. 133). These developments made hospitals more attractive to the middle and upper classes. Hospitals became "workplaces for the production of health" (ibid. 146), where patients were treated only during the acute phases of their illnesses. Moreover, "the demands and example of an industrializing capitalist society, which brought larger numbers of people into urban centers, detached hospitals from traditions of self-sufficiency, and projected ideals of specialization and technical competence" (ibid.). In this era, U.S. hospitals symbolized the wealth of new and expanding American cities, where a "demonstration of show, even conspicuous waste, became a lasting aspect" (Stevens, 135).

Hospitals were among the most luxurious and costly structures ever built—even in the Depression years of the 1930s. A significant boom period occurred after World War II, driven by the Hospital Survey and

Construction Act of 1946 (Hill-Burton), which steered federal funds to the states for this purpose.

An early instance of unintended consequences followed defeat of national health insurance in the 1940s. Advocates of more government funding for biomedical research seized upon this defeat to promote research as the best health insurance Americans could have. The 1950s and 1960s were a golden age, when "the postwar economy was booming, and community hospitals added new technology, larger facilities, and a burgeoning work force of professional and technical workers to assist physicians in the care of their patients" (Brannon 1994, 1). As increased knowledge fostered greater medical specialization, this heyday of the medical research enterprise resulted in labor- and capital-intensive technological change within the hospital (Strauss et al. 1997). Money from the government and pharmaceutical and medical manufacturers created a group of medical superstars. By the 1970s, the technologic imperative was well entrenched. In what has been called the "medical arms race," every hospital board felt it had to have its own computed tomographic scanner and heart catheterization laboratory. Medical successes, fortified by American faith in the sciences, fostered enthusiasm for ever greater investment not only in research but in hospitals and medical schools.

Medicine as a profession had had a rocky start. In 1910, distinguished educator Abraham Flexner wrote a pivotal report (sponsored by the Carnegie Foundation for the Advancement of Teaching) that attacked medical schools as inadequate, ill-equipped, and incompetent to train students as physicians. The report forced most of the schools to close, and universities took over medical education.[2] Historians contend, however, that neither the teaching change nor American veneration of scientific achievement, although important, are enough to explain the rise of the medical profession. Historians point to a number of factors to explain how a financially insecure group that was weak and bitterly divided in the nineteenth century became transformed into a prosperous, united, and respected profession in the twentieth, able to move medical care from the home into the marketplace. "Doctors exploited progressive belief in science over populist support of self-reliance. Having increased demand, they then controlled supply—by ending sectarian quarrels within medicine; restricting entry to the profession through licensing laws and limited admission to recently reformed medical schools; and establishing their authority over medication" (Geiger 1983, 26). Unlike other countries where doctors were employees of the hospital, in the United States only doctors could order the admissions that filled the beds. Hospitals provided places where medicine was practiced by independent entrepreneurs who had established their professional sovereignty within a unique structure:

In Europe and most other areas of the world, when patients enter a hospital, their doctors typically relinquish responsibility to the hospital staff, who form a separate and distinct group within the profession. But in the United States, private doctors follow their patients into the hospital, where they continue to attend them. This arrangement complicates hospital administration, since many of the people making vital decisions are not the institution's employees. . . . Instead of a centralized system of hospitals under state ownership, America developed a variety of institutional forms—a kind of 'mixed economy' in hospitals—with both public and private institutions of several kinds under independent management. . . . Both internally and as a system, American hospitals have had a relatively loose structure because of the autonomy of physicians from hospitals and of most hospitals from government. (Starr 1982, 147)

Thus, in contrast to the single authority structure of typical corporations, power in hospitals is complicated by their shared governance among administrators, physicians, and trustees—a balance that has fluctuated, as Perrow has demonstrated (1963), based on which group has been most crucial to organizational goals. From the late 1800s to the 1930s, trustees were dominant because physicians and administrators depended on community elites for both capital and social legitimation. From the 1930s to the post–World War II period, physicians seized the high ground because they controlled the admission of patients and were critical in the production of medical services. Then, throughout the postwar period, administrators gained ascendancy as health care became more organizationally complex.

In its heyday, physician dominance was buttressed by the hospital medical staff organization, which exists to this day. This system dates back to 1917, when the American College of Surgeons (ACS) established specific standards and placed authority for those standards on medical staff. Quality assurance standards were built around monthly case reviews by department committees. When the Joint Commission on Accreditation of Hospitals was formed in 1951, it inherited the original ACS hospital standardization program. Not only do medical staff continue to monitor quality but more significantly, the system evolved into a political entity through which physician influence on the hospital could be channeled. The result has been a struggle between lay persons and physicians for control of hospitals, "a struggle in which privatization and the profit concept have strengthened the need for lay administrators at the same time that they have increased the dependence of hospitals on their physicians for attracting 'paying' patients" (Straus 1988, 185).

There is, however, a difference between corporations that physicians control and corporations that control physicians—a difference that is epitomized in the attacks on the traditional medical staff organization as a dinosaur that has outlived its usefulness. "The duplicate management structure is detrimental to quality improvement and to the quick adjustments hospitals will need to make for survival in the future," critics charge.[3] As the Joint Commission has relaxed its standards for the organization and meetings of medical staff committees, many hospitals have begun to revamp the committee structure. But tradition is not yielding without a struggle, and "battles over space, equipment, and personnel can lead to bitter, deep-rooted lack of respect between technical professionals and management professionals" (Thompson 1984, 10). Toomey (see Note 3) has observed the physicians' hierarchy of loyalty is first to their profession and patients; second to their practices and employees; third to their specialty and its organizational and educational structure; fourth to their own personal and financial well-being; and, last to the hospital.

To the extent that this characterization is accurate, it is substantially the result of the economic independence from hospitals that physicians maintain.

> Hospitals provided capital and support staff, including nurses and a wide range of technical support personnel, such as radiologic technologists and laboratory technicians. While (increasingly) the role of physicians shifted from the direct providers of care to the coordinators of the production of complex services using resources provided by hospitals, there was no corresponding shift in clinical accountability to the administration of the hospital. Rather, physicians remained accountable to their peers and their patients. (Salmon et al. 1990, 264)

A physician interviewed for my research explained that

> the cumbersome three-party triad remained tolerable over the years because of the expressed overwhelming concern of the physician staff for patient welfare and for its own autonomy and the administration's insistence that it does not practice medicine, but exists only to contribute the support needed by the physicians to carry out their mission of patient care. Additionally, the board of directors understood its dependence on the advice of the administrator (and his attorney), and perhaps one or more leading physicians and took few independent initiatives.

THE EVOLUTION OF HEALTH INSURANCE

Technological advancement and expanded services were already contributing to the rising health care dollar when the economy collapsed during the Great Depression. As unemployment increased and the wages of those workers who retained their jobs fell sharply, only the wealthiest members of society could afford health care. The rest were likely to postpone seeing a doctor and feared that a major illness requiring hospitalization could destroy them financially (Brannon 1994, 15). The solution to this crisis became another watershed. Hospitals devised a method for reimbursing their costs by establishing a system of insurance, which they named Blue Cross.[4] Starting in 1929 as an insurance plan for 1,250 school teachers signed up by Baylor University Hospital in Dallas, Texas, Blue Cross grew to a membership of six million by 1940. Blue Cross plans covered only hospitalization at a single community rate, regardless of risk related to specific groups and individuals. As Sager points out, cost reimbursement was not designed with profligate or evil intent but rather for financially starved nonprofit entities that had never spent extravagantly. He continues:

> Few expected that reimbursing their costs would markedly change their behavior. How then did this happen? Nonprofit hospitals' responses to cost reimbursement were modulated in important ways by simultaneous changes in economic conditions, physician-hospital power relations, patients' expectations, and medicine's capacities. In a sense, cost reimbursement arrived on the scene at exactly the wrong time. (Sager 1997, 226)

Before World War II, hospital administrators had little authority. They typically supervised housekeeping functions and kept rudimentary accounts. Trustees made the major financial and physical-plant decisions; physicians allocated available medical resources. "Cost reimbursement worked on this penurious environment like a rainstorm on dried seeds in a desert. Hospital trustees and managers accustomed to counting syringes and bedpans suddenly and unexpectedly had access to vast resources" (ibid. 226–27). Furthermore, an incentive now existed to enlarge diagnostic and therapeutic technology, buoying demand "as an endless bounty for pharmaceutical firms and hospital equipment and supply companies" (Salmon et al. 1990, 265). In the late 1930s and early 1940s, Blue Cross organizations worked with physicians to establish Blue Shield plans to cover physicians' services, providing further nourishment for those dried desert seeds:

> Both Blue Cross and Blue Shield were captives of the doctors and hospitals. Through their state and local medical societies and their dominance of the boards of directors of the Blues, doctors controlled the scope of coverage and the amounts they and the hospitals were paid. Portrayed as a public service, Blue Shield was also a minimum income security program for doctors. Participating doctors had to accept the amounts the plans set as full payment only for low-income subscribers; they were free to levy additional charges on others. (Califano 1986, 43)

The success of Blue Cross and Blue Shield evoked competition from commercial insurance companies. At first contesting the unfair advantage of the Blues, insurance companies soon began to perceive themselves as more closely aligned with the doctors and hospitals whose bills they paid than with their subscribers. "Before these consumers realized what was happening, or anybody took much notice, the health insurance sector of the health care industry was harnessed to minimize competition, control prices, direct usage, and ease bill collection for doctors and hospitals" (ibid.). A system was now in place whereby premiums rose with hospital costs. Physicians benefited from this system as the third-party insurer became a source of greatly increased income. "Because of the hospitals' financial need to keep their beds filled, they opened up access to physicians on generous terms and became dependent on the physicians' good will" (Starr 1982, 332).

A concurrent development was the decision to channel health insurance through employment. When price and wage controls were established during World War II, health insurance became a trade-off for wage increases. "As a fringe benefit, health insurance benefited the employer as well as the worker, solved problems in the marketing of private insurance, gave the providers protection against a government program, and offered the unions an alternative to national health insurance and a means of demonstrating concern for their members" (ibid. 333). By the end of the war, twenty-six million Americans were enrolled in group hospital plans. Throughout the 1960s and 1970s, business and labor continued to extend health insurance coverage and benefits—replacing deductible and copayment plans under which employees shared part of the insurance cost with "first-dollar coverage plans." The cost of this expansion was hidden in the products consumers bought but "families blanketed in the rich first-dollar coverage plans thought they never had to pay for doctors or hospitals . . . (while) our biggest corporations and unions had, with little or no appreciation of the ramifications, granted to doctors, hospital administrators, medical laboratories and pharmaceutical manufacturers the power to tell the patients what services, tests, and drugs, to buy, regardless of cost" (Califano 1986, 46). The rapid growth of the health insurance system hastened yet another unintended consequence by "unleashing forces that would eventually help bring about the government intervention its leadership hoped to avoid" (Starr 1982, 331).

THE UNIVERSAL-CARE COMPROMISE:
MEDICARE AND MEDICAID

Three months after taking office in 1945, Harry Truman became the first American president to give universal health care his full support. Truman was motivated by his dismay on learning that one-third of the men reporting for the draft during World War II were physically unfit to serve

(Poen 1979). Truman's proposal—a single-payer system that would cover all Americans—met passionate opposition from the American Medical Association (AMA), which protested that doctors would become "clock watchers" and "slaves." Nor did Truman's assurance that doctors and hospitals could choose whatever method they preferred for payment and delivery of health care services mollify the AMA. The doctors remained convinced that "a voluntary sickness insurance system developed with features peculiar to the American way of life is better for the American people than a federally controlled compulsory sickness insurance system" (Fishbein 1946, 87). Organized medicine's position was buttressed by the 1946 election that brought a Republican majority to Congress:

> Truman was unable to muster the support he needed to pull his legislation out of committee. His opponents in Congress used Red Scare rhetoric honed by the AMA. In 1947, a House subcommittee investigating national health insurance reached a "firm conclusion" that "American Communism holds this program as a cardinal point in its objectives," and that "known Communists and fellow travelers within federal agencies are at work diligently with federal funds in furtherance of the Moscow party line." (Greenberg 1993, 130)

Despite the opposition of organized medicine, the president remained loyal to his populist goal, making national health insurance pivotal to his proposal for a Fair Deal during the election of 1948. He defended his plan as "100 percent American," arguing in a radio message, "Is it un-American to visit the sick, aid the afflicted, or comfort the dying? I thought that was simple Christianity" (Peon 1979, 130). Truman's words did not sway the AMA. Disappointed by the unexpected defeat of Republican Thomas E. Dewey, the AMA leadership mounted the most ambitious lobbying effort that had ever been seen in the United States, levying a special twenty-five-dollar assessment upon each of its members and hiring a high-powered public relations agency to conduct a campaign that accelerated the branding of Truman's proposal as socialized medicine and part of a communist plot.

The AMA's campaign had the full support of the conservative coalition in Congress, which would defeat every attempt at government health insurance until 1965. In what Marmor has called "the dogged defeat."[5] Truman lowered his sights and went after the more modest goal of a health insurance program for social security recipients.

It would, however, be another fourteen years before this approach became the Medicare program. The initial idea was that Medicare would be the first step in coverage that eventually would include most of the population. Most important, it was clearly understood that Congress would not interfere with the doctors and hospitals providing Medicare-financed care:

> The overwhelming Democratic victory of 1964 seemed to guarantee that hospitalization insurance for the elderly would pass in 1965. President Johnson's commitment to Medicare was plain in the electoral campaign, and the new Congress of 1965 acted so as to prevent further delays in the Great Society's agenda. . . . Outside of government, national pressure groups made enormous and costly efforts to shape the discussion of Medicare. The Medicare proposals sent to Congress reflected the continuing attempts of those within the government bureaucracy to articulate and balance the pressure groups' rival claims. (Marmor 1988, 369)

Anticipating AMA objections, physicians' services were excluded from the original bill. A felicitous turn occurred when the senior Republican on the Ways and Means committee, responding to growing public support from the aged constituency, proposed a voluntary insurance plan, subsidized out of government revenues, that would cover major medical risks and include doctors' services and drugs. The portion paid by the aged would be scaled to their Social Security benefits. In what Starr has called an "ingenious move," Representative Wilbur Mills proposed combining the administration's and the Republican measures and adding a third program to support services for the poor.

> The result was what one observer described as a three-layered cake. The first layer was the Democratic plan for a compulsory hospital insurance program under Social Security. This became Part A of Medicare. The second layer was the revised Republican program of government-subsidized voluntary insurance to cover physicians' bills. This became Part B of Medicare. And the third layer, called Medicaid, expanded assistance to the states for medical care for the poor. (Starr 1982, 369)

Negotiators of the new program had yielded to pressure that doctors be paid their "customary" charges. Also, bargaining between government leaders and the hospital industry resulted in adoption of Blue Cross's "reasonable cost" method of hospital reimbursement (Somers and Somers 1967; Feder 1977). The resultant inflationary pressure is clear on hindsight:

> Vague definitions of key legislative terms—"reasonable costs" and "customary charges," in particular—proved to be significant loopholes that allowed energetic gaming strategies on the part of providers. Unusual allowances for depreciation and capital costs (such costs were taken into account in determining provider reimbursement rates) contributed to a built-in inflationary impetus. The use of private insurance companies as intermediaries preserved physician autonomy and weakened government controls on reimbursement. (Marmor 1988, 11)

The legislation not only turned over to insurance companies the tasks of paying and auditing physicians and hospitals but gave the hospitals the right to choose which insurance companies they wanted to be their auditors. It also gave the insurance companies the right to determine "reasonableness" of costs and "customary" services. (After all the opposition, Medicare *eventually* became a bonanza for physicians and hospitals, when managed care entered the scene and both entities found their rates being negotiated downward. Ironically, senior citizens had become a profitable segment of the market, combining a significant need for health care with insurance through Medicare and private programs.)

EXPANDING MEDICAL CAPABILITY

Meanwhile, in the 1960s, the federal medical research budget grew from $200 million to $1 billion. In 1965, President Johnson convinced Congress to pass the Heart Disease, Cancer, and Stroke bill, which created regional medical centers to provide sophisticated hospital care in every section of the country. As former secretary of Health, Education and Welfare Joseph Califano correctly asserts, the expansion of the National Institutes of Health and the creation of these centers increased the richness and intensity of medical care provided in hospitals across America.

> The prevailing attitude was: if such care is far more expensive, so be it. Medicare was picking up the tab for the elderly and big business had agreed to pay the bill for its employees, so plenty of money was available. The vicious circle kept spiraling costs upward with each turn: research funds created a demand for more specialized researchers and scientists, who created new demands for more research funds to support their work, and their spectacular discoveries made the American people willing to pay for more research and to train more specialists. After all, this investment in research had produced vital-organ transplants, psychiatric and anti-cancer drugs, electric-shock therapy to revive hearts that had stopped beating, surgical operations that reattached partially severed fingers, hands, and arms, psycho-surgery that altered the mind, stunning advances in fetal medicine and the treatment of premature babies, and the ability to extend life for thousands who would have died of heart disease, cancer, stroke, or respiratory complications just a decade earlier. (Califano 1986, 54)

While Medicare and Medicaid were initially seen as "health restoration" measures, it is unlikely that many legislators understood the extent of chronic illness that they would be called upon to meet. Since then, it has become clear that the arsenal of modern drugs, procedures, and machines currently available constitute "halfway technologies"[6]—they do not really cure although blessedly they compensate for the incapacitating effects of disease or postpone death for varying lengths of time. Although these technologies entail enormous cost, the continuing expansion of health facilities, and the need for highly trained personnel, more than one sage has observed that, for those who suffer from incurable diseases, halfway is a long way to go. It has since become abundantly clear that the arsenal of modern drugs, procedures, and machines cannot "restore" health to the chronically ill. They can, however, mitigate some effects of disease and postpone death—although at enormous cost.

Few would dispute that government involvement through Medicare, Medicaid, and support for medical research, coupled with the growth of employer-provided third-party insurance (Blue Cross/Blue Shield and commercial insurers) has enriched American health care. However, along with the blank check for American hospitals and doctors came the enormous growth in hospital staffing, wages, and purchases of new equipment and supplies, as well as the steady increase in hospital and physician fees.

As enhanced care raised the standards of appropriate treatment, however, malpractice suits increased. Earlier court decisions held that a physician need only meet the standard of care of the local community to avoid liability for malpractice. Scientific invention, medical technology, specialization, Medicare and Medicaid, and the Great Society's regional heart, cancer, and stroke centers nationalized the standard of care for physicians. "An increased number of diagnostic tests became routine procedure just to meet those standards." Huge judgments added to the cost surge: "First, in attempting to forestall lawsuits, doctors and hospitals felt compelled to run one test after another, especially since they weren't paying for them. Second, malpractice insurance premiums soared, in 1984 costing doctors $3 billion, and hospitals at least another $1.5 billion" (Califano 1986, 55).

Yet another contributing factor to ballooning costs was the hospital building boom made possible by the Hill-Burton Act of 1946, which for the first time made considerable federal funds available to establish, expand, and upgrade community hospitals. Designed to attract physicians to less-populated areas and to increase public access to medical and hospital care, this program created a situation of supply and demand that became clear only in retrospect. Bed availability was causing physicians to admit patients they had formerly treated at home:

> The simplest fact of hospital operation is the magnetism of an empty bed when payment for its use is assured. . . . A half-century ago, only the most desperately ill were hospitalized; cases of pneumonia, tonsillectomies, deliveries, heart attacks, fractures were treated at home or in the doctor's office. Today not only are these cases hospitalized, but so are cases of multiple-tooth extractions, psychoneurosis, epilepsy, diabetes for insulin stabilization, or any obscure condition for diagnosis. All this is made possible by an increase

in the relative supply of beds, and reciprocally it creates pressures for continual expansion of the bed supply. (Roemer and Shain 1959, 364)

THE GROWTH OF THE
NURSING PROFESSION

Neglected in the discussion so far, in direct disproportion to its importance,
is the role of the nursing profession vis-à-vis the hospital. It is important to
remember that "Until the 1920s, most people were nursed in their own
households, sometimes by a practical nurse, typically an older woman
who had acquired experience through the care of friends and neighbors as
well as her own family members" (Brannon 1994, 62). The first three hospital-based training programs in the United States (culminating in a *nursing diploma*) appeared in 1873, although most were founded between 1900
and 1920, accompanying the surge in hospital building. That most schools
were established by hospital authorities and physicians made them financially dependent and organizationally subordinate to their founders.[7] Hospital nursing schools were seen as a source of cheap labor for patient care.
Most accounts of this period stress the exploitative nature of the system,
where apprentices worked for long hours on hospital wards, receiving
meager room and board. Formal instruction was commonly given in the
afternoon or evening after a long work day. A significant structural condition, with repercussions to this day, was the authoritarian hierarchy of the
hospital:

> Physicians and hospital superintendents, the patriarchs of the institutional
> household, dominated apprentice nurses, who were expected to defer to
> their authority and to demonstrate appropriate social behavior, such as
> standing when they entered the wards. Although apprentices were consid-
> ered the handmaidens of physicians with responsibility for carrying out their
> medical orders, apprentices also labored under the immediate authority of a
> female nursing hierarchy in the training school. (Brannon 1994, 66)

The entire structure, exemplified in the nursing superintendent or matron, was based on the need for order and strict discipline. Much has been
written, especially by the nursing community, about the "power asymme-
try" and "institutionalized subservience" in the nurse-physician relationship that continued even after training. Many factors account for it: the
hierarchical structure of the society in which the two professions developed; the fact that university training made physicians the sanctioned
group of healers; the formation of the American Medical Association, le-
gitimizing doctors as primary healers; and the social roles of males and

females in the family and the larger society at the time. Moreover, the introduction of trained nurses to do bedside care involved conflicts not only with physicians, who were afraid that nurses would undermine their authority, but with older nurses, as well as with the administration (Rosen 1963). The lowered status of nurses is partially attributable to the need for the matron to establish her own authority:

> If the new matron was to undertake what she considered to be her duties, she had to carve out an empire of her own. She had to take over some of the responsibilities of the medical staff and some of the responsibilities of the lay administration. In addition she had to centralize the administration of nursing affairs. (Abel-Smith 1960, 25)

Despite the shift to university nursing schools, which began between 1910 and 1920 and offered a *baccalaureate degree,* and to community colleges which, dating from as of 1952, offered an *associate degree*—expected to enhance the nursing profession—nurses continue to feel undervalued in proportion to their increased responsibility for the management of patient care.[8]

Until the 1930s, most graduate nurses entered private-duty nursing, a market that collapsed when the middle class could no longer afford this indulgence. Then, as hospitals began to expand, and as they were increasingly criticized for exploiting nursing students, they began to hire graduate nurses to staff the wards. These nurses found themselves thrust back into an onerous situation reminiscent of their apprentice days, with heavy workloads and an authoritarian, hierarchical structure. In addition, wages were low and jobs insecure, dependent as they were on the hospital's census. Further, nurses' aides and practical nurses were being added to the occupational hierarchy. Nurses aides had been trained in the late 1930s by the Works Progress Administration and then by the Red Cross during World War II. When a number of graduate nurses left the hospital to serve in the military, practical nurses—who had still been doing private-duty nursing—replaced them. After the war, nurses returning to civilian hospitals found themselves sharing a stratified work force with these two groups.

Three major studies that appeared in the late 1940s had an impact on the organization of nursing labor: one by Eli Ginzberg, chairman of the Committee on the Function of Nursing (1948) (the Ginzberg Report), and the second prepared for the National Nursing Council (1948) by Esther Lucille Brown (the Brown Report). Both reports addressed the troublesome relations among registered nurses (RNs), practical nurses, and aides. Both proposed that the title of "professional nurse" be restricted to RNs and eventually to RNs with baccalaureate degrees from college and university programs. Both also agreed that each rank be assigned distinct tasks or "nursing functions," and that all would be organized into teams under the supervision of RNs. No less influential was a manual by nurse-educator Eleanor Lambertsen (1953) that became a guide to team nursing in the 1950s and the 1960s.

Despite the popularity of the team nursing concept, especially as the means to professionalize nursing, the next two decades saw yet another transformation, the introduction of "primary nursing." A new generation of nursing leaders claimed that team nursing had actually deprofessionalized nursing, and that a reunification of tasks would reprofessionalize the occupation (Brannon 1994, 104). Under this reorganization of work, RNs would no longer supervise teams of auxiliaries but would now have complete responsibility for bedside care. As illogical as it appears, the displacement of ancillary caregivers by registered nurses was launched during the 1970s, just when cost-containment was becoming a primary concern. Brannon offers a convincing explanation for this apparent anomaly. The replacement of team nursing with primary nursing, which became firmly established by the mid-1980s, did not stem simply from the drive toward professionalization. More to the point, nursing's interests coincided conveniently with those of managers. RNs were, of course, more expensive but "the differential overall was relatively narrow, and moreover, RNs could perform a wider range of nursing and nursing-related tasks without supervision" (ibid. 132). Despite the assurances contained in yet another outpouring of literature emanating from nurse-educators now promoting primary nursing, occupational autonomy and equal status with physicians remained elusive. To the contrary, not only was the workload of RNs intensified but their accountability to physicians and administrators was increased, as was paperwork:

> not only does part-time employment, common for many RNs, mitigate against continuous responsibility, but nurses work only one shift during a twenty-four hour period. Although primary nurses were formally accountable for each patient's care, in practice an "associate" nurse took care of the patient when the primary nurse was off duty. To maintain responsibility, the primary nurse was supposed to write detailed "nursing orders" in nursing care plans, so that the associate nurse could follow the primary nurse's directions. (ibid. 129)

In addition to bedside care, much of the RN's time was taken up with maintaining a worksheet (an explicit recording of the tasks required for each patient)—information to be passed on during shift report. Full responsibility also meant consulting the Kardex, a file containing the physician's medical orders, medications due, changes in treatments, diet, and so forth, as well as a current record of the care plan. Not surprisingly, "RNs were frustrated by the incongruity between the ideology of primary nursing as professional upgrading and job enrichment, and the reality of work intensification and job enlargement" (ibid. 143). Physicians remained the dominant professionals in the hospital while managers maintained bureaucratic control.

More recently, the clinical expertise demanded by specialized equipment and by more problematic chronic illnesses has led some nurses to avail themselves of advanced degrees that designate them "clinical nurse specialists" in nephrology, neurosurgery, infectious-disease control, orthopedics, etc. Combined nursing specialties, such as pediatric dialysis or pediatric immunology, reflect the growing sophistication required by developments in biotechnology. These expanded roles have increased the nurses' autonomy and made inroads on the physicians' domain. The coronary care unit is a case in point:

> Once the nurse became recognized as the essential figure in the coronary care unit, the physician increasingly deferred to her in matters related to the technical details of the unit, and to her expertise and knowledge, collaborating with her in the best interest of the patient. This new collaboration and interdependence between medicine and nursing has led to increased delegation to the nurse of authority to act in the absence of the physician, and has made it difficult to determine where the doctor's function stops and the nurse's begins. (Berwind 1975)

Obviously, this has also increased hierarchical divisions within nursing between clinical nurse specialists and ward nurses. Furthermore, by the late 1980s, auxiliaries were being reintroduced to hospital wards, and by the 1990s team nursing made a reappearance, this time under the aegis of "patient-focused care," discussed in Chapter Two.

"CORPORATIZING" HOSPITALS

In the nineteenth century, as hospitals became safe and attractive places, small for-profit hospitals sprung up in Europe and the United States. In Europe they faded from the scene as government assumed the responsibility for providing health care. By contrast, the for-profit industry flourished in the United States:

> In the early 1980s, for-profit chains were the darling of Wall Street with a 20 percent growth rate. During 1982, a recession year for most businesses, stocks of the top four hospital chains rose 30 percent. Profits of the twenty largest chains went up 38 percent in 1983 and 28.5 percent the following year. In 1984, Hospital Corporation of America's chief executive officer was the second highest paid executive in the nation, and the head of National Medical

Enterprises beat out the movie moguls as the highest paid executive in Southern California. (Dalek 1997, 198)

The open-ended system for paying hospitals and the expansion of services had made health care a lucrative investment. Ironically, having contributed to the overbuilding of hospitals, hospital corporations were in a position to take advantage of the situation. The chains' access to capital through sale of stock has enabled them to purchase financially troubled hospitals (other for-profits, public, and non-profits) and to construct new ones. In addition to the receptivity of Wall Street, there are two important forces affecting the growth of hospital chains: a change in the ideological climate with the election of President Reagan and changes in state policies to promote privatization, rationalization, and competition in health care (Estes et al., 1994).[9]

A word of explanation regarding the nomenclature of hospitals. The term "community hospital" was introduced by the American Hospital Association to denote nonfederal, acute-care institutions, regardless of their location, size, or level of care. Although Stevens, in her historical account, questions attaching the notion of "community" to the thriving market that hospitals have become, she grants that they have provided centers for training, employment, and voluntary work for community residents (1989, 137–38). And while the notion of for-profit hospitals seems antithetical to the American value of community service as originally conceived in the Hill-Burton hospital building act, it is consistent with the capitalism that propels the economy. Americans (usually from the unfortunate vantage point of a hospital bed) gradually have come to see that the business of hospitals is business.

Arnold Relman, professor of medicine at Harvard and for many years editor of the *New England Journal of Medicine*, was the first physician to warn his colleagues about the dangers of the "medical-industrial complex." His disquiet over physician and for-profit ownership of hospitals, nursing homes, kidney dialysis businesses, laboratories and pain clinics— and of the "corporatization" of medicine—has been echoed and enlarged upon by other thoughtful observers (1980).[10] Relman asserted that the small "proprietary" hospitals and clinics owned by physicians (primarily for the purpose of providing a workshop for their practices) were quite different from the vast and growing network of private corporations engaged in the business of supplying health care to serve its own entrepreneurial ends. Between 1990 and 1996, nearly 200 of the more than 5,000 not-for-profit hospitals in the United States converted to for-profit status. In 1996 alone, more than 60 not-for-profit hospitals made the switch (United States General Accounting Office 1998).

The historical distinctions between "for-profit" and "not-for-profit" status are important. "Voluntary hospitals" (the term used to denote not-for-profit, nonpublic hospitals), have received financial breaks—such as tax exemptions and access to tax-exempt bond financing—and have benefited from eligibility for federal grants and loans. Concern has been raised about the potential loss of community benefits resulting from conversions, as well as charitable groups' use of conversion proceeds for non-health-related activities. Both types of hospitals rely on surplus income to survive and grow. Nonprofits call this money "reserves" or "excess of revenue over expenditures"—funds held to cover future costs. For-profits call it "profit."

Legally, the distinction takes on greater import: Nonprofits are prohibited from "private inurement" (distribution of excess revenue), while for-profits can distribute some or all of the profit to owners. Hence, the apprehension of those who foresaw danger in the commercial trend. By 1998, a number of states had passed laws governing the sale of community hospitals, but in states where there is no oversight uncompensated care has decreased dramatically. With due regard for a businesslike, efficient management of health-care facilities, vexation over this issue centers on the implications of operating a facility funded with Wall Street dollars: Does private enterprise's attention to sales and total volume foster services that are profitable to the exclusion of those needed by the community? Starr's monumental book on the transformation of American medicine ended with discomfort over the "rise of the corporate ethos" and the decline of the ideals of professionalism and voluntary work, which previously had softened the underlying acquisitive activity. Noting that business school graduates were displacing graduates of public health schools, hospital administrators, and doctors in the top echelons of medical care organizations, Starr (1982, 448) could see that the restraint previously exercised by these ideals was growing weaker.

The ensuing years have brought a succession of consolidations that neither Relman nor Starr could have predicted. When their publications appeared in the 1980s, National Medical Care, with its network of prestigious, academically connected physicians, dominated the dialysis field and had expanded into the sale of dialysis equipment and supplies and into other types of care, such as respiratory and obesity centers. Its stock had risen from $1 a share in 1974 to $25 in 1981. Hospital Corporation of America, then the largest chain of investor-owned hospitals, owned and operated 385 hospitals in the United States and five others overseas. Its stock had risen from $1 in 1974 to $38 in 1981. Humana Corporation, by using the strategy of building doctors' offices next to their hospitals—thereby ensuring a constant flow of patients from doctors who appreciated not only the convenience but the reduced rent—was then the most profitable of all the hospital chains, with 1983 revenues of $2.3 billion from 89 hospitals.

The warnings of Relman, Starr, and their fellow prophets pale in comparison to what has followed. By the mid-1980s, for example, the author of *The Medical-Industrial Complex*, no longer needed to define his title but instead could begin with "the story of the explosive growth of . . . corporate medicine," focusing on "medical moguls," monopoly, and prescription for profit (Wohl 1984; Estes et al 1994). By the late 1990s, a series of rapid-fire acquisitions had made Columbia/HCA Healthcare (itself a merger of two conglomerates) the nation's—indeed the world's—largest health care company with 342 hospitals and other medical facilities in 36 states and Europe, and assets valued at $20.2 billion (*USA Today* 1997). In one quarter alone in 1996, Columbia/HCA reported a $364 million profit (*San Francisco Chronicle* 1996).

From its earliest days, Columbia had successfully won physicians' loyalty by wooing them with ownership interest—a way to ensure that doctors would send patients to Columbia hospitals rather than to rivals (Gottlieb and Eichenwald 1997). The company was aggressive: purchasing office buildings doctors owned or buying out their lease agreements to make it easier for them to move into company offices, which were often next to Columbia hospitals (Eichenwald 1997). Despite the questionable legality of offering referrals as incentives, Columbia/HCA Healthcare managed to remain within the law well into the 1990s. News reports lauded the genius of chairman Richard L. Scott (referred to as "the Bill Gates of health care") and of his system for grading hospital chiefs for their return on assets, profit margin, productivity, and such. According to reports, Chairman Richard L. Scott often returned scorecards to each hospital chief with handwritten comments, such as, "Good job on surgery growth" (Lagnado 1997).

Columbia/HCA's huge expansion was halted in 1997, when it became the subject of a massive federal investigation into possible Medicare fraud and Scott was replaced. The corporation announced that it would sell various holdings (a large pharmacy benefits-management company, a managed-care company, and an information-technology company), cancel $218 million worth of hospital construction projects it had planned in five cities, and review for possible cancellation projects worth between $200 million and $300 million (Sharpe and Lagnado 1997). Only after Columbia's alleged infractions started to be reported daily in the press did financial analysts begin to ask if the corporation had perhaps used tactics suitable in manufacturing but not in health care—for instance, buying up hospitals in order to close them down ("Nightly Business Report" 1997).

As is obvious from Columbia's divestiture of its holdings, in addition to the consolidation of multihospital corporations ("horizontal integration," in economic terms) there has been a simultaneous growth in the development of organizations with different levels and types of services ("vertical integration"). For example, at its height, National Medical Enterprises (formerly National Medical Care) owned hospitals, nursing homes, psychiatric hospitals, recovery centers, and rehabilitation hospitals. After it was forced to pay $380 million in fines and penalties to settle various federal and state charges of health-care fraud, it "rose from the ashes" (Meier 1997, 1), installed new management, and changed its name to Tenet Healthcare Corporation (Tenet, the second largest giant in the consolidating hospital market, was in the midst of talks of merger with Columbia, which were suspended when the latter's fraud investigation was launched.).

In addition to mergers and acquisitions, some institutions have sought innovative arrangements in order to ease the financial burden. For instance, during 1995 and 1996, the Medical University of South Carolina considered a lease agreement with Columbia/HCA. Under this agreement, the company would have purchased the hospital's equipment and then would have made annual payments for leasing the real property, academic support, capital improvements, and research centers. Furthermore, the company was to operate the facility, retaining all profits after making the prescribed payments to the university. The proposed agreement was delayed due to a legal challenge from a competing medical group, which, coupled with strategic questions raised by Columbia/HCA's problems, effectively halted implementation.

In an even more surprising development, two renowned institutions— the University of California San Francisco (UCSF) and Stanford hospitals— combined in 1997, after two years of planning and negotiations. Both entities (and their satellites) were governed by a private nonprofit corporation called UCSF-Stanford Health Care. Much of the debate on this marriage had centered on the fact that UCSF hospital is unionized and public while Stanford hospital is nonunion and private. Critics objected, for example, to Stanford's insistence that the new corporation be exempt from public-meeting laws and other forms of public accountability. California legislators finally effected a compromise whereby the new hospital would hold public meetings and make records public. Collective bargaining or other contract negotiations, sale of property, pending lawsuits and the terms of health care contracts, however, remained private. Academic leaders at both universities "reasoned that by combining resources, they could avoid duplication of costly capital projects, and could negotiate more favorable deals with health plans for complex care such as cancer treatment and organ transplants" (Russell 1997).

Two years into the merger, it was revealed that UCSF Stanford Health Care had finished its fiscal year with an $86 million operating loss, attributed in no small part to Medicare funding cuts and the changing nature of the health care market. Stanford trustees were calling for separate accounting and management of the respective hospitals. Attempts to consolidate medical departments to cut costs had met opposition from competing faculty chiefs. The two top executives of the merged entity resigned and a consulting group with a cut-and-slash-reputation was hired as interim management. Within months, Stanford announced its withdrawal from the merger. The process of dissolution began—expected to cost "as much as $40 million in one-time charges and $25 million a year afterward" (Russell 1999, A20).

Thus have the exigencies of the marketplace created turmoil and blurred the traditional distinction between public and private:

> Given the long-term historical role of the private, nonprofit sector in the U.S. health and social services since the earliest days of the Republic and the rapid organizational changes of the 1980s, vertical and horizontal integration have blurred boundaries between the heretofore distinct nonprofit and for-profit health-care sectors. For-profit entities have nonprofit subsidiaries, and vice versa, and conceptual and structural complexities have multiplied, rendering impossible the simple differentiation of *public* from *private*. (Estes et al. 1994, 6)

Increasingly, financial reporters are paying attention to the trend among nonprofits to trim indigent services, market themselves, pay hospital-based physicians for their "productivity," and generally to seek higher margin lines in much the way the for-profits do (Langley 1997).

CONCLUSION

In sum, the professional dominance physicians historically enjoyed within the hospital has gradually been chipped away. Not only are nurses more knowledgeable and, in some cases, more assertive, but there is now a vast army of health-care professionals with whom the physician shares the stage: technical specialists in encephalography, echocardiography, nuclear medicine, and the like on whom the physician relies for diagnosis; respiratory and physical therapists who carry out the doctor's general directions but consider themselves professionals with specialized skills; bioengineers who are responsible for keeping machines calibrated and maintained; purchase managers who question the purchase of equipment formerly requisitioned relatively freely. Reflecting the ever-growing complexity of the contemporary hospital are two additional factors: the increasing presence of business-school graduates at the administrative and business level and the expansion of companies selling software on everything from cost-figuring to Medicare billing and in-house record keeping. The increased complexity of hospital organization has created a ripe field for outside consultants. Large management consulting firms and national accounting firms now have health and medical divisions and, as one reporter has noted in an article about health specialization of lawyers, "merger mania in the health care industry may not do much for patients, but it's working wonders for the legal profession" (Holding 1995). As Stevens has written,

> there is growing array of new communities—vested interests, with diverse purposes, in constant conflict. The idea of a hospital as the embodiment of medical expertise has given way to the exercise of monopoly power by numerous groups. Hospital management and planning become the outcome of a continuing process of bargaining, negotiation, and consensus-building among differing points of view, both inside and outside the institution. (Stevens 1989, 142)

Without question, the huge expansion of managed care has abetted this transformation. But even before managed care, the mushrooming of the U.S. health care arena in the last century mirrored the capitalist system that guides the economy. Capitalism, praised by George Will as "an enveloping culture of restless striving by individuals broadly emancipated from constraints on seeking the satisfaction of their multiplying appetites" (1997, A27), has a darker side in which it can be predicted that "multiplying appetites" will, at times, be at odds with the traditional medical code of "First, do no harm." Some of the means to impose a diet on the health care arena are discussed in the next chapter. Some have yet to be devised.

NOTES

1. For a social history of American hospitals, *see* Rosen (1963); Rosner (1982); Rosenberg (1987); Stevens (1989); Starr (1982); Brown (1979).
2. For an excellent history of the evolution of medical education, *see* Ludmerer (1985).
3. Robert Toomey, quoted in: "Traditional hospital medical staff structure may be doomed" (1993).
4. For a social history of Blue Cross, *see* Miller (1997). Rothman (1991) also cites the essays in the *Journal of Health Politics, Policy and Law*, 16 (1991) for "an insightful history of Blue Cross which focuses on New York but takes the story well beyond that."
5. See Marmor (1996). Marmor (1973) presents an instructive analysis of this subject. *See also* Hirshfield (1970) and Numbers (1978)
6. The term "halfway technologies" appeared originally in a 1972 report of the Panel on Biological Medical Science of the President's Science Advisory Committee but was popularized by Lewis Thomas (1974).
7. Regarding this relationship, Brannon cites three excellent sources: Melosh (1982); Reverby (1987); and Ashley (1976).
8. For a humorous account that chides nurses for their complicity in the continuation of an imbalance in power, see Allen, Brady, and Vonfrolio (1995).

For a review of the literature on role conflicts between nurses and physicians and on the nature of physician-nurse interaction, *see* McMahan, Hoffman, and McGee (1994). *See also* Kramer (1974).

9. *See also* Estes (1990) and Schlesinger, Marmor, and Smithe (1987).

10. Some say the concept was first introduced by Ehrenreich and Ehrenreich (1971). Salmon (1990) says that the term was coined by Robb Burlage in 1967 for Health PAC. For thoughtful assessments of this subject see Estes et al. (1984), Ginzberg (1988), Gray (1983), and Light (1986).

2

The Arrival of the Era of Accountability
Rationalization, Regulation, and Restructuring

There is a certain relief in change, even though it be from bad to worse, as I have found in traveling in a stage-coach, that it is often a comfort to shift one's position and be bruised in a new place.

—*Washington Irving*

Aesculapius, in Greek mythology the god of healing, is represented in art as a strong, earnest youth bearing a serpent-entwined staff. A legacy of the "first physician" is the survival of this staff, in modified form, as a symbol of health—at one time the emblem of the United States Department of Health, Education and Welfare. The goddess of health in Greek mythology is Hygeia, Aesculapius' daughter, whose staying power is indicated by her survival of her name in the word "hygiene." Much less importance in Greek mythology, however, is given to Aesculapius' sister, Panacea, the goddess who personified the cure-all. Can we assume that the ancient Greeks, in their wisdom, were acknowledging the elusiveness of a panacea?

To some extent, the history of American health care represents a search for one panacea after another—a patchwork of "cures" for what ails the system—related in no small part to American optimism and the value Americans place on technological progress and on the expertise required to apply technology. At times, this has led health policy leaders to assume, erroneously, that movement is necessarily progress; it has, moreover, led them as well to place their confidence in the newest expertise available. In the latter half of the twentieth century, the result has been an emphasis on the engineering (and re-engineering!) of the hospital organization, as well as a firm belief that computer-generated information will provide hospitals with the "facts" they need to be accountable. The direction taken in the health care arena is also a function of American pluralism. Many attempts to order health-care delivery have been obstructed by the federal structure of U.S. government, resulting in unequal distribution of benefit among states, counties, and cities. As a continent of considerable size, variation in geography, population, traditions, values and attitudes inevitably prevail, and are reflected in clashes of interest, and the power of interest groups.[1] Furthermore, in keeping with the American economic system, the philosophy of free enterprise and the profit motive have exerted a forceful influence, creating a highly competitive and complex private health care structure existing together with the public structure.

The changes in health care financing noted in Chapter One—the emergence of health insurance in the 1930s, the Hill-Burton hospital construction program in the 1940s, the enactment of Medicare and Medicaid in the 1960s—had a profound effect on the evolution of American health care. Subsequently, changes in the law—the demise of charitable immunity, the birth of the corporate negligence doctrine and the malpractice crises of the mid 1970s and early 1980s—intensified hospitals' interest in policing the work of the physicians who practiced within them (Jost 1995). Furthermore, structural changes—the growth of hospital conglomerates, the enlarged role of employers as health-benefit payers, the burgeoning of managed care, and the increased replacement of sole medical practice with the physician-as-employee—have undercut the luxury of self-regulation. Finally, the rising cost of health care has motivated consumer groups to join economists, health policy reformers, and major insurance purchasers (industry and government) in the call for more regulatory programs.

A variety of interested parties, public and private, now oversee hospitals, of which only the main agencies and programs are discussed in this chapter. Each panacean development has contributed to arena growth in the form of vast mechanics for financing, administrative overhead, and the expenditure of energy, resources, and money. Administrative personnel in hospitals have an appreciation of these factors only to the extent that enforcement of specific directives affects their work—the average hospital worker less so. But that the attempts to rationalize and regulate health-care decision making exerts an impact on all hospital personnel, and most significantly on patients, is without doubt.

REGULATORY ATTEMPTS TO RATIONALIZE DECISION MAKING

Technology Assessment

Congress created the Office of Technology Assessment (OTA) in 1972 as an advisory arm. OTA was expected to help legislators anticipate the consequences of technological change and examine the impact of technology on people's lives. Although the agency undertook studies on a host of areas—from energy to genetics to space—a significant portion of OTA's research centered on biomedical technology.

Articles on the demise of this agency twenty-three years later emphasize its inadequate funding: about $23 million annually. One commentator belittled the amount as "a tiny fraction of a percent of the federal budget (equal to the income tax contribution of 4,000 average taxpayers)." (Susman 1996, 154). Another reports the figure as $22 million, contrasting it with "the $2.3 billion budgeted this year for Congressional salaries, buildings, and assorted operations" (Greenberg 1995, 171). Considered Congress's own think tank, the OTA was respected by elements of the scientific and health policy community as,

> a rare instrument of scholarly enlightenment in the grubby realm of politics. With a staff of about 180, OTA's reports, 20–30 a year, are written in-house after consultations with specialists who are considered among the most knowledgeable, whether from the U.S. or abroad. An earned reputation for density is the bane of OTA literature, while a dedication to comprehensiveness has sometimes taken precedence over timely enlightenment for legislative purposes. A 2-year gestation is not unusual for an OTA report. (ibid.)

Faced with closure under the budget-cutting determination of the Republican congressional majority, OTA's defenders argued that it may have saved far more money than it cost to operate. One example was the 1989 proposal to screen elderly Americans for high cholesterol.

> "Everyone was in favor of screening," recalls Clyde Behney, who headed the OTA's health education, and environment division. "Health organizations wanted it; congressmen wanted it; the elderly wanted it. Yet when we analyzed what was involved we realized that not only was screening going to cost taxpayers $5 billion in Medicare funds, we also could not show that such screening would result in any health benefit to the elderly." The result: Congress turned down legislation to fund screening. (Susman 1996, 154)

For the critics, Jerry Taylor, an environmental resources expert at the Cato Institute in Washington, D.C., commented, "To suggest that the OTA could provide some service that could not be produced through academic research groups, independent think tanks such as RAND, the Brookings Institute, the American Enterprise Institute and the National Academy of Sciences, the National Institutes of Health, the Government Accounting office, the Congressional Research Service, and the Congressional Budget Office is just laughable." On the other hand, there were those who were indignant at the demise of the agency, for instance Peter Montague, editor of *Rachel's Environment and Health Weekly*: "The loss of the OTA simply means that Congress is going to be dumber than it used to be—if you can imagine that." What may have hurt the OTA was its lack of recognition among the rank-and-file members of Congress, as shown by a Senate aide: "If you polled members of Congress about what the OTA accomplished, most of them would just stare blankly—if they even knew the office existed" (ibid. 155).

Equally dedicated to evaluating novel biomedical technology—thereby rationalizing decisions about appropriate use—was the National Center for Health Care Technology (NCHCT), established in the 1970s within the Public Health Service. This agency, too, received paltry funding and was dismantled by the Reagan administration. Replacing it was the Office of Health Technology Assessment (OHTA), with even less financial support. The Institute of Medicine (IOM) had argued forcefully for technology assessment, saying that its absence had resulted in the employment of ineffective, costly, and occasionally harmful interventions. The IOM credited OHTA with $200 in Medicare savings accrued for each $1 spent on the program. OHTA supporters point out that assessments were the bases for coverage of such beneficial technologies as liver, lung, and heart-lung transplantation, laparoscopic cholecystectomy, and magnetic resonance angiography, as well as the Medicare initiative that provided coverage for a trial of lung volume reduction surgery for emphysema. OHTA (renamed the Center for Health Technology) continued to operate in the 1990s but with a greatly reduced staff (Holohan 1996). Assessments for Medicare and the Department of Defense programs remain within its purview—a large scope but more circumscribed than the original intent of both the OTA and the NCHCT.

Health Systems Agencies

Another notable rationalization attempt was The National Health Planning and Resources Development Act, which was passed in 1974. It established some 200 health systems agencies (HSAs) across the country, which were to serve as a restraining hand on profligate spending.

Unfortunately, in many areas HSAs generated more heat than reason. Regulatory strength relied on the enactment of state certificate-of-need (CON) laws, which required that the state agency review and approve investments in new health facilities (except doctors' offices), services, and expensive equipment. Not surprisingly, since HSAs were composed of providers (physicians and hospital administrators) and consumers, most became controversial forums. Fights emerged over which hospital should enlarge its plant, which should purchase a computed tomography (CT) scanner, and so forth. In a number of situations, legal cases ensued which then lumbered their way through the courts. Certificate-of-need control of large technologies essentially fell by the wayside:

At present this strategy is in great jeopardy because it was simply too costly to obtain creditable information with which to limit the distribution of big new technologies. Information about the supply, use, and costs of special equipment and services was reported as sketchy, and consistent review standards were viewed as virtually nonexistent. Thus, the goal of direct technology control is being dropped in several states in which it was attempted. (Moloney and Rogers 1979, 1415)

Raising another issue, Tannen speaks to the "myth of consumer control" of HSAs. The requirement that all planning agencies were to have a majority of consumers on their boards did not lead to consumer domination.

Consumer members are not a homogeneous group; included in this category are insurance companies, business and labor organizations, public officials, and community leaders. Although "consumers" technically constitute a majority on HSA boards, grassroots community representatives are a minority which moreover lacks the technical experience or financial support that other representatives (consumer or provider) have; they are therefore less powerful. (Tannen 1990, 29; Marmor and Monroe 1979)

Nevertheless, HSAs accomplished one aspect of their mandate. Between 1970 and 1988, the number of hospitals in the United States decreased by 10 percent even though the population had grown by 21.5 percent. "For ten years, the health system agencies had put so much pressure on hospitals that many had been forced to merge or close, usually, those that were the least 'cost-efficient' because they served disproportionate numbers of uninsured or underinsured poor patients. At that point, the CON process reached a point of diminishing returns" (Leyerle 1994, 50). This underscores the point made above—that federally determined criteria stressed how well the agencies contained health costs, not how effectively they dealt with the local problems of access, quality, or health status. In 1981 the health planning act was repealed.

Professional Standards Review Organizations

Where HSAs erected barriers to independent decision making on the part of hospitals, professional standards review organizations (PSROs)—established in 1972 by amendment to the Social Security Act—took a more aggressive look at medical decision making.

PSROs were expected to control cost *and* regulate quality by making the medical profession responsible for the "appropriate use" of health resources and facilities. Local medical societies or other groups of physicians, supported by federal funds, were to review the records of discharged Medicare patients to determine whether care was medically necessary, of recognized quality, and provided in the proper facility or level of intervention. PSROs soon found this beyond their grasp. "Peer assessment of quality care" became enmeshed in a thicket of controversy over what defined "quality." More attainable was the goal of reviewing cases to determine whether a diagnosed problem justified hospital admission and length of stay, called "utilization review."

This regulatory program was supposed to identify and sanction physicians who overused services. "Using the term 'peer' to describe those who carry out the review process was a vain attempt to placate doctors who were accustomed to exercising autonomy in their work: the reviewers were usually lower-level personnel, such as nurses" (ibid. 52). A QA/I professional interviewed in my research who had worked for a PSRO became disheartened by the ineffective response to discoveries of egregious care. She recalled, "You could recommend sanction after a long, detailed process of evaluation or you could send the doctor a letter saying, 'Hey, that was lousy.' There wasn't much in between."

One aspect of PSRO work foreshadowed subsequent problems with establishing practice guidelines (discussed in Chapter Three). More than 100,000 individual criteria sets were developed by hospitals to measure the quality and appropriateness of hospital care for patients with heart attacks. "Such criteria were developed by committees of physicians (3 to 7 per committee) who spent 1 to 2 hours in each of 2 to 3 meetings developing them. Multiplying these numbers means that 2 million physician-hours (100,000 × 5 physicians × 2 hours × 2 meetings) were spent at $50/h, or $100 million, in developing practice guidelines, or appropriateness standards, for patients with heart attacks" (Brook 1989, 3029–30).

The Reagan administration tried to phase out the $174 million program, hoping that government withdrawal of support would convince private business and insurers to take on the responsibility. Instead, legislation was enacted in 1982 reducing the number of PSROs by consolidating geographic areas. In keeping with the deregulatory philosophy of the Reagan years, Medicare oversight became privatized, with organizations vying for government contracts in each state.

Along with this change came a new title, Utilization and Quality Control Peer Review Organizations (PROs), and new entrepreneurial opportunities. Many PROs not only have benefited from government contracts but have increased their power by soliciting and obtaining contracts from businesses and insurers to review non-Medicare patients' utilization of hospital services. An important aspect of the new PRO role was the enlargement of its purview. Hospitals and physicians were now required by the Health Care Financing Administration (HCFA) to cooperate with PROs as a condition of participation in and reimbursement by Medicare. Each PRO has worked out its own criteria.[2]

Generally, the reviews of Medicare oversight in the 1980s are mixed. According to one expert, at the height of the PRO program in the late 1980s, "the hospital records of one out of every four Medicare discharges were reviewed by PRO reviewers and over one hundred doctors were sanctioned because of quality concerns" (Jost 1995, 832; 1989). Others strongly disagree with this assessment of the program's merits. A QA/I coordinator interviewed in my research said, "looking at isolated cases is like looking for a grain of sand in a sand castle." Two government policy experts concurred, proclaiming, "A growing body of research shows that physician review of hospital medical records to determine quality of care has only modest reliability. . . . Actions by PROs based primarily on such reviews tend to lead to acrimonious disagreements that diminish the chance that physicians will accept or learn from them" (Jencks and Wilensky 1992, 900; Goldman 1992; Rubin et al. 1992).

Although comparing physicians in the same specialty in the same institution was sometimes helpful, one quality analyst recalled, "You can imagine the diplomatic skills of the individuals given the responsibility of presenting that data." As a result, the HCFA decided to reshape its Medicare review by replacing a police posture with an assessment of trends and patterns that would shape clinical practice. A recommendation to this effect by the Institute of Medicine (Lohr 1990) dovetailed with the trend in health care to adopt models from American industry that stress improving processes rather than using inspection to search out "bad apples" (discussed in Chapter Three). The new approach, the Health Care Quality Improvement Initiative (HCQII), began in 1993. Henceforth, PROs would change from watchdogs to collaborative resources. Two data systems were to be used. One was the National Claims History (NCH) file, a system of bill-payment records comprising all claims paid by Medicare (physician, hospital, home health, and outpatient) and containing more than 1 billion line items a year. The other was the Uniform Clinical Data Set (UCDS), which contained detailed clinical information on a 10 percent sample of discharged patients, describing their demographic characteristics, history, findings, and treatment. UCDS, which was initiated in 1989, uses algorithms—i.e., rules of procedure or sets of instructions, providing conditional logic for solving a problem or accomplishing a task (U.S. Department of Health and Human Services 1995). HCFA had two purposes in mind for this system: as medical records were abstracted, a large data base of clinically meaningful information would be created and, at the same time, algorithms would flag cases for review. An expert in the arena, when interviewed in 1993, described the results as follows:

It didn't work very well because the number of data elements was really large and enormously burdensome cost-wise. It was taking anywhere from 45 minutes to an hour to abstract your average medical record. Also there were a lot of issues around which elements are meaningful and necessary. The algorithms were giving high false positive rates for physician review. They were costing a fortune in cases going to physicians that were then determined to not be a quality issue. Retrospectively, I think it's not surprising that the UCDS was not going to work. The idea of having algorithms that would address any type of medical and surgical problem that might be a reason for admissions to a hospital was a pretty hefty undertaking.

By 1995, HCQII had evolved into the Health Care Quality Improvement Program (HCQIP). Bruce Vladeck, Director of HCFA, announced that HCQIP's goal was to stimulate the creative involvement of physicians in quality improvement activities. "This redirection also emphasizes quality measures based on practice guidelines and parameters rather than the more subjective judgments of individual physicians reviewing individual cases" (Vladeck 1994, 1896). Hospitals were told that a new system, called Medicare Quality Indicator System (MQIS), was replacing the UCDSS. Director Vladeck promised:

> When mature, MQIS will include quality indicators for access, appropriateness, outcomes, and patient satisfaction. It will cover preventive, acute, and chronic services in both fee-for-service and managed care settings. . . . The MQIS will profile patterns of care based on practice guidelines sponsored by medical specialty societies or the Public Health Service's Agency for Health Care Policy and Research. When guidelines are unavailable, indicators will be based on expert consensus. (ibid.)

HCFA awarded contracts to two private organizations, referred to as Clinical Data Abstraction Centers (CDACS), leaving each PRO the choice of utilizing this data service for state projects or requesting specific categories of records from hospitals on its own. In the words of a PRO representative, the procedure is "warm and fuzzy":

> We design projects that are based on evidence-based or consensus guidelines and then we market it to the hospitals. It's all voluntary. We solicit the hospitals to collaborate on the projects. Once they agree to do that, then we use the claims data to select their cases for that particular project. For instance, one of our projects is antibiotic treatment for community acquired pneumonia. We have a formula for deciding what the sample size needs to be and we select the cases, send the record request to the hospital. They copy the records and send them to us. We pay for photocopies, we do all the work free. We do the abstraction, and the analysis, put together a packet with the feedback information and then send it back to them and follow up appropriately—present information to their staff or answer any questions, explain it. We are funded by HCFA to do this.

Hospitals are now given 30 days to provide the records—as one QA/I coordinator put it, enough time to "clean" the records; that is, to make sure everything is well documented and all loose reports (radiology, laboratory, electrocardiogram, etc.) are incorporated. The same PRO representative underscored the contrast to the past:

> There's nothing punitive. If they don't send us the charts in 30 days, it's not like in the old review where we would deny the cost of the claim. This is supposed to be a collaborative process and we want them to have the time to get the records to us. The more records they can get, the better the sample.

Studies have covered such indicators as the rate of preoperative antibiotic prophylaxis for major joint (hip and knee) replacement; the prevalence of advance directives in the medical records of patients and the impact of this variable on the number of invasive procedures performed; and the use of anticoagulation medication for chronic atrial fibrillation. The labor expense required to pull the charts (and clean them!) is borne by the hospital, but those that are sincerely bent on improving care are provided with greater insight into appropriate and inappropriate treatment. As this system has settled in, shared understanding of the feasible has evolved. By 1998, a QA/I specialist described it as follows:

> What they do now is studies on the major things that HCFA finds are costly for Medicare patients. So they had about 11 studies, that will be cut down to about 5 that they'll be concentrating on. Basically their studies are retrospective chart review on issues that have either newer or more controversial kinds of changes in practice. And almost all of them center on medications because that's something that they can apparently abstract pretty easily. For instance, the literature will say that patients with congestive heart failure should have certain kinds of medications. So they'll survey a database, and say the state has 25% of people doing this, and the literature says it should be 50%, and your hospital is doing only 10%. This is supposed to clue you in that maybe you'd like to do an improvement project. Which indeed we have in regard to aspirin and myocardial infarctions (MIs)—heart attacks in laymen terms. We worked on that and put it on a pre-printed order so that it didn't get lost or forgotten, which was what was happening. When the patient passed from the ER doctor to a cardiologist, the cardiologist would think that the ER doctor had already done that and the ER doctor, in the haste to take care of the acute MI, hadn't. So they met and came to some conclusion of who would take the responsibility.

Clearly, there are pros and cons to each system. When HCQII began in 1993, a noteworthy paper documented the review of 50 cases of serious medical errors identified by California's PRO under the old system (Feldman and Rundall 1993). The senior author was uniquely qualified to undertake such a review, having served as medical director of the San Francisco PSRO, subsequently California Medical Review Inc. This analysis identified significant barriers to effective collaboration between hospital medical staffs and PROs. The paper listed: (1) a lack of collegial interaction between hospital management and medical staff, (2) delays of weeks—even months—in completing medical records, (3) a disclaimer on the part of hospital administrators and their attorneys of responsibility for medical error or negligence, and (4) a defensiveness on the part of medical staffs with regard to any action or procedure performed by physician colleagues and called into question—even in situations of unequivocally poor performance. The authors found that "hospitals have failed to identify and act upon episodes suggestive (or in some cases clearly indicative) of iatrogenic injury at their time of occurrence" (ibid. 146). They warned that the new PRO approach, replacing case-by-case review in favor of pattern analysis (called "trending" in the arena) would leave identification and correction of poor quality of care primarily in the hands of hospital peer review committees, adding: "In our judgment, hospital peer review as it is currently practiced is not an effective means of identifying and correcting quality of care problems" (ibid.). The authors concluded with a strong statement: "In the hospitals included in our review, a gap has appeared between the intent to provide adequate care and the reality of that care" (ibid.). PROs defend the current system by claiming that it makes more of an impact on physicians by not being punitive.

Another part of HCQIP consists of national projects, the first of which was launched in 1991. Called the Cardiovascular Cooperative Project (CCP), it was an attempt to reach consensus on appropriate treatment for patients suffering from acute myocardial infarction (AMI). For these patients, hospitals were required to report use and prompt timing of aspirin, beta blockers, and Angiotensin-Converting Enzyme (ACE) inhibitors, and avoidance of calcium channel blockers in cases of left ventricular systolic dysfunction. Eventually, hospitals and medical staff would be held accountable for deviations. A national steering committee was convened, with staff from HCFA and The American Medical Association as joint chairs. This committee comprised more than 35 physicians, health service researchers, and others representing many physician specialty groups and other health care organizations (Lambert et al. 1994). Their charge was to identify the elements that should be abstracted from the record, what the algorithms should cover, and how the information should be compiled. After much deliberation and review, a document emerged, containing 10 clinical indicators of AMI care derived from American College of Cardiology and American Hospital Association guidelines. Pilot projects were initiated in four states—Alabama, Connecticut, Iowa, and Wisconsin—and information was gathered on 16,124 AMI discharges from June 1992 through February 1993. The two companies that had been employed as data abstraction centers collected and processed information from medical records and sent the raw data to HCFA.

PROs began to receive the first installments of data on this project in the fall of 1995, enabling them to make presentations to hospitals through seminars, individual meetings, telephone conference calls, and letter campaigns. Thomas Marciniak, a physician and HCFA's chief clinical advisor for CCP, lauded the improvements in the process of AMI care in an interview, presenting as evidence a 10 percent relative reduction in mortality and reduced length of stay. He announced a "positive trend" in the nation but even he had to admit the difficulty of attributing improvement to any one source. He explained: "What has to be determined is what caused the improvement—CCP? National Institutes of Health? Drug companies? Professional societies? Others trying to improve quality of care?" ("Preliminary CCP results . . . " 1997, 2)

Three years later, the enormous challenge of influencing physician practice was underscored by a study of the use of ACE inhibitor therapy in patients discharged after acute myocardial infarctions. Researchers reported that even though prescription of ACE inhibitors (as recommended in the guidelines of the American College of Cardiology / American Heart Association) increased from 25 percent in 1994 to 38.7 percent in 1996, less than half of the patients most in need of the drug were discharged with this life-saving therapy (Barron et al. 1998).

Thus far, the CCP is the only project that is nationally mandated. Other national projects have been developed—for instance, one on congestive heart failure—but hospitals have the option of not participating. Under HCFA's "Sixth Scope of Work" (launched in late 1999), PROs will convene expert panels, develop the clinical abstraction tool, and put together a compendium of best practices. The emphasis on performance improvement is symbolized in yet another name change: PROs, formerly PSROs, have been renamed QIOs by HCFA—designating their role as Quality Improvement Organizations. Since hospital participation in studies is voluntary, marketing of the QIO "product" is a significant component of their operation.

RATIONALIZING THROUGH PROSPECTIVE
PAYMENT: DIAGNOSIS-RELATED GROUPS

The Social Security amendments of 1972 set limits for the first time on the fees that would be reimbursed under Medicare. But previous attempts to rationalize health care decisions pale in comparison with the impact of the 1982 Tax Equity and Fiscal Responsibility Act (TEFRA), which adopted a Medicare/Medicaid reimbursement system based on "diagnosis-related groups (DRGs)." Despite assurances that the "processes of patient care in terms of quality and cost are inextricably linked" (Fetter et al. 1977, 146), the major goal of the new system was to tighten the efficiency of hospital care by reducing unnecessary costs via better accounting systems, better organizational arrangements, and more responsible and astute management. The system identified six factors as most closely associated with hospital use and clustered them into DRG categories: primary and secondary diagnoses, surgery (if any), age, sex, and presence of complications. The official title of the program, Prospective Payment System (PPS), signals its purpose: to set limits on how much hospitals would be paid for each DRG, based on statistical averages of the services that are delivered to a patient in each diagnostic category. The amount paid is based on the average cost of treating a particular condition and DRG into which a discharge is classified, regardless of the number of services received or the length of the patient's stay. The incentives of this program are clear: profit rewards for hospitals that provide services below the DRG rate and serious overruns for those that exceed it.

The DRG scheme stemmed from a marriage of econometric analysis and computer capability and was devised to delineate "case mix," that is, "a way of defining a hospital's 'product' or output by identifying clinically homogeneous groups of patients that utilize similar 'bundles' of treatments, tests and services" (Hospital Research and Educational Trust 1981). Researchers at the Yale University Center for Health Studies developed the system in the late 1960s and early 1970s. Initially, their aim was modest: The definition and categorizing of case types was intended as a tool for utilization review and quality assurance applications (Coburn and Harper 1983). Very soon, however, the Yale researchers were offering their scheme as a means of comparing the consumption of resources and the costs of care among different institutions. Finally, their mission was enlarged to include hospital budgeting (cost finding, projection, and control) and some of the originators began to promote the system overseas. As they argued, under the traditional structure of a U.S. hospital, no department is responsible for assuring that individual patients are financially well managed. In contrast to prevailing costing mechanisms—which did not permit a physician to make the connection between the way he or she is treating a certain patient and pounds of laundry per day or raw food costs per meal—the Yale researchers proposed a means of enlightening doctors on the financial implications of their medical decision-making (Thompson et al. 1979). No longer would the administrator be alone in concern for hospital finances. Armed with information on the cost and value of any kind of case that might be delivered, "meaningful dialogue among clinicians, administrators, planners, and regulators can proceed in rationalizing of observed differences" (Fetter et al. 1980, 22). (Provided, of course, that clinicians are as interested as the other parties in availing themselves of this information or, for that matter, are convinced of its relevance to their clinical decisions.)

In 1980, the state of New Jersey picked up the DRG system as a means of prospective billing for all third-party payers, after a disappointing trial with various regulatory cost-control methods. According to a nurse-educator closely involved with the New Jersey experience, the Yale research provided the immediate impetus for the state's transition to case-mix billing. After dividing the range of diagnostic codes into broad disease areas, the developers decided to use length of stay (LOS) as a predictive measure since it was not only an important indicator of utilization, but was "*easily available*, well standardized, and reliable" (ibid. Emphasis added). Shaffer's explanation of this decision portrays the state of the art in the 1980s. Actual costs would have been an ideal measure. "If, for example, a nurse paid $22,000 annually works with a patient fifteen minutes using equipment worth X dollars, and administering X drugs, an ideal accounting system could account precisely for the dollar amount assigned to such treatment" (1983, 391). Such data did not exist, and the practical implementation of the program was perceived as too urgent to await the computer capability that could spew them out.

Despite objections from critics who felt evaluation of the DRG experiment in New Jersey and other selected pilot states was far from definitive, the scheme became part of the Social Security amendments of 1983, after a brief consideration. In the federal plan, however, the appeals process, which in New Jersey created a backlog of rate adjustment cases, was eliminated. Appeals were left to state discretion. Also, each region's DRG rates are adjusted by the market-basket index, which takes into account the area's salaries, cost of living, and other related factors. Furthermore, the rates are updated annually to reflect changes in the diagnostic codes within each DRG as well as any market-basket changes.

First, they were the impetus for installation of the Computer-Based Patient Record (CPR), now called the Electronic Patient Record (EPR), since assignment of principal and secondary diagnoses cannot be done manually with any degree of efficiency. Second, they offered potential insight regarding operating costs.

DRGs became the catalyst for the business transformation of hospitals. In the early stages of its implementation, I interviewed a hospital budget analyst, who extolled: "DRGs give us reason and justification for something that should have been done long ago. For the first time, every institution will know what its unit costs are (e.g., how much per type of surgery, or how much per type of disease)."

In ironical juxtaposition to Aesculapius' mission of healing (noted at the beginning of this chapter), a small Trojan horse or a slight Achilles heel had entered the city of health professionals in the form of a new business lexicon. Addressing the American Hospital Association's 1983 annual convention, a hospital management consultant made a persuasive case for the new payment plan, explaining that henceforth the key to operating profitably will be to manage a hospital along "product lines." (Lest readers be confused by this language, the journalist who reported on this speech explained that the hospitals' "products" are discharged patients) (Wallace 1983, 56). Emphasizing the vital role of physicians in controlling resources under DRGs, the consultant said that an administrator must have data in hand before asking a physician to change his or her practice patterns. His advice:

> Start by asking which DRGs represent the highest volume of Medicare admissions. Of the high volume DRG admissions, which ones are the most and least profitable? . . . Take a look at the least profitable DRGs and ask which physicians are admitting this group of patients. Here you start to see the big spread in the practice patterns of some of the physicians on your staff. . . . Compare the high-cost physicians' length-of-stay patterns with national averages. Look at how your physicians use ancillary services. And look at whether these doctors are treating highly severe cases compared with other patients in the DRG. Then you'll have something to talk about because you'll know where the money is going and why. (ibid.)

It was clear at the outset that DRG data would be subject to inaccuracies. The project director of an experimental project on DRGs told the audience at the 1983 AHA convention that her group found that about 20 percent of the patients in this project had been grouped into the wrong DRG. The discrepancies arose from: (1) the medical-records personnel relied on discharge data rather than on the patient's full record; (2) the physician was too late in providing the medical information; or (3) medical records personnel were not trained in how to classify the data (ibid.). Teaching physicians how to document for optimum reimbursement remains important, as do hiring adequate staff and teaching them to be proficient at DRG coding. The multitude of advertisements in healthcare journals for accounting firms and computer programs that address this issue reflect this continuing problem. And a consulting industry has arisen devoted to assisting hospitals on the most beneficial DRG use. "Software programs with names like Optimizer and Strategist offer hospitals a step-by-step guide to exacting everything they can claim under the DRG system" (Lagnado 1997, B2). One quality analyst I interviewed described a "DRG options training course" she took in 1997 (well after the instigation of the system) and the subsequent job assigned to her. Although "horribly labor-intensive," the hospital found it necessary for three analysts to do concurrent review of every Medicare patient to "make sure that complications—any kind of dehydration, blood loss, anemia, those kinds of things—are actually written in the chart, just those little kinds of things that you know the doctor is meaning but he may not be writing." She explained further: "You know how hospitals always say, 'my hospital is different because our patients are sicker?' The data do not show that for our hospital and it's just because we're not taking credit for the right kinds of documentation."

More worrisome than inaccuracies is the potential for maneuvering within the system. Donald Simborg, a policy-oriented physician, warned early on that hospitals would deliberately adjust their reporting to achieve a more advantageous reimbursement and that the practice of "optimizing" discharge-abstract reporting would be worked into computer programs—prophesies that have proven abundantly true. In a landmark editorial, he called this phenomenon "DRG creep":

> There are legitimate medical vagaries and uncertainties in many diagnostic situations. When does abdominal pain and duodenal scarring on an upper-gastrointestinal-tract series become the more costly 'probable duodenal ulcer'? When does 'probable transient ischemic attack' become the much more costly 'possible stroke'? . . . Minor diagnostic nuances and slight imprecisions of wording have little practical clinical importance, yet under DRG reimbursement they would have major financial consequences. (1981, 1603–4)

The practice of upgrading the seriousness of a medical condition now has an official label, "upcoding," and by 1997 it was sufficiently worrisome to warrant an investigation by the Department of Health and Human Service's Office of the Inspector General. A New York health-care consultant described upcoding as "a sport" for hospitals, adding "every hospital does it, or they die" (Lagnado 1997, B2). In a cost-cutting move, the government had scrapped its contracts with PROs to do Medicare review in 1993. Subsequently, Simborg's examples of DRG creep have taken on much larger proportions. For example, Columbia-Presbyterian Medical Center, in its monthly column on the "DRG of the Month," described how to document malnutrition in a patient with a bleeding ulcer: "Treating the ulcer alone pays only $15,705 under a DRG 155, the item noted. Bringing in a nutrition consultant to document malnutrition—'severe, mild, moderate, or protein-calorie related'—and the charge becomes DRG 154: $34,114" (ibid.). While the term "upcoding" implies manipulation, "good coding," as a manager of a Medical Record Department explained to me, is critical to the reporting and analysis of clinical data. She makes an impressive case for this position:

> A good manager of what is now more frequently called the Health Information Management Department will tell you that the only way to accurately code is to review the entire record to capture all physician-recorded diag-

noses. Dependence on what a doctor documents as a final diagnosis on a face sheet would bankrupt the institution. The example I use when talking to physicians, especially emergency (ER) doctors, is the patient who comes in with a fracture of the cervical spine, no procedure noted, and falls under DRG #243, $4,600. However, if there was insertion of skeletal tongs, usually done in the ER, and PERHAPS documented by two small words ("tongs inserted") somewhere in the record, the DRG is #234, $7,700. And if there is a co-morbid condition, it is $13,000. It was the review of the record that documented nurses were taking care of a patient with tongs, and then documentation that tongs were removed, that gave us the information to take back to the ER doctors.

Obviously, it is impossible to do a scientific evaluation of the effect of DRGs on patient care, let alone the quality of that care. A double-blind crossover study of DRGs alone cannot be done since there is no control group of Medicare patients treated without DRG restraints or without all of the other changes of the last decade that, designed to reduce costs, have affected health care delivery. That there are myriad difficulties in assessing the system based on retrospective analysis is made abundantly clear by as series of reports from a well-respected research group (Kahn et al. 1990; Draper et al. 1990; Keeler et al. 1990; Kahn et al. 1990a; Rubenstein et al. 1990; Kosekoff et al. 1990; Kahn et al. 1990b; Rogers et al. 1990).

But a number of things are abundantly clear. Starting with DRGs, the cost-control incentive now has teeth, and sharp ones at that. Certainly, under the fee-for-service system, none of the decision-makers had been concerned with cost. For the physicians who prescribed treatment, ordered tests and procedures, and decided when and for how long to hospitalize a patient, the incentive was to provide more services. They wanted access to the most advanced technology and hospital administrators and boards of directors took pride in being at the forefront. Patients preferred to be treated in hospitals that were in the vanguard and were insulated from the true cost of their care. DRGs became the demarcation between the old era and a new one in which all of these parties were catapulted into a competitive, business world where hospitals were rewarded for tracking "resource consumption," ultimately fostering the growth of managed care.

REGULATORY OVERSIGHT

A variety of regulatory agencies share oversight for different aspects of the hospital. Adherence to laws pertaining to such considerations as fire, environmental pollution, and safety of workers, while integral to the maintenance of the institution, are sometimes within the purview of QA/I departments, sometimes covered by risk management departments. QA/I personnel are, however, generally responsible for compliance with the statutes and regulations pertaining to licensing and certification, which vary from state to state.

Licensing and Certification

The federal government has delegated overall review of adherence to certification standards to the Joint Commission on Accreditation of Health Care Organizations (JCAHO), discussed below. The federal government also contracts with each state (in California, a representative of the Licensing and Certification Division of the Department of Health Services) to conduct an inspection in response to a complaint or when there is a change of status (e.g., the addition of a new program). From time to time, the federal government may also ask the manager of this division to send a team to a particular hospital to validate the quality of its recent JCAHO review. Since staff is largely inadequate to handle such a review, teams of nurses and physicians are mobilized for each project.

Most ominous to the QA/I department is an unannounced visit from the state inspector representing the state Licensing and Certification Division. Previous reluctance to provide documents regarding quality reviews of physicians has been eliminated, at least in the case of Medicare patients, by statutes that stipulate that refusal will result in either civil contempt proceedings, notification to HCFA of refusal to comply, or referral to the District Attorney for misdemeanor prosecution and/or unfair business practices action. These options have encouraged the state's inspection and/or photocopying of documents. An inspector whose visit I observed described his role as follows:

> We have the authority to walk in any time of day or night. And I have been wrongly chewed out by administrators for going down in to a facility at 7:00 in the morning when they were not available because it was convenient for me, and torn to pieces and reported to my office, how can you dare let him wander into my hospital without my authority? And we had to gently—my supervisor had to gently remind them that I have that authority. But, out of courtesy, to make the relationship peaceful, the ground rules are we will report to Administration first. So we're taken in hand and then we're taken on a protected environment. It doesn't close our eyes and it doesn't limit our question to the area involved. We can lateralize. We can call HCFA and say, 'I've got something that's very rotten in Denmark and we want a validation,' but that has to go through authority. Also the facility can challenge us, saying, 'You asked for this chart. Why are you asking for x, y, and z?' We have to justify our request.

He explained further that he is less interested in what is found regarding questionable treatment in a particular case than in whether the case was reviewed by peers. As to validation samples, this inspector described a hospital committee that was reviewing deaths six months to two years late. In his words:

> Three months, you know, is justified. It takes time to get the records together, the doctor has to sign it, laboratory work has to come back, blah, blah, blah. Three months is still extraordinarily long. Six months is unreasonable. Two years is absolutely unforgivable. That's where we interface in saying you're not doing it timely.

Asked whether his department then follows up on this type of situation, he answered, "Theoretically we're supposed to go back to see if it's working. But we don't have the time to do that." He sadly described himself as "the cop in the middle of the street, better than not being there at all."

The arrival of an inspector from the State Licensing and Certification Division in response to a patient complaint elicits rapid mobilization of QA/I personnel, since the patient's chart must be produced in twenty minutes. One that I observed concerned what the inspector, a retired physician, told me was a frequent complaint: "My father was in the emergency room four times in a week and they wouldn't admit him and finally when they admitted him it was too late." This situation—clearly a quality-of-care issue—was scrutinized for QA/I process: Was emergency readmission a screen that would send this case to peer review? Since, according to the inspector, angiograms are "notorious for failure," was the emergency angiogram followed up by further tests? The inspector asked for evidence that there is automatic peer review for readmissions as well as the nursing report that caught (should have caught) this case.

Over the years, a number of attempts have been made to tighten controls on health care practices in the interest of the public. Jost (1995) cites as examples the corporate negligence doctrine, which holds hospitals liable for negligent credentialing and supervision; the federal Health Care Quality and Improvement Act, which requires reporting of adverse credentialing actions to a federal data bank and sets the rules for certification programs; continuing medical education requirements imposed by medical boards; and, in some states, the addition of "token" consumer members to medical licensure boards. Jost notes, however, that although these programs represent efforts to impose external regulatory controls on professionals, they nevertheless retain important elements of self-regulation: "PROs and medical boards were still dominated by physicians and applied standards prescribed by physicians" (ibid. 834). Medicine has managed to remain a closed club in which physicians are given licenses after passing a state examination and in essence assured of keeping them for life, sometimes after being found guilty of malpractice. The inspector from the California Licensing and Certification Division quoted above confirmed the looseness of oversight:

> We tend to stay away from practice issues. We tell families if it's a practice issue, the physicians have to show us they have a mechanism for reviewing the work. We look at the credential files of the physicians and say, how was that physician appointed to the hospital? Was there a quality assurance review of his or her work in the preceding two years? And they'll say 'yes.' I'll say, 'show me there's some numerical evidence of it.' Hospitals are very sophisticated. A credential file they'll show you may be one of many.

Asked if he meant hospitals keep double books, he answered, "I would say double books is a minimal. I would say five separate credential files on a physician are not unusual." He stipulated further that committee notes have to have appropriate meeting comments and show that the physicians are reviewing a percentage of cases, adding:

> There's a lot of self-justification. You'll see at the bottom, 'standard of practice met.' One Chief of Surgery told me, 'we've had 500 charts and there's no problem with any of them.' And I would take a deep breath and say, 'you're a liar. Tell me how you managed it.' And he finally admitted, 'Well, we talk to the physician.'

Writing in the *New Yorker*, a physician, looking back on his residency, provides a vivid account of morbidity and mortality conferences (called "M. & M."). These physician meetings take place, usually once a week, in most academic hospitals and in some others and are taken seriously, especially by surgeons. "Here they can gather behind closed doors to review the mistakes, complications, and deaths that occurred on their watch, determine responsibility, and figure out what to do differently next time" (Gawande 1999, 48). With exquisite care, the author describes the ritual of these meetings, who sits where, who speaks and who does not—the hierarchy of addressing errors. Ultimately, the author recalls how he was not confronted with his error at the meeting but rather was taken aside in the hospital's hallway where his superior went over the missed steps in detail. By the author's account:

> I felt a sense of shame like a burning ulcer. This was not guilt: guilt is what you feel when you have done something wrong. What I felt was shame: *I* was wrong. (ibid. 49)

This description offers a rare insight into the way peer pressure and self-regulation work in hospitals. Occasional jars to this system of self-regulation have occurred, of course. In late 1998, for instance, the Health

Professions Commission financed by the Pew Charitable Trusts proposed that every physician, nurse, and other kind of health worker in the United States be required to demonstrate every few years that they are competent by passing a written examination and by allowing state regulators to watch them work and inspect their patients' records at least every six years. The commission also recommended that consumers make up at least one-third of the members of every state board that regulates doctors, nurses, and other practitioners ("Regular competency tests urged . . ."). Nevertheless, for the most part when problems occur, as the above-mentioned Chief of Surgery told the inspector, "We talk to the physician."

Standardization and Accreditation

Among the business organizations devoted to improving quality and accountability, two are especially noteworthy for health care. First is the International Organization for Standardization (ISO), housed in Geneva, Switzerland, which is promoted by the International Society for Quality in Health Care (ISQUA) for many reasons, not the least of which is the goal of comparability of service standards in an increasingly federal Europe as well as the hope that standards for health care delivery be based on common international principles. ISQUA does not propose that ISO replace existing systems for accreditation of hospitals nor that it be confused with statutory licensing, which is legally required by the state as a minimum condition of operation. Rather, the focus of ISO standards is on the *quality* of process, assessed mainly through customer satisfaction. Certification of compliance with ISO standards (called ISO 9000) is achieved through the assessment of independent auditors, qualified by ISO-recognized training. In addition to the expense of preparation for external assessment, the cost for ISO certification depends on the number of days required until success is achieved. Thus, it can be even more costly than accreditation surveys. ISO 9000 does not tell you how to run your business; it helps businesses define and document their own quality procedures. ISO certification has not as yet made a significant impact on hospitals in the United States.

The second program is the Malcolm Baldrige National Quality Award, named after the Commerce Secretary who served in the Reagan administration and met an untimely death while practicing for his favorite sport, rodeos. The bill establishing this award was renamed in his honor eleven days after his death, passed by the Congress, and signed by the president fifteen days later—unusual speed in an administration dedicated to the proposition that "government is not the solution." In truth, Edward Meese, Reagan's Attorney General, had said that the government had no business giving awards and "in official Washington, it is generally accepted as fact that if the bill had not carried the name of Malcolm Baldrige so the president could honor his old friend, Reagan would not have signed it" (Dobyns and Crawford-Mason 1994, 163). Baldrige standards focus on such matters as leadership, strategic planning, human resource development and management, and business results. The award is administered by the National Bureau of Standards (later named the National Institute of Standards and Technology, NIST), an established agency that was formed in 1901 to do basic scientific research and define physical measurements, such as the size of batteries. Criteria even to apply for the Baldrige award are very stringent. As one QA/I coordinator commented, "It's not the award that is of value—it's what you have to become to be considered for the award. As a business, I think it could help us be much, much better." Although the JCAHO has worked to bring its own standards into line with Baldrige criteria (Cesarone 1997; Carr and Jackson 1997), they have had an uneven impact on American hospitals—sought by a few but unknown to many more.

"Uneven" would in no way apply to the impact of the Joint Commission itself, described to me in the very earliest stages of my research with fear, awe, and, in some cases, loathing. The JCAHO today evaluates and accredits more than 17,000 health care organizations in the United States, including more than 5,200 hospitals. To fully appreciate these statistics, one must look back to the early twentieth century when in an estimated 75 percent of American hospitals, patients were not examined upon admission, no history was taken nor diagnosis made, and no follow-up work was performed to determine the results of treatment (Joint Commission 1990; Davis 1973). Not only were medical records useless but no attempt was made to determine a physician's competence to practice in a hospital and most hospitals lacked a clinical laboratory, X-ray, and other services needed for preoperative and postoperative evaluation of surgical patients.

In this climate, another watershed event occurred at the Third Clinical Congress of Surgeons of North America in 1912. Following the adoption of Franklin Martin's resolution establishing the American College of Surgeons, Allen Kanavel presented a resolution (at the request of Martin) that a system of standardization of hospital equipment and hospital work be developed. Hospital standardization became one of the college's stated objectives when it was founded in 1913. By 1917, backed by a grant from the Carnegie Foundation, the college developed a one-page list of requirements called the *Minimum Standard for Hospitals* and established the Hospital Standardization Program (see Figure 1). To the late-twentieth-century eye, these standards seem minimal indeed.[3]

College representatives then conducted field trials, which were expected to bring approval to at least 1,000 hospitals. Unhappily, only 89 of the 692 hospitals of 100 beds or more met the standards. Some of the most prestigious hospitals in the country had failed the test. In a move that current American politicians might envy, the surgeons took a bold stance: "Although the College made the numbers public, it burned the list of hospitals at midnight in the furnace of the Waldorf Astoria Hotel, New York, to keep it from the press" (Roberts et al. 1987, 937).

As news of the program's success spread, more and more hospitals sought approval; by 1950, 3,290 had been accredited—over half of the hospitals in the United States. The time had come to move beyond the original sponsorship. In 1951, the American College of Physicians, the American Hospital Association, the American Medical Association, and the Canadian Medical Association joined the American College of Surgeons to form an independent, nonprofit organization, then called the Joint Commission on Accreditation of Hospitals. (The Canadian Medical Association withdrew in 1959 to participate in its own program and in 1987 "Hospitals" was changed to "Healthcare Organizations" to reflect the enlarged sphere of the organization.)

> By 1950, the size and scope of the program had increased significantly, and the College, which had already invested $2 million in the Hospital Standardization Program, was having difficulty in supporting the effort alone. In addition, the increasing sophistication of medical care, the growing number and complexity of modern hospitals, and the rapid emergence of nonsurgical specialties after World War II required that the standards be revised, expanded, and updated, and that the scope of the survey be extended. (ibid. 938)

As has been true since its origin, the Joint Commission is a nonprofit organization to which requests for accreditation surveys (every three years) are voluntary. Although some hospitals choose to be accredited by other entities, such as state medical associations, for the most part the Joint Commission was free to build a powerful organization until the first serious threat to its existence came in 1985. At that time, the organization's board of commissioners met to decide whether it was becoming unnecessary in light of increased federal and state regulation of quality. Instead of abolishing the organization, the commissioners decided to revamp it under a plan that came to be known as the Agenda for Change (see Chapter Three). Then, in 1993, another threat was perceived when the organization was not mentioned in the 1,300-page Clinton administration health care reform bill. Proposed instead was a national quality council and government oversight ("Future role of Joint Commission . . ." 1993, 189). Ironically, the Joint Commission survived and became all the stronger when the Clinton health reform bill failed.

Threats to the organization did not "stop the money from rolling in" (Burda 1994, 18). According to the Joint Commission's tax filing, profits were over $5 million on record revenues of $84.4 million in 1993. Partially attributable to income from educational programming and publications

The Minimum Standard

1. That physicians and surgeons privileged to practice in the hospital be organized as a definite group or staff. Such organization has nothing to do with the question as to whether the hospital is "open" or "closed," nor need it affect the various existing types of staff organization. The word "staff" is here defined as the group of doctors who practice in the hospital inclusive of all groups such as the "regular staff," "the visiting staff," and the "associated staff."

2. That membership upon the staff be restricted to physicians and surgeons who are (a) full graduates of medicine in good standing and legally licensed to practice in their respective states or provinces, (b) competent in their respective fields, and (c) worthy in character and in matters of professional ethics; that in this latter connection the practice of the division of fees, under any guise whatever, be prohibited.

3. That the staff initiate and, with the approval of the governing board of the hospital, adopt rules, regulations, and policies governing the professional work of the hospital; that these rules, regulations, and policies specifically provide:

   (a) That staff meetings be held at least once each month. (In large hospitals the departments may choose to meet separately.)

   (b) That the staff review and analyze at regular intervals their clinical experience in the various departments of the hospital, such as medicine, surgery, obstetrics, and the other specialties; the clinical records of patients, free and pay, to be the basis for such review and analyses.

4. That accurate and complete records be written for all patients and filed in an accessible manner in the hospital—a complete case record being one which includes identification data; complaint; personal and family history; history of present illness; physical examination; special examinations, such as consultations, clinical laboratory, X-ray and other examinations; provisional or working diagnosis; medical or surgical treatment; gross and microscopical pathological findings; progress notes; final diagnosis; condition on discharge; follow-up and, in case of death, autopsy findings.

5. That diagnostic and therapeutic facilities under competent supervision be available for the study, diagnosis, and treatment of patients, these to include, at least (a) a clinical laboratory providing chemical, bacteriological, serological, and pathological services; (b) an X-ray department providing radiographic and fluoroscopic services.

Figure 1. *Bulletin of the American College of Surgeons.* January 1920. American College of Surgeons. Chicago, IL. Reprinted with permission.

and to big increases in accreditation survey revenues, this represented a 22 percent increase over 1992's total revenues of $69 million. Income from survey fees alone had risen more than 26 percent, reflecting a 6 percent surcharge that the Joint Commission placed on accreditation fees in 1993 in order to help fund the research and development of its indicator monitoring system. The tax filing also revealed that the JCAHO had paid the consultant firm Gold and Liebengood $96,000 for lobbying work on its behalf during the Clinton healthcare reform debate.

Then, late in 1994, a surprise public attack on the agency came from the American Hospital Association (AHA) and the American Medical Association (AMA), organizations that control half of the seats on the JCAHO's board and at that time contributed a combined $280,000 annually to its operations. The AHA called for sweeping changes in the internal operations of the JCAHO, pointing to "survey inconsistency, rapidly increasing costs to hospitals for JCAHO surveys, inconsistent education programs and variability among Joint Commission surveyors" (American Hospital Association 1994). Simultaneously but independently, the AMA House of Delegates resolved to examine the implications of withdrawal from the JCAHO as well as the alternatives for working with other health care organizations involved in certification and accreditation of health care organizations (American Medical Association 1994).

According to one report, an AMA delegate described the accrediting body as "unresponsive to complaints that it had become too burdensome and expensive for the benefits yielded" (Burda and Morrissey 1994, 2). As seven state hospital associations added to the rising chorus of dissatisfaction by announcing they were looking for alternative means of accreditation, the JCAHO proclaimed a self-improvement effort in regard to such issues as its telephone and mail responsiveness, the survey process, and standards changes. In a move to deal with yet another bone of contention, the commissioners severed their ties with Margaret O'Leary, wife of the director, who served as a consultant to the organization. A physician specializing in emergency medicine, O'Leary also had written books under contract to the JCAHO, which had been marketing them to accredited facilities—seen by some hospital executives as a conflict of interest (Burda 1995, 13).

The next blow came when the American Hospital Association conducted a hospital executive opinion poll in 1995 that confirmed what was already well known within the hospital world: hospitals seek accreditation from the JCAHO more for financial considerations than out of concern for the quality of patient care. Their rationale is based on "deemed status," meaning that only accredited hospitals qualify for Medicare and many state Medicaid and commercial insurance programs. By virtue of JCAHO's imprimatur, hospitals do not have to submit to separate inspections from each insurer. A side effect of the hospital poll was evidence of growing concern within the AHA leadership that "a conflict of interest exists between the Joint Commission's basic function of optimizing organizational performance and the function of Medicare deemed status (right to operate)" (Pugh 1995, 82).

Despite its woes, the JCAHO managed one victory during this period of controversy. Initially, the AHA had supported the state hospital associations that were looking for alternatives sources of accreditation. Eight months later, the AHA board formally voted against support (Burda 1995, 28). But another setback soon eclipsed even this small triumph. In 1996, the agency lost a five-year legal battle to exempt its $23 million corporate headquarters building complex from local real estate taxes. The JCAHO had claimed that it deserved exemption as a public charity because it served the public interest by improving the quality of health care services at accredited facilities used by the public. The Circuit Court Judge of DuPage County, Illinois, ruled that "the JCAHO operated more like a business than a charity, concluding that the JCAHO'S activities directly benefited healthcare facilities, not the public, and the organization generated 'a substantial surplus of funds' from survey fees, not from any public or private donations" (Burda 1996, 46).

RESTRUCTURING HEALTH CARE

Relman's characterization of the cost-containment era in health care as the "Revolt of the Payers" (1988, 1221) speaks volumes. As hospital administrators and QA/I professionals juggle the requirements of oversight agencies—adjusting to Medicare's Diagnosis Related Groups (DRGs), remaining on top of all of the elements subject to examination by the state, the Joint Commission, and HCFA—another massive transformation spurred by the payer revolt has occurred. The economic upheaval caused by DRGs is a ripple compared to the tsunami that has become known as "managed care," which by 1997 dominated the health care market. What is salient for this study is the effect this development has exerted on cost cutting and the subsequent concern regarding its impact on the quality of hospital care. Whatever else can be said about managed care, no one would question that rationalization of health care is now in full swing. The golden egg that had been known as fee-for-service is not only tarnished and but has become demonstrably more hard boiled.

The name of Paul Ellwood, Jr., is indelibly associated with the history of managed care, specifically with its origins in health maintenance organizations (HMOs). A sympathetic profile that appeared in the *New York Times Magazine* in 1996 portrays him as setting out to create a system of competition between health care providers based on price and quality. Instead, he has witnessed the evolution of a system based almost entirely on price. Many recipients of health care would agree with the reporter who said, "And while the incentives under the old system were for doctors to do what many would describe as too much, the incentives today are for doctors to do what many would describe as too little" (Belkin 1996, 68). Ellwood was the chief architect of the Nixon administration's HMO strategy, which the president presented in 1971.

"Managed care organization" (MCO) is an umbrella term for HMOs, preferred provider organizations (PPOs), and point of service plans (POS). PPOs offer a network of providers who agree to provide services at a discount to enrolled members. PPOs encourage members to go to providers within the network by using incentives such as deductibles and copayments. Members who prefer to use nonnetwork physicians may do so but then must pay more. POS enrollees also can decide whether to use network or non-network providers. HMOs, however, require members to use designated physicians, hospitals, and other health care providers. HMOs control utilization by requiring members to choose a primary care physician, a "gatekeeper," who provides or coordinates all of their medical care, except in emergency situations. (POS plans encourage but do not require members to choose a primary care physician who then serves as the gatekeeper.) Of the three types, HMOs have stirred the most controversy and are most often associated with the concept of managed care—so much so that the terms are frequently used synonymously.

Prepaid plans, precursors to HMOs, first developed on a large scale around the turn of the nineteenth century, mostly in the U.S. Northwest. They accompanied the opening of the West by railroads and the ensuing industrial development (Mayer and Mayer 1985, 590). One of the most powerful forces leading to organized delivery of health care was the practice of recruiting people to work in isolated areas in the 1800s, as the owners of plantations in Hawaii, the lumber camps in Michigan, Wisconsin, and Washington State, and the mines in Minnesota sought to provide health services to attract and retain workers. "Physicians were on contract or salary; hospitals were owned or some number of beds was contracted for" (Friedman 1996, 957). Then in 1927, in "the medical shot heard around the nation" (Mayer and Mayer 1985, 591), Dr. Michael Shadid sold shares to the farmers of Elk City, Oklahoma, at $50 each for the construction of a community hospital. Each share entitled the holder to medical care provided by the hospital. In 1934, the Farmer's Union assumed sponsorship of the program and Community Hospital became the Farmer's Union Cooperative Association.

Not-for-profit plans such as the Ross-Loos Medical Clinic in Los Angeles (1929), the Group Health Association in Washington, D.C. (1937), Kaiser-Permanente Medical Care Program (1942), and others in New York, Puget Sound, and Cleveland were seen as progressive approaches to rationalizing health care delivery. Close examination of the Kaiser-Permanente example sheds light on why large corporations were attracted to the HMO. As with plantations, mines, and lumber camps, the drive sprang from the need to provide medical care to Kaiser Industries workers at remote construction sites. "Maintaining the health of the workers through preventive care and providing early medical intervention to quickly return the worker to his job proved to be good business practice" (Salmon 1990, 88).

From his writing and consultation through Interstudy, a Minneapolis health think tank, and as advisor to the Nixon administration, Paul Ellwood had invited private corporations to lend their "industrial know-how" to his concept of extending HMOs throughout the country and had called for corporate involvement in profit-making HMOs (Ellwood 1971, 291). "The historical significance of Ellwood lies not in his conceptualization of the HMO itself but in his ability to put the 'idea whose time has come' into a strategy for eventual corporate control of health services delivery, to raise the profitability of the industry, and to contribute to increased worker productivity" (Salmon 1990, 87).

When Congress passed the Health Maintenance Organization Act in 1973, President Nixon envisioned that government and corporate support of HMOs eventually would make these programs available to 90 percent of the population and would enroll 40 million or more people. But in 1980, when President Reagan took office, there were still only 236 in the country, serving just over 9 million people (Leyerle 1994, 56). Observers point to many factors to account for the initial slow start. Opposition by physicians and hospitals, consumer uninterest, the Watergate-disrupted federal bureaucracy, and the economic recession of 1973–75 and its aftermath, all played a part.

Nevertheless, the promise of the HMO program sharpened, once and for all, the relationship between capitalism and health care (1) by helping legitimize profit-making through corporate entities in the delivery of health services, and (2) by bringing to the surface corporate resentment over the inflation in fringe benefit packages for workers and the effect of health insurance premiums on profit margins (Salmon 1990, I, 59). A group of large firms formed the Washington Business Group on Health to address the ever-rising costs, attributable, they believed, to the health care system. In the 1980s, Chrysler, Ford, and General Motors announced that their health care expenditures had climbed to more than $3 billion. Chrysler claimed that almost $600 of the cost of every one of its cars could be attributed to medical care (Jensen 1991, 110). Chrysler's chairman and chief executive officer asked Joseph Califano, Jr., former secretary of Health Education and Welfare in the Carter administration, to join Chrysler's board and chair its health care committee. This decision led to a computerized audit of hospital admissions and charges that uncovered widespread overutilization, inefficiency, waste, and fraud. After obtaining union backing, Chrysler approached local hospitals to assure reduction in length of stay. Califano's summary of the results of Chrysler's strong stand—"The gospel lesson is that hard-negotiating buyers, who treat health care like the other products they purchase, can change the system" (Califano 1986, 26)[4]—could serve as the motto for the managed care movement.

There is a brutal logic to what followed. In the past, insurance companies profited by managing risk: "In any given year, some 10 percent of the population incurs 80 percent of the medical costs in this country; hence any company thrives to the extent that it can identify and avoid members of this group while insuring the others" (Poplin 1997, 319). This practice is called "cherry picking" in the insurance industry. Providing health insurance through place of work virtually removes the burden of insuring people who are seriously ill: "You simply cannot be employed full time if you suffer from the effects of a crippling disability or disease." Only later did it become evident that "the system wasn't meant to care for sick people; it was meant to make and manage money" (Glasser 1998, 36).

It must be emphasized, moreover, that most Americans cannot be said to have chosen a health plan. Rather, they are enrolled in one that was made available through their place of employment. In 1996, approximately 43 percent of employed Americans were being offered only one insurance plan by their employers; 23 percent a choice between only two (Etheridge et al. 1996; Davidson et al. 1998). A survey conducted by Louis Harris & Associates Inc. and the Harvard School of Public Health in 1998 revealed an added dimension to this spread, finding that 22 percent had a choice of plans that were essentially the same ("Industry Insights" 1999, 4). So much for competition, as understood by the originators of managed care! "This means that they [employees] effectively face a private, single-payer system" (Reinhardt 1998)—a sardonic reference to the American rejection of a public, single-payer system. When coupled with the reminder that the recurrent theme of capitalism is "whoever pays the piper ultimately calls the tune," we have managed care in a nutshell (Poplin 1997, 332).

For a brief period, it had appeared that government would manage managed care. Many explanations have been offered for the quick demise of President Clinton's 1993–94 national health insurance program, the Health Security Act. In 1995, the *Journal of Health Politics, Policy and Law* devoted an entire issue to the role played by the institutional and structural features of the American political system. A contributor laid some of the blame on President Clinton and his administration (Rockman 1995). Some analysts argued that reform failed because of the opposition of business and various interest groups (Baumgartner and Talbert 1995; Judis 1995; Martin 1995). Others attribute the failure to class relations (Navarro 1995); still others to fragmentation within the health policy community (Patel and Rushefsky 1998). A *New York Times* obituary captured the essence of the legislative collapse: "Though unfinished, the history of health care legislation is a striking measure of the complexity of legislating major change in an era of intense partisanship, with a public that distrusts Washington as never before, a campaign technology applied to whipping around voters' opinions, and news reports that emphasize conflict, not explanation" (Clymer et al. 1994, A1). Clinton's health care reform measure was a bonanza for pollsters, pundits, number crunchers, lobbyists, and advertising agencies—resulting in the privatization of the HMO approach. A business commentator reminded her listeners that it was big firms such as Dupont and American Telephone and Telegraph that had pushed government to "do something" about costs. But, she said, "big business viewed the Clinton plan as a mandate and they do not like that word" (Kaplan 1996). Not to be overlooked are the established insurance firms and the new managed care companies, who sponsored the "Harry and Louise" advertising campaign that masterfully belittled the Clinton plan (Skocpol 1996; Hacker 1997). Last, Ira Magaziner, who drafted the plan, failed to convey the message that it placed equal weight on quality and access, not just cost:

> Magaziner's inspiration was to recognize that managed care was inexorably taking over health care; his plan sought to take advantage of managed care's ability to hold down costs, while regulating the quality and availability of the care it provided. . . . Many potential supporters didn't understand it and fell sway to fraudulent claims that the plan would eliminate fee-for-service medicine. (Managed care was already undermining fee-for-service medicine—Magaziner's plan would have left every citizen the option to pay extra to avoid managed care). (Judis 1998, 22)

Corporate America had already learned the Chrysler lesson, that if they put pressure on physicians and hospitals they can push costs down without the help of government. So the advertising campaign opposing the Clinton plan, at around $50 million (Finkelstein 1997, 23), was money well spent. Corporations were already following the lead of the Washington Business Group on Health and pooling their health-insurance buying power. In 1994, some of the San Francisco Bay Area's largest businesses banded together in a coalition called the Bay Area Business Group on Health in order to negotiate *en bloc* with different health plans for the best rates. The California Public Employees Retirement System (CalPERS), which was then purchasing benefits for 920,000 Californians, announced that it had obtained an average premium cut of 1 percent for 1995; and the Health Insurance Plan of California, a purchasing pool created by state law to make health insurance more affordable for small business, negotiated average cuts of 6 percent (Barnum 1994). Similar alliances were forming all over the country.

It should be noted that what is now known as "managed care" originally was called "managed competition"—a truer representation of the intent of the HMO as set forth by its champions, dubbed the "Jackson Hole Group" after Jackson Hole, Wyoming, where they conducted their think tank (Enthoven 1978; Enthoven and Kronick 1989; Ellwood et al. 1992). "'Capitation' is the cornerstone of managing care through HMOs, which refers only to a payment mechanism—paying a provider a specific sum of money for the ongoing care of a person or group of people for a particular period of time. The sum set is set in advance of the actual period of service, and it therefore represents a prediction, or at least an agreed-on estimate, of the amount of money that will be required to provide that care" (Berwick 1996, 1227). As envisioned by its originators, health plans would compete for market share by negotiating with groups of doctors and hospitals for reduced rates of payment. Competition would be based on quality and price (quality was very much part of the original conception) and consumers would drive the market. Certainly, in the words of a first-hand observer of the limitations of health care delivery, "the good ole days were not good for everyone",[5] and this seemed to be a way to destroy the "medieval guild structure of American medicine" with "accountable health plans" (Millenson 1997, 242).

Proponents appear not to have foreseen the Gold Rush mentality that would propel the market—or, if they did, saw it as a healthy correction. What has followed, however, is tremendous flux: an increase in the number of mergers, acquisitions, and divestitures, and extensive movement of enrollees and physicians from one plan to another. Moreover, arising from the early freedom accorded HMO development is a raft of consumer-protection measures instigated by state legislatures and the Congress to counteract, in piecemeal fashion, excesses such as: (1) "gag clauses" against physicians (barring them from presenting to patients all treatment options, including those available outside the HMO); (2) 24-hour restrictions on hospital stay for new mothers to counteract too-early discharge from the hospital; (3) limitations on malpractice grievances; and (4) denial of emergency room care (Annas 1997). The advertising campaign launched against the Clinton health plan had claimed it would entail too much government management. Consistent with the history of American health care reform, legislation such as a federal "Patients' Bill of Rights" (and similar bills on the state level that improve patients' ability to challenge treatment decisions by HMOs and press for enlarged access and broader networks) are attempts to address *incrementally* the balance between market-driven health plans and government intervention. Not surprisingly, even such incremental change will not go unchallenged. According to reports filed with the secretary of the U.S. Senate, insurance companies spent $60 million lobbying against new regulations for managed care in 1998. "The $60 million lobbying outlay was four times the $14 million-plus spent by medical organizations, trial lawyers, unions and consumer groups to press for passage of the so-called Patients Bill of Rights and is enough to pay the salaries of everyone in the U.S. transportation secretary's office or finance for almost two months the childhood immunization program of the Centers for Disease Control and Prevention" ("$60 million tab . . . " 1998, A5).

One can gauge the impact of any new wrinkle in health care by tracking subscription offers for newsletters designed to ease one through the transition. An introductory letter to *Capitation Abstracts & Analysis* advises health care professionals that they need to find the strategies that will make capitation most profitable for their organizations and then asks: "But did you know that more than 100 publications write about capitation?" Another, for the *Digest of Managed Health Care*, asks: "Too much information? Too little time?" and offers to keep subscribers informed "about the dynamic changes brought on by managed care." Nevertheless, shifting attitudes and adjusting *modus operandi* for this reform require much more than information and time. It has become evident that the revolution wrought by the managed care movement far exceeds all efforts that preceded it.

Take, for instance, the changed structure of health care delivery. In a national survey conducted by Louis Harris and Associates, 44 percent of adults covered by employer-provided health insurance in 1997 reported they were in HMOs (Kaiser Family Foundation and The Commonwealth Fund 1998, 38). Hospitals and physicians accept the discounted fees offered by HMOs because they are guaranteed a certain volume of patients. Most HMOs contract with a number of medical groups. Thus, doctors have an incentive to join big groups—the bigger the group the stronger its position in negotiating fees. Similarly, HMOs have been a driving force behind the shift to less-expensive outpatient care, forcing hospitals to face the harsh reality of empty beds. This has accelerated hospital mergers, acquisitions, and joint ventures. Not only is there the expectation that joining together will result in economies of scale (increased purchasing power, more rational distribution of costly technology and services) but these consolidations offer enhanced ability to compete for managed care contracts. Moreover, in the name of cost saving and efficiency, there is now a new layer of administration, for-profit entities called medical services organizations that contract with MCOs to negotiate contracts with hospitals and payers. They do the billing, the computerized monitoring of physicians' decisions, and handle approval of patients' tests and surgery. Also experiencing growth are physician practice-management companies that buy doctors' practices and then sign contracts with them, essentially "hiring" them. The doctors are paid a salary that represents a share of the practice's total revenue and a portion of its profits (if any). As these companies themselves merge, their size enables them to demand higher fees from MCOs. Meanwhile, MCOs are merging into ever-larger companies, putting them in a better position to offer lower prices to employers because they have more clout to negotiate doctors' and hospitals' fees downward.

Another noteworthy development was Medicare's managed-care "risk contracting program," started in 1982. It allows qualified HMOs to contract with Medicare and accept a preset, monthly capitation payment for enrolled beneficiaries. By accepting a risk contract, the HMO gambles that its volume of reimbursement from Medicare will offset expenditures incurred by high users of health services. The number of Medicare contracts has increased substantially since 1992, totaling 346 in June 1998 (Medicare Payment Advisory Commission 1998, 30). "Risk plan enrollment accelerated significantly after 1991, reaching an annual rate of 36 percent in 1995. Since then, the rate of increase has fallen each year although it remains above 20 percent today, representing a nationwide inflow of more that 50,000 new enrollees per month" (ibid. 37). Further, from 1991 to 1997 Medicaid managed-care enrollment jumped from 9.53 percent to 47.82 percent (Health Care Financing Administration 1997). Thus has health care in the 1990s become an arena of tough contracting, frugal use of referrals to specialists, and what detractors have described as "ruthless" efficiency.

At the same time, investors in managed-care companies have found themselves in a volatile market. The first decade of managed care was marked by huge growth, but the ascendancy of some managed care companies has been exceeded by the rapidity of their decline.

Oxford Health Plans Inc. is a case in point. Oxford, which served about 1.7 million members, mostly in the Northeast, was highly regarded by Wall Street. It was considered "consumer friendly" and was the first plan to develop multidisciplinary care teams to coordinate patient care in the hospital and at home, the first to provide direct access to specialists for patients with chronic illnesses, and the first to base a portion of physician pay on measurable clinical outcomes (Kleinke 1997). In 1996, Oxford began covering alternative medicine such as acupuncture, massage, yoga, and herbal remedies. In 1997, it announced a program to allow members who were operated on to rate the hospital, surgeons, and nurses in a report card that would be given to other patients facing the same surgery. Another innovation Oxford introduced the same year was the "personal service agent"—a single person to call whenever the patient has a question, responsible for getting them an answer within 24 hours ("HMO lets patients rate . . . " 1997, A4). By the end of the year, Oxford experienced its own stock market crash after announcing it expected a $53 million third-quarter loss "due to what it said were overestimations in its number of members and computer billing snags" and after "New York's insurance regulator slapped a $3.0 million fine on Oxford for alleged violations of the state's insurance statute and regulations" ("Oxford Health fined . . . " 1997). Oxford's decline remains a subject of debate: some say it under-priced its membership fees; others point to its grossly inflated CEO salary, purported to be $23 million plus (Winslow and Paltrow 1998, A1).

Fluctuations in the competitive marketplace have disrupted continuity of care as subscribers, now called "covered lives" in the managed-care industry (and, unhappily, "capitated lives" in some quarters), find themselves without the plan they counted on. Scrambling for an alternative plan, many have discovered their doctors are no longer authorized or that the rules have changed governing referrals, prescriptions drugs, and certain services.

Motivated by the promise of cost-saving, the government encouraged the elderly to sign up for Medicare and Medicaid risk-contracted HMOs. Medicare subscribers were happy to eliminate the out-of-pocket expense of supplemental insurance (called Medigap policies), and were attracted to plans that paid for prescription drugs, eyeglasses, dental care, and some preventive care not covered by regular Medicare. Approximately six million seniors were enrolled in Medicare managed-care plans in 1999 (Miller 1999, 24) and, according to the California legislative representative for the American Association of Retired Persons, 38 percent of the state's seniors took the HMO option (Abate 1999, D2). Big HMOs expected to turn a profit by covering this population, but "soaring drug prices, federal Medicare budget tightening and management miscalculations have dashed their dreams" ("HMO's Medicare cuts . . . " 1998, B1). In some communities, Medicare HMOs that found themselves "over-extended, over-subscribed and under-paid" have pulled out and left subscribers—retirees who could not afford fee-for-service medicine—without coverage for the preventive and acute care required by the exigencies of their chronic illnesses (Kilborn 1998, A1). (Note 2)

Oxford Health's financial decline drew the attention of financial reporters to the fact that oversight of managed care plans is so fragmented, state by state, that no single authority has jurisdiction over large HMOs operating in several states (Paltrow 1998, A14).[6] For instance, the principle regulator of HMOs in California is the California Department of Corporations; in Pennsylvania, HMOs are licensed and regulated by the state insurance commission. Nationally, although the Joint Commission on Accreditation of Healthcare Organizations (JCAHO) began its own plan to accredit HMOs, for the most part oversight of managed-care plans has been taken over by the National Committee for Quality Assurance (NCQA), a private, not-for-profit organization organized in 1991 and dominated by representatives of large employers and health plans (Iglehart 1996). The NCQA accredits managed-care plans that voluntarily request a review of their operations and develops performance measures for plans through the Health Plan Employer Data and Information Set (HEDIS). Several observers have questioned the conflict of interest in the way NCQA is financed: "About half of its budget comes from accreditation fees, which may create an incentive against setting standards too high" (Kuttner 1998, 1635). Critics have proposed that separate bodies should perform accreditation and quality review. Critics have raised another issue:

> Many of the measures of quality extolled by the champions of this movement are benchmarks that are mainly relevant to healthy populations. In my interviews with the medical directors of HMOs, I kept hearing the same seven or eight examples. Are the standard immunizations and screenings being carried out for the vast majority of appropriate plan members? Are case-management protocols being followed for conditions, such as asthma, diabetes, and hypertension, for which best practice is well established and not controversial? (ibid. 1636)

The emphasis is clearly on preventive care and the health of whole population of enrollees, rather than the care of sick individuals.

> Since the great majority of enrollees in any employment-based health plan are healthy and likely to remain so, regardless of health care, it is very easy to concentrate quality efforts on serving their minimal needs, knowing that they are relatively easily met and that the results for the plan as a whole will be greatly dominated by the experience of the healthy. Deficiencies in the care of sick patients, particularly those with serious, chronic diseases, could easily be overlooked or swamped by minor (and inexpensive) successes among the healthy. (Angell and Kassirer 1996, 884)

Another observer says it well: "Prevention means long-term but the public expects 'someone to take care of me when I'm sick.' Also, managed-care executives think in quarters; coronary artery disease does not move in quarters."[7]

Late-night TV comics can joke that Joseph and Mary had to go to a manger because they belonged to an HMO but lives have been seriously affected by the transfer of clinical-decision-making to MBAs and cost accountants. Critics, calling the movement "unmanaged care," "mismanaged care," and "managed cost," decry "HMO empires" for their avarice, hyperinflated executive salaries, and the huge stock options showered on chief executives. Critics also complain that companies are profiting by denying payment for needed treatment. Physicians complain that they spend more and more time arguing with the companies for approval; patients that they spend more and more time waiting for referrals. Nor does it help the managed-care cause for the public to learn that at a large Medicare HMO "medical directors view a constantly updated, electronic ticker-tape of the firm's stock price that flashes on their office wall while they decide whether to approve drugs and procedures" (McCall et al. 1997, A29). Defenders respond that the managed-care system has made health care affordable, reduced incentives for treatment enjoyed under fee-for-service, lowered costs in an industry that was losing money, and kept in check the rising portion of the gross national product that had been consumed by health care. They also point out that Medicare HMOs have a better rate of preventive screenings—for instance, for breast and colorectal cancer—than does traditional Medicare fee-for-service, partially attributable to their extensive computer systems for tracking patient care ("Study says . . . " 1999, A7). Further, some argue, "there is an urgent need for managed care to second-guess decisions by physicians to subject patients to needlessly risky surgery and needlessly costly tests" (Weinstein 1999, 1).

For most of the 1990s, MCOs were able to turn a profit. By 1997, however, the industry had entered a troublesome new phase: "struggling with the consequences of its extraordinary expansion this decade, forced in many cases to raise premiums, lay off doctors and close clinics" (Kilborn 1997; Hall 1996; Hendren 1998). One way they had controlled cost was by negotiating with pharmaceutical companies for price and restricting members to certain formularies. Now that too was being questioned by members. Overall, MCOs had priced aggressively to appeal to their business purchasers and had successfully attracted young, healthy people. But there are still segments of the population that are harder to "manage":

> The spectacular success of managed care proved to be the cause of its equally spectacular failures. Cherry picking is another name for a Ponzi scheme, and sooner or later it falls apart. Even a company blessed with tens of thousands of healthy subscribers eventually finds itself obliged to pay for the occasional premature birth at $1500 a day, or the occasional employee who develops a brain tumor or whose wife is diagnosed with ovarian cancer. There are car accidents and near drownings. There are late complications of diabetes, the forty-year-old struck down with a heart attack, the previously undiagnosed melanoma, the complications of hypertension. The odd executive may need a hip replacement because of an old football injury, or a chief financial officer a heart transplant after what should have been a routine viral illness. (Glasser 1998, 37)

By the end of the 1990s, it was becoming clear that the managed care movement had probably squeezed as much as possible out of the health-care dollar. MCOs were responding by hiking premiums; businesses by passing on costs to employees. It was also clear that small businesses could not negotiate rates downward with the same clout afforded big corporations. More and more were slashing benefits, driving increasing numbers into Medicaid or adding to the ranks of the uninsured. Free-market advocates are hard put to argue with this observation: "Initially, managed-care companies may create efficiencies and negotiate discounts, and still provide generous services. But after consolidating, the only remaining way to boost profits is to limit choice and to reduce access and quality" (Finkelstein 1997, 26).

Physicians also were feeling increasingly threatened. In 1990, a Louis Harris survey had found that 81 percent of the physicians polled would accept a 10 percent reduction in fees in return for "substantially increased physician autonomy, with less utilization review and less regulation" (1990). Undoubtedly, a later poll would have found physicians striking a bargain for an even greater reduction. Yet there has been very little organized resistance from physicians to the relationship between managed care and quality. Thus, a decision in 1999 by 600 doctors in California to reject a contract with Aetna U.S. Healthcare came as a surprise to the community. The doctors' group, the San Mateo Independent Practice Association, said that Aetna was not paying enough for provision of quality care to the 20,000 Aetna members who visit them (Abate 1999). Could this be the beginning of a trend?

THE CONSEQUENCES

By the end of the twentieth century, the extent of "horizontal integration" (consolidation of multihospital corporations) and "vertical integration" (organizations with different levels and types of services) had far exceeded expectations. During 1997, the health care industry witnessed the second largest number of mergers and acquisitions (M&As)—in excess of 630—of any industry. Announcing a 1999 conference, Deloitte & Touche asserted, "That number is projected to increase by as much as 20 percent in 1998. While M&As have become vital to the success of many healthcare organizations, the cold reality is that more than 60 percent will fail."

Market and reform pressures have spurred the growth of a new breed of cat, "Integrated Delivery Systems" (IDSs)—networks of hospitals, insurers, physician groups, HMOs, outpatients clinics, and other medical services. Their stated purpose is "to cost-effectively provide a population with a full 'continuum of care'—from prevention through check-ups, tests, surgery, rehabilitation, long-term, and home care" and to be "accountable for costs, quality of care, and customer satisfaction" (KPMG 1994, 1). But the fortunes of IDSs too have fluctuated, not only in market performance but in overcoming physician morale problems and consumer backlash ("IDS survival strategies" 1997). Moreover, vertical integration limits choice: "When financing and delivery of care is integrated, competition for consumer preference occurs only once, and that is to select the integrated system. This raises concerns at the market, provider, and individual levels" (Shactman and Altman 1995, 14).

Almost two decades ago, Starr observed that public financing of health care through Medicare and Medicaid made it attractive to investors and set in motion the formation of large-scale corporations. The consequences have only accelerated since then:

> Paradoxically, the efforts to control expenditures for health services also stimulated corporate development. The conservative appropriation of liberal reform in the early seventies opened up HMOs as a field for business investment. And in ways entirely unexpected, the regulation of hospitals and other efforts to contain costs set off a wave of acquisitions, mergers, and diversification in the nonprofit as well as profit-making sectors of the medical care industry. Pressure for efficient, business-like management of health care has also contributed to the collapse of the barriers that traditionally prevented corporate control of health services. (1982, 428)

Other observers concur:

> Large, integrated networks can present a conflicting set of incentives as they seek to maximize the number of covered lives, minimize the amount of utilization, and maximize the quality of care. They tend to be for-profit because access to equity and capital markets is necessary to build such huge organizations. Both the capital needed to assemble these systems and the flow of capital they generate provide a different kind of health organization. Rather than being governed by a board of directors from the local community, they are more likely to be run by MBAs whose attention is focused on financial markets and payments to stock and bond holders. Their sheer size in terms of capital and employment is likely to make them a potent political force. (Shactman and Altman 1995, 14)

Consolidation in health care organizations mirrors that occurring on the larger American corporate scene, notably in the banking, airline, automobile, and telecommunications industries. The 1990s have become known as a decade of mergers and acquisitions in the interest of increasing shareholders' value. Very little has been heard about the role of antitrust laws during this period of "merger mania." Thus it took no small amount of courage for St.

Luke's Hospital in San Francisco to file an antitrust suit early in 1999 against one of the largest conglomerates in California, Sutter Health. According to a reporter who is following this legal action, Sutter is a $2.7 billion corporation that would qualify for the Fortune 1000 if it were a for-profit corporation rather than a nonprofit charitable trust (and therefore largely unregulated). Sutter operates the three sites of California Pacific Medical Center (CPMC), formerly Presbyterian, Children's and Ralph K. Davies hospitals. The suit charges that St. Luke's could be driven out of business through a contract with San Francisco's largest medical group, Brown and Toland, which requires that the medical group admit all of its insured patients to CPMC. With 2,000 doctors, this group represents almost half the doctors in the market area. St. Luke's claims it can put a person in a hospital bed for $945 while it costs $1,450 at a CPMC hospital—leading St. Luke's to question why it is not getting those admissions. Although the subject of the suit is the 24 percent of their patients with HMO coverage, the hospital's dispute over the whole system of contracting is potentially precedent-setting (Abate KQED). St. Luke's position, according to an insightful article in the *San Francisco Chronicle*, is that CPMC is siphoning millions of dollars in revenues that St. Luke's needs to stay afloat. By extension, St. Luke's lawsuit draws attention to the increasing problem of access to care, exacerbated by the current emphasis on market competition. The hospital serves approximately 340,000 people, many of them poor and non–English-speaking. The statistics cited in the newspaper illustrate the effect of the new arrangements on charity care:

> Statistics gathered by the Office of Statewide Planning and Development bear out St. Luke's claims that it does more than other hospitals to treat patients regardless of ability to pay. For 1996, the most recent year data were available, St. Luke's dispensed $3.3 million in charity care, or 2.2 percent of its total revenues of $148 million. Statewide, all hospitals averaged a 1.1 percent donation to charity care in that reporting period. By contrast, CPMC told the state it handed out $1.2 million in charity care, or just two-tenths of 1 percent of its total revenues of $522 million. The charity figures actually understate St. Luke's care to low-income patients, because they leave out the fact that nearly 40 percent of its patients are poor enough to qualify for Medi-Cal. (Abate 1999a)

In the past, hospitals paid for nonpaying patients by using "creative accounting," shifting the burden of the costs onto private patients. That they no longer can do this makes the St. Luke's lawsuit all the more salient. By relieving the public institution, San Francisco General Hospital, of some of its caseload, St. Luke's performs a community service not evident to the taxpayer. Nevertheless, this is not the emphasis of the lawsuit. Rather, it is that being driven out of business "would lessen competition in the hospital market" (Abate 1999a, D4).

A telling indication of the extent of market incursion on health care is the extension of market language to include "product differentiation" and "branding." In a bizarre incidence of the "branding of America" (Hambleton 1987)—a phenomenon that has burgeoned since corporate logos moved to the outside of apparel and owners started naming ball parks after corporate sponsors—AiC, in 1997, designed a conference on "Product Differentiation Strategies for Managed Care." The brochure for this event offered participants a chance to learn how to "gain market share and minimize risk." Included in the cover letter's usual "You won't want to miss this important industry event!" was the 1990s truism: "Products and pricing are so similar from plan to plan that MCOs must differentiate themselves to gain a competitive edge!"

And in 1999, HealthCareAmerica sponsored "the *first* National Executive Conference" on "Branding, Positioning, and Competitive Strategy for the Healthcare: A Brand New Day in Healthcare." Their announcement asserted that "gaining a competitive advantage by developing and establishing a strong brand identity and the brand equity that follows has become a critical issue for healthcare organizations." One session, entitled "What Do Coke, Milk, and Health Care Have in Common? Not Enough," focused on how healthcare should learn from the advertising industry:

> When was the last time you saw an advertisement that described Coca-Cola as the 'best tasting, brown colored, carbonated sugar water that comes in convenient, recyclable aluminum cans and bottles?' Informational advertising will tell you the soft drink tastes good. Conceptual advertising will make you thirsty for it. Healthcare, like any other industry, needs to connect and motivate.

Another session presented "a panel of executives from companies such as Procter & Gamble, Disney, Gillette, Simmons Company, and others, sharing their wisdom to help healthcare executives think creatively about their own brand equity challenges." Yet another offered a case study of the venerable Mayo Clinic, whose name in other times would not have been considered in these terms: "Many would argue that Mayo Clinic, unusually enough for a healthcare organization, already had a brand name with considerable brand equity, that customers / patients came to them from far and wide because of the existing strength of their brand. Nevertheless, they recently rethought and refocused their approach to brand management."

A major consequence of this highly competitive and hugely complex private structure is that it has now joined with government in placing regulatory constraints on health care services.

> The DRGs mechanistically create new, universal, standardized, statistical norms of practice, with the primary goals of reducing utilization and costs—

and with no necessity for looking at a living, breathing patient. But the system itself is not to blame; like all bureaucratic mechanisms, it is 'value neutral.' Thus it serves the ideological and economic interest of anyone who has the power to use it. (Leyerle 1994, 64)

So too does the private system serve ideological and economic interests. Although both DRGs and HMOs work simultaneously to control providers and to ration services, "HMOs are far less efficient than DRGs, since they require massive duplication of functions and still permit wide variations in the ways physicians practice medicine around the country. They cannot completely 'standardize' practice because individual HMOs create and enforce their own goals, based on diverse professional norms and values regarding patient care" (ibid.). While HMOs alone cannot completely standardize practice, conglomerates such as Sutter Health, by purchasing many hospitals in a region, do potentially have the power to affect the standard of care in that region profoundly. In addition, Leyerle raises the compelling point that rather than reduce health care costs, administrative surveillance and control mechanisms (public *and* private) have significantly increased health care costs for the United States as a whole.

It may be that our pluralistic health care system is now so complex that any and all regulatory strategies will ultimately fail to achieve their cost-control objectives. In fact, acceptance of a health care financing and delivery system as complex as we now have as a given in our regulatory equation is probably a mistake. Efforts to regulate such a system must be complex also and, over the long term, expense generating. In fact, there is substantial evidence to support the point that the relatively high expense of the American system, as contrasted with the system of most other developed countries, is more due to its overall complexity than to the alleged waste and inefficiency of health care providers or any of its other components. (Kinzer 1988, 28–29)

One can hardly look back on the old days of unbridled fee-for-service and conclude that it was without serious faults. Another long-time observer, Emily Friedman, argues persuasively that trade-offs between cost and quality in both fee-for-service and managed care have varied enormously. She points out that sometimes cost has won; sometimes quality has won.

This does not mean that high cost implies good quality or that low cost implies good quality, for that matter. However, when the cost / quality trade-off is unbalanced, one consequence is that patients usually bear the brunt of the failure. The ethical issues of balancing cost and quality under fee-for-service payment have to do with inappropriate care, profiteering, patient disempowerment, violation of the Hippocratic promise to do no harm, and the violent maldistribution of resources in a society that could do many other things with the money that is being misallocated or squandered. These same issues arise under managed care. The fact is that managed care is no more a magic bullet than fee-for-service incentives are inherently evil, and vice versa.

Furthermore, it is fruitless to depict either fee-for-service or managed care approaches as monolithic, implying that they do not vary internally but only from each other. Fee-for-service incentives and structures can be good or bad. It depends on the specific circumstances, including the structure of the provider, the ownership of the plan and providers, the incentives (financial and otherwise) involved, and the patient populations. (Friedman 1997, 176)

So where does this leave accountability for quality of care in hospitals? The complexity of the overall system, the intricacies of the regulatory mechanisms, the competitive drive for profit, and the restructuring brought about by managed care—all of these factors combine to create the need for oversight of quality of care while simultaneously making effective oversight a formidable proposition. The administrator of a small, rural hospital, interviewed in this study issued the following complaint:

> I certainly don't want to be interpreted . . . I don't think any hospital administrator would want to be interpreted as feeling that quality assurance is not important. However, we, like many others, are very frustrated by all of the people out there who are getting involved in this process and expect us to respond to their particular interpretation of what QA is. We've got the Joint Commission, we've got the state of California, we have the insurance companies themselves. Now we're getting into the HMOs and all the managed care people. They all have a special set of criteria that they want you to meet. And they don't want to line up. I mean, I wish they'd all go off some place and talk and be in each other's heads and come back with a list and say, this is what we want you to do. I think that's our biggest frustration.

Writing in 1995, the editor of *Health Care Management Review* looked back at the articles he has published on governance and ownership of hospitals, managed care, and physician practices, and observed, "In a large sense, the world is changing without hard evidence of whether it will work well" (Brown 1995, 5). QA/I personnel are expected to provide a good part of this evidence through the mechanisms that have been established to monitor and improve the quality of hospital care. We turn to these next.

NOTES

1. For an analysis of the role of interest groups in the defeat of the 1993 health care reform proposal, see Johnson and Broder (1996). *See also* Alford (1975). For a more general discussion of the relationships that link politicians with corporations and the "modern methodologies of persuasion," *see* Greider (1992).

2. For a discussion of utilization methods and criteria, see Restuccia (1995).
3. The Joint Commission's Comprehensive Accreditation Manual for Hospitals for the year 2000 contains close to 1000 pages, covering 564 standards, including text on the intent of each standard and examples of evidence of compliance.
4. Millenson provides a lively account of the role played in the 1990s by benefits managers who banded together into the Business Health Care Action Group (BHCAG), pushing the entire Twin Cities (Minneapolis-St. Paul) health care system to manage the cost and quality of care provided. In 1992, the participating BHCAG members included fourteen companies whose workers and their families added up to 150,000 lives. The emergence of the BHCAG as a "powerful and sophisticated buyer" is significant: "The coalition specified in detail exactly what *it* wanted to purchase rather than leaving it to the medical professionals to define the health care services they would sell." Millenson (1997, Chapter 11; quote is from p. 240).
5. Dr. Mark D. Smith, addressing the International Congress on Performance Measurement and Improvement in Health Care, November 14, 1997. Dr. Smith is President and CEO of California Healthcare Foundation, established to improve access to affordable, quality health care for underserved individuals.
6. "Regulation of HMOs is far from perfect," *Wall Street Journal* (April 29, 1998), A14. One serious flaw in the regulatory picture is that under a 1987 U.S. Supreme Court ruling, employer-paid HMOs fall within the federal Employee Retirement Income Security Act of 1974, or ERISA. Workers who receive coverage from their employers cannot recover damages from an HMO for inappropriate denials or delays of care. HMOs that lose an ERISA grievance pay only the cost of the benefit denied, no penalties. "If ERISA rules applied to bank robberies, convicted thieves would simply have to give the money back" (Court 1999). Because of ERISA, HMOs have claimed that they are merely extensions of employee benefit plans and thus protected from state laws that have anything to do with health insurance. One by one, a few state legislatures have challenged this loophole. *See* Findlay (1997).
7. See note 5 above.

3

Formalizing the Accountability Endeavor

Forging a Path from Quality Assurance to Quality Improvement

> *Striving to do better, oft we mar what's well.*
> —*William Shakespeare*

The drive for accountability, manifested in the QA/I process, is based on the assumption that health care is an industry. According to *Webster's International Dictionary*, an industry is a group of productive and profit-making enterprises or organizations that have a similar technological structure of production and that produce or supply technically substitutable goods, services, or sources of income (for example, the auto, air-transport, poultry, or tourist industries). It does not take a dictionary to tell us that a "good" industry is one that is efficient and does not operate at a loss.

Rationalization of industries—planning, programming, product monitoring, accounting systems, and performance assessment—began with the late-nineteenth-century expansion of the railroad industry (Chandler 1980). The acknowledged pioneer of organizational efficiency—the first "management consultant"—was Frederick Winslow Taylor, who was driven by a religious sense of mission (Kanigel 1998; Bendix 1956). Early in the twentieth century, Taylor advised factory owners not only on how to cut labor costs by firing nonessential employees but also how to maximize productivity among those they retained. Taylorism has been described as "the Protestant Ethic in skeletal form, stripped of spiritual and even ethical flesh."

> Taylorized work was pure technique, devoid of any connection with worker's mind or soul.... Taylorism seeped into offices, schools, even

81

kitchens. . . . Time-and-motion study played a central role in making offices seem more like factories and schools seem more like prisons. . . . Ultimately, Taylorism survived most significantly as a set of rhetorical tendencies and tacit assumptions—an impulse to mask concentrated power in spurious technical language, a belief in a disembodied ideal of 'productivity' as the highest aim of human aspiration. (Lears 1997, 26)

Scientific management fit neatly with American progressive philosophy and the attendant value placed on societal improvement.

"During the 1920s and 1930s, the pages of journals such as *Modern Hospital* were filled with discussions advocating the use of corporate cost-accounting and capital-budgeting techniques and the systematization of personnel practices in order to achieve greater administrative control over hospital operations" (White 1994, 43). In the 1920s, a prestigious, privately funded commission, the Committee on the Costs of Medical Care, was established. Research reports from this commission provided detailed information on national health expenditures and the first reliable breakdown of the "medical dollar" (Starr 1982, 262). A CPA on the committee proclaimed, "Hospitals are in many respects typical of all business enterprise. Procedures of scientific management in a hospital are much the same as those in a hotel or other place of business" (Rorem 1982, 19).

Most organizations operate under the value of efficiency and have a long history of budgetary control, efficient resource allocation, and a philosophy of scientific management. Hospitals, however, are quite another matter. Under the full-care, hospital reimbursement system that existed prior to 1984, quality was the "taken-for-granted, dependable, and unquestionable value on which hospital practices and policies were organized and evaluated. . . . If considered at all, efficiency clearly was secondary to the value of quality" (Geist and Hardesty 1992, 76). Medicare's fixed-priced prospective payment system, using DRGs, became a turning point in the balance of these values. At the time DRGs were introduced, definitions of quality varied. To administrators, quality was evidence of the organization's best possible care, its professionalism, and the use of appropriate management strategies for coordination of services. To physicians, quality involved autonomy, skillful decision making, and concern for their reputation. To nurses, quality meant professional competence and—although this had been waning long before the 1980s as nurses' days became more and more filled with documentation—attention to patient's needs. To employers, the primary payers of health insurance, quality meant curtailing overuse of medical care while maintaining enough care to keep the workforce healthy. To insurance companies, quality meant realizing a profit while maintaining the satisfaction and loyalty of subscribers.

As hospitals have moved into the new accountability era a redefinition of quality has emerged, designed to fit the basic economic tenet of health care as an industry: improved efficiency will lead to improved care. What is not considered in this equation is the massive, invisible work necessary to achieve this goal. Within an extremely complicated health care system, QA/I is a no less intricate arena comprising people who must establish mechanisms for achieving quality, evaluate and monitor them, and then negotiate with hospital personnel in order to fit QA/I demands into daily hospital work. Attending a gathering of quality professionals, I was struck by a comment made by the guest speaker, a corporate trainer whose topic was "New Tools for Communication." She said, "I speak to a lot of groups and I have encountered no other industry that requires so many shifts in communication or where they occur so suddenly. One minute you're talking to a housekeeper regarding infection control, the next to a manager regarding the latest accreditation standard." In a convoluted way, quality professionals are caught in a paradox—using quality improvement tools inherited from corporate America, all the while adding to the financial crisis, since the work of QA/I is itself costly.

FINDING THE RIGHT PATH

"I come from Boston where roads were made in the directions the cows walked. A lot of people in health care right now are managing change in the direction that the cows are walking." So said a health educator interviewed for this study. We now need a QA/I lexicon defining such terms as "outcomes research," "continuous quality improvement," and "benchmarking." But even with such a guide, these terms will mean different things to the various players in the health care arena. By what cow path did we get here?

As early as 1956, Paul Lembcke had called attention to the need for medical audit, which he defined as "the evaluation of medical care in retrospect through analysis of clinical records" (*see also* Lembcke 1959, 1967). In the 1970s, the Joint Commission mandated a system of medical audits, requiring that each hospital set criteria for high-quality care, determine what exceptions to the criteria were acceptable, examine a representative number of charts to see if the criteria were met, and note the variances or failure to meet them. Since physicians conducted audits, the process came to be known as "peer review." While the concept was sound, there were impediments to effective audits:

> Problems with the system were manifold. One of the most irritating aspects was that we got locked up in a ritual. There was more emphasis by Joint Com-

mission surveyors and everybody else on how an audit was performed, on the process, than on improving quality. Was there a proper meeting to set criteria? Were minutes kept? How many criteria were set? Was that really enough? Were they ratified? We almost lost sight of the purpose: that we were trying to measure performance. One of the traumas of the Joint Commission survey was that the surveyors would immediately sit down and ask to see some of our audits, and then would criticize how we did them. This wasn't necessarily the fault of the surveyors. They only had a limited amount of training on audit, and were given instructions, which were heavily weighted toward the cumbersome and redundant PEP system Performance Evaluation Procedure for Auditing and Improving Patient Care. Much of the protocol in the Joint Commission approach missed the point.

The topic, for example, was at first expected to be a diagnosis or surgical procedure—appendicitis, pneumonia, a caesarian section. But we discovered that this is not where the majority of patient care deficiencies lie. The problems are mostly in systems, many of which affect patient care only indirectly: the method of getting an X-ray report from radiology to the nursing station and onto a patient's chart, the procedure for administering cardiopulmonary resuscitation in the emergency department, . . . the procedure for dispensing medication, and so on. Yet according to the accreditation surveyors such audits were unacceptable for credit.

Another shortcoming was the method for setting criteria. It was an extremely painful process. The rules were that in a large hospital like ours, a peer group must set the criteria—internists for internal medicine, pediatricians for pediatrics, surgeons for surgery of course, and nurses for nursing. Each department had its own audit committee, which would meet periodically. First, the committee would set a topic. This would take forty-five minutes of arguing about the technical problems in choosing this or that diagnosis or procedure. When they finally arrived at a topic, they'd have to define the objective—what aspect of, say, pneumonia were they going to consider. Then they'd set the criteria, they'd toss them on the table, one after the other: such and such should be done in such a circumstance. There'd be dozens of them (in one case, they ended up with eighty-five) and often the criteria would be poorly defined, such as "severe headache." This made it very difficult for the people in the record room who were responsible for checking through fifty, sixty, or more charts to see if the criteria had been met. So the doctors were asked to be more restrictive, to define the criteria more precisely, and this involved more arguing and took more work. (Skillihorn 1980, 31–32)

Over the years, hospitals had devised mechanisms other than medical auditing to understand whether they were doing things right; for example, patient care conferences and medical committees to review tissue, infections, morbidity, and mortality. Although not required in all states, risk management programs were established by most hospitals during the 1970s and 1980s. "Risk managers" look at hospital policies and procedures in relation to changing external requirements, such as consent procedure for blood usage or liability related to the Americans with Disabilities Act. They also retroactively track unexpected events, "incident reports," sent to them by hospital personnel. Responsibility for different aspects of quality of care—infection control, utilization, risk management—remained separate in some hospitals, combined in others.

As the workload steadily increased because of the differing reporting schemes of external reviewers, new quality departments or components were established. Quality coordinators were urged to cut through the maze of constantly changing regulations and bring order to the quality of a hospital system that had become extremely complex. Their first decade was one of trial and error, as new professional roles evolved. Some quality staff came from medical records departments or regulatory agencies; in California they were drawn primarily from nursing. A quality coordinator, interviewed for this study, assessed the suitability of nurses for the job: "They're organized, they're used to fluid situations—they get good at molding and changing their day." Most departments experimented with concurrent review of charts for every admission, looking for discrepancies from established indicators. Called "quality screens," typical red flags were: readmission due to possible early discharge, operative complications, medication errors, and returns to surgery. Quality analysts were expected to use clinical judgment in reading between the lines but, as a medical-records manager observed, "God help the QA person who questioned a physician on *anything*."

Hospitals that found concurrent review too labor-intensive turned to retrospective review. Every quality coordinator interviewed for this study bemoaned the ongoing challenge of plowing through piles of journals and newsletters that addressed QA/I problems, and choosing from among multiple seminars devoted to the subject. "It's trying to assimilate it all and to try to take heart . . . to do the reading that allows you to make the decision is next to impossible. I have to skim and know what I'm trying to find because I just don't have time." During this period, quality analysts devised "studies," usually audits of 20–30 charts with a set of criteria that medical staff had put together. For a diabetes study, for example, they would review charts for level of blood values, medication ordered, and diet change; for a study of angioplasty (reconstruction of a blood vessel by balloon dilation) they would review for patients who had had a heart attack or had required bypass surgery within 48 hours of the original procedure.

The Joint Commission was telling hospitals, "look at your scope of care and see what's most important to you," but their manual of quality criteria had now become exceedingly complex. As documentation of peer review became more stringent, physicians turned to the nurse-turned-quality analyst, who, in her traditional role as handmaiden, was expected to attend peer review meetings, bring appropriate cases to the physicians' attention, and hand-record and transcribe the minutes so that compliance with accreditation standards was documented. One told me, "The physicians are coddled a lot by their analyst and they like that."

By 1993, quality coordinators were complaining that, as one expressed it, "We do a tremendous amount of work for very little payoff in terms of: What kinds of actions were taken based on our review? Did they implement new policies or change practice? Did they counsel among themselves?" The appraisal of one coordinator was echoed by most of those interviewed for this study: "The quality process has come about as the result of regulation where it became a paperwork versus a real process." Adhering to the directives of the Joint Commission and to state standards, each QA/I office observed for this study contained mountains of binders for every medical service, documenting that a program was in place and that there were two indicators of important aspects of care—say, infection rate following cholecystectomies or rate of caesarian sections—that were being reviewed on a regular basis. One director characterized the situation as follows: "There's kind of an overkill, looking for the bad apple out there. Because the physicians didn't police themselves well in the past, the policemen are being very aggressive—there's a lot of baton swinging." All coordinators interviewed spoke of the difficulty of adapting to yearly changes in the regulations, especially those of the Joint Commission. As one said, "There's a communication lag. They make a change and it's easy for them to implement but we have to respond. So you feel like a chameleon, always mutating, like an amoeba inching your way around."

A hospital administrator referred to QA/I personnel as "worker bees." More accurately, they were expected to be the messengers of increasing complicated (and ever-changing) regulatory demands, and more likely to be seen as killer bees by some of the medical staff. For the most part, however, their work remained invisible to staff and patients. New clerical and administrative job categories in hospitals had expanded rapidly as huge numbers of people were required to handle the increasing categories of things that must be added to the official records and as surveillance had become dispersed and fragmented. "Like a factory assembly line, where no worker can recognize a product as his or her own, surveillance is divided into many different tasks. The heart of this process is to redefine and recreate the patient chart, transforming it from a working tool that simultaneously protects the authority of providers to a surveillance mechanism for bureaucratic managers" (Leyerle 1994, 77).

As the scope of work has increased, and the need for expertise has been increasingly recognized, some—but not all—quality personnel have attained greater professionalization by seeking (through formal examination) certification from the National Association for Healthcare Quality or the American Society for Quality, a professional organization with a health care division. Nevertheless, the main task for QA/I personnel is something no certification can provide for them: rationalizing the amorphous and conferring reason on the irrational. This is a process of reaching agreements and understandings with other hospital personnel, especially nurses and physicians, and continually renegotiating them as unexpected problems appear. It also means building upon previous relationships or in some cases overcoming previous resentments, working with competing turf rights, and surmounting "the way we've always done things."

MASTERING THE TECHNIQUES

Remarking on the doubling of America's health care costs in the 1970s, and then, as if to mock the cost-containment efforts that followed, the doubling of costs again in the 1980s, a book heralding the new age of accountability described the physician, the patient, the administrator, and the payer alike as, put simply, *frustrated* (Berwick et al. 1990). The authors' prescription— that health care organizations apply modern quality-management techniques as their primary operating strategy—arose from the National Demonstration Project on Quality Improvement in Health Care, which brought together twenty-one health-care organizations and an equal number of industrial quality-management experts in 1987. The project convinced its participants (or so this document proclaimed) that the answer to the question, "Can the tools of modern quality improvement, with which other industries have achieved breakthroughs in performance, help in health care as well?" was a resounding YES. More specifically, they proclaimed, "We are confident that, with time, resources, and committed leaders, quality improvement methods will flourish in health care as they have in other industries, and that all of us—patients, clinicians, managers, payers, and society at large—will profit" (ibid. 158).

By the 1990s, QA/I personnel had been given an extensive armature to accomplish their daunting task. One reference describes more than 50 quality tools designed to solve a particular problem or achieve a certain goal (Tague 1995). Of these, the ones described in the next section are most dominant.

Continuous Quality Improvement

Of pivotal importance was the introduction in 1986 of the Joint Commission's Agenda for Change, shifting the focus from individual cases to the hospital's organizational structure. After following the cow paths in a somewhat helter skelter fashion, quality professionals now had a clearer route to follow, called continuous quality improvement (CQI).

The warm reception afforded this technique arose in part from the frustration of working with the old regulations. Many had seen medical audits as a useless waste of resources, a failure. Department audits ignored the fact that the patient is not taken care of by a department but by a team, often a huge one. Even Joint Commission representatives could say, in retrospect, "In too many cases, these studies became paper exercises conducted to meet Joint Commission or Professional Standards Review Organization requirements. . . . Preoccupation with the audit requirement rather than quality of care had left hospitals at the periphery of meaningful quality assurance activities" (Roberts et al. 1987, 939).

A parallel to CQI in the education arena is, however, instructive. Discussing the current popularity of multi-intelligence theory, one observer suggests it "has proved powerful not because it's true but because it chimes with the values and presuppositions of the school world and of the larger culture" (Traub 1998, 22). Similarly, the philosophy of CQI dovetailed nicely with the need for nonmedical hospital staff to participate in decision-making and with the dominant American values of egalitarianism and democratic participation, with a little of the trendy attention to "diversity" in the mix.

The Joint Commission had taken its cue from the work of an American, W. Edward Deming, whose training and management system focused on worker involvement, goal setting, and communication within the corporate structure, as opposed to competition among workers and management control (Deming 1986; Walton 1986). A prophet without honor in his own country, Deming had taken his philosophy to Japanese industry after World War II, where it was more cordially received. An American admirer has said that Deming is one of the most revered Americans in Japan, second only to General Douglas MacArthur, and that the walls of the Toyota plant contain three pictures of honor: Mr. Toyota, the Emperor, and Dr. Deming.[1] Indeed, since 1951, the highest medal for economic achievement in Japan has been the Deming Prize.

Expanded in the 1950s (Juran et al. 1979; Juran 1964), Deming's theories are credited with helping Japan revolutionize its manufacturing. It was not until the 1970s, however, when U.S. manufacturers began to feel pressure from Japanese competition, that the principles were applied in the United States. The Ford Motor Company became an ardent convert, as did Westinghouse, Hewlett-Packard, Honeywell, and the 3M Company. Called Total Quality Management (TQM) by industry (although Deming himself never used this term), much of the philosophy is based on the idea that more than 90 percent of error *cannot* be traced to a faulty piece of material, a poor worker, or a broken machine. Error, rather, comes from the system created by management (Crosby 1979; Ishikawa 1985; Scher-kenbach 1986).

One of the leading proponents of the suitability of TQM to health care contrasted it to the "Theory of Bad Apples," which emphasizes inspection. Previously, quality control entailed a search for outliers—statistics far enough from the average that chance alone is unlikely to account for deviance. "Bad Apples theorists publish mortality data, invest heavily in systems of case-mix adjustment, and fund vigilant regulators. Some measure their success by counting heads on platters" (Berwick 1989, 53; *see also* Baltalden and Stolz 1993; Baltalden and Buchanan 1989; Blumenthal and Scheck 1995; Laffel and Blumenthal 1989). TQM was designed to replace the old notion that "managers think, workers do" and the old concept of quality control. "Inspection is like scraping the toast after it's burnt. You maybe should adjust the toaster first" ("Forum" 1993).

In no time, TQM became a big business for consultants, prompting one commentator to suggest that TQM was adding substantially to hospitals' operating costs—the precise ailment that it was supposed to cure. (Burda 1991). Disciples of Deming and Juran warned that the health-care market was becoming saturated with poorly trained TQM consultants who were selling programs that were highly unlikely to work. Nevertheless, the clearest sign that there was money to be made in TQM was the movement of quality-consulting firms from other industries—for example, Philip Crosby Associates—into the hospital market. Close on their heels were the big accounting firms, prompting Brent James, director of medical research at Intermountain Health Care in Salt Lake City, to say, "these firms are learning at the expense of their customers" (Burda 1991, 27). Evoking images of the old snake-oil salesman, Matthew Kelliher, director of quality management at Harvard Community Health Plan in Brookline Village, Massachusetts, delivered a telling barb:

> Consultants that used to sell productivity are selling quality improvement systems. Consultants that used to sell team building are selling total quality management. Consultants that used to sell cost accounting are selling cost-of-quality systems. (ibid.)

The criticism did not stop the movement. Hospitals not only continued to spend considerable money hiring consultants but some got into the business by offering workshops to others.

By the time the Joint Commission adopted TQM, it had been renamed "Continuous Quality Improvement" (CQI)—"continuous" meaning that an organization is never finished improving a product or service. The principles remained the same: problems should be identified by workers themselves, who then should interact with each other in multidisciplinary, creative ways to change its source, develop indicators to assess the change, and periodically monitor the effectiveness of actions in order, in CQI language, to "maintain the gain." Indeed, the CQI argot is a wondrous thing. Middle managers are told to be "coaches," not "bosses," told further that people need to feel part of the genesis of a solution in order to feel that they have "ownership." The creed is the PDCA cycle: Plan, Do, Check, Act. CQI also emphasizes identifying "internal customers"—Deming had said that everyone has a customer, meaning it can be the person down the production line—and "nominal group technique," a weighted ranking that allows a team to rank a large number of issues without creating "winners" and "losers."

For a time there was a religious fanaticism in the belief that "walking the talk," would lead to "lateral integration" of departments. In those early days, hours were spent constructing the language of "vision statements." A typical hospital vision statement (they became interchangeable over time) begins, "We are committed to be a nationally recognized high performance team that is dedicated to a tradition of excellence and building an organization where: Quality is our organizing principle—patient care is our passion." This statement then listed other objectives along the lines of dedication to patients, fulfilling the medical staffs' personal and professional aspirations, and being an organization where employees and volunteers look forward to coming to work each day. In keeping with the CQI canon, the vision statement is usually accompanied by a "mission statement" (more long hours working on proper wording and on the difference between a mission and a vision). The mission statement of the above hospital states: "Our mission is to enhance and support the quality of life of our patients, their families and the community through the provision of high quality, nationally recognized patient care services. We are also committed to medical education and research programs that distinguish our organization and contribute to the quality of our patient care."

The link to the value Americans place on self-help—epitomized in Alcoholics Anonymous and its successors, as well as groups that foster "enforced self-improvement," "empowerment," and "personal transformation"—is obvious enough to need no amplification. Also apparent is the tie-in to the feminist movement with regard to respect, collaboration, and cooperation. Nevertheless, creating this paradigm shift was a formidable task for CQI believers. For the entire first year of my research, QA/I personnel in the two hospitals where I did the most intensive observation were constantly re-educating staff, who clung to the old Joint Commission reporting system based on indicators, instead of realizing that standards now required that they identify a problem and organize a multidisciplinary team to address it. As the concept caught on, typical CQI projects included availability of medical records (a universal problem, certain to evoke laughter from any assemblage of QA/I personnel), coordinating starting time of surgery, reducing the number of groin bleeds after cardiac catheterization, and improving control over designated blood.

One of the CQI projects observed in my research is a good example of the lengthy process entailed in using this tool. Addressing coordination of surgical starting time, the team used all of the paraphernalia of CQI—a facilitator, a transcriber, brainstorming sessions, butcher paper, flip-chart tear sheets (inscribed with color-coded marking pens and then taped to the wall), and preparation of diagrams and graphs. The process is best described in the QA/I director's own words:

> We sent out a physician satisfaction survey from which we learned that physicians were upset about the operating room (OR) time delays. So we established a team to include an OR technician, a short-stay person, a management person, a staff nurse, an admitting person, a management engineering person, an anesthesiologist, and some surgeons. We met every single week for six months. We decided to brainstorm . . . a lot of these people are intimidated by the surgeons there because it's new but I asked, 'what is an OR start time?' And I had 16 people in the room and 16 different answers. The surgeon thought it was the cut time, the anesthesiologist thought it was the anesthesiologist's time, the technician thought it was the time to go pick up the patient. Other people thought it was the time they came in from the outer part of the OR to the big double doors. Another group thought it was the time they went into the small doors into their little room. And it was all the same people that were working together for 25 years. . . . We decided that the OR start time is the time that the patient passes through the portal—now we call it "portal time." So then we asked, "what are the reasons that the patient is not going to pass through that door at the time that we have now decided it's going to be?" They came up with 58 causes. We did the usual CQI things: we categorized the causes, then we put them on a fishbone diagram (the diagram is shaped like a fish) with cause and effect arrows providing the skeleton. Then we broke down into subcommittees.

One result was a streamlining of the admitting procedure, which required hardwiring the computer system, followed by a protracted discussion of whose budget would cover the $600 for this upgrade. The committee also discovered that 50 percent of the time the anesthesiologist was late, whereas 50 percent of the time it was the surgeon—and, more significant, one particular surgeon was consistently late, delaying the schedule for the entire day. Although this finding came as no great surprise to anyone, one nurse pointed out: "Sometimes, these protracted meetings are the only way to get that kind of message across."

Throughout CQI projects, team members must be convinced, cajoled, manipulated, coerced, rewarded, etc. As in any organizational situation, reactions within the group may run the gamut from enthusiasm to personal antipathy toward a fellow-member who "gets on my nerves." Success requires a strong facilitator, such as the nurse who told me, "I look at it like 'this meeting is costing us $400 in our time. We need to come out of this with $400 worth of value.'" Nevertheless, many QA/I personnel came to view CQI as a road to legitimacy and larger acceptance of the importance of their work. The statement of one quality coordinator is revealing: "As I told the board, quality is from the basement to the board room, not just my little office in the basement." Another coordinator expressed the mixed feelings evoked by using the CQI process: "We reported the results of our CQI task force on 'advanced directives' (obtaining written consent regarding predetermined wishes on end-of-life decisions, a federal law) to the administrative team and it went very well. R. had graphs made of our compliance before and then after, which was much more powerful than if we had just given them raw numbers." Later in the interview, this coordinator, who had acted as facilitator of the group, alluded to "unspoken constraints." Pressed to explain, she said, "Members brought old messages along with them. . . . The representative of the ER and the one from Admissions were very protective of their staff, worried about being encroached on." When I commented that the ER representative had stood apart, never sitting, during the last meeting I attended, the facilitator answered, "She told R. afterwards that she felt she had sold her staff, her colleagues, down the river." The facilitator also remarked that everybody had made a point of being at the meetings early on, "and the longer and longer this dragged out, I found myself losing interest! And people didn't feel the commitment to it that they did early on." Her conclusion was that, "Yes, I think it can be adapted. I think that the tools, using the diagrams and the flow charts worked. But I don't think it has to be as formalized as we at X Hospital tend to make it. . . . You can become so fixated on that fishbone diagram or whatever, that you lose sight of what the purpose is."

Certainly, CQI is still embraced in some hospitals, with some success. Yet one wonders how slavish adherence to the CQI book can survive in any business after the merciless lampooning it has received at the hands of Scott Adams in his popular Dilbert cartoons. A memorable one, for instance, shows a consultant who has been sent to "Elbonia" to teach total quality management explaining, "In the old days, quality was just an empty word meaning 'good.' Eventually it evolved into a complicated method for transferring your money to business consultants." In another, the consultant is pointing to a fish skeleton he has drawn on a huge sheet of poster paper. He tells the Elbonians that the diagram helps identify the root cause of problems. Hearing his wise conclusion, "in your case, the root problem seems to be that you're a nation of imbeciles," the Elbonians have the last word: "True, but *you're* the one who had to draw a dead fish to figure it out."

Countering the glowing reports given at conferences on successful CQI projects are the stumbling-blocks. Two years after observing CQI at the height of its popularity in one hospital, I asked a QA/I analyst if the process was being used. A number of the proponents who had received intensive CQI training at the hospital's expense, she said, had either left or been discharged as part of the cost-cutting impetus. No CQI projects were operating, mainly because the reduced staff were too busy with a targeted review by the Health Care Financing Administration (HCFA) and the California health department, arising from allegations of substandard care that had reached the press. Moreover, the CEO had been replaced by a man whom she described as a "terror," whose "tone at meetings is if you don't do this, you're fired"—the antithesis of the CQI philosophy! She concluded, however, that "things like CQI don't go through the system without touching some people"—a comment given emphasis by another QA/I professional: "CQI may have been a Joint Commission fad, but I'll tell you teamwork and using the staff to help build your systems is the only way to improve." The strengths and weaknesses of CQI and whether it can work in health care continue to be debated (Stern 1997; Nerenz 19976; Marquerez 1997; Goldman 1997).

Critical Pathways

A big thrust in the new business paradigm in hospitals has been to reorient personnel to a "process management model," defining work as a process with inputs, outputs, customers, and suppliers (Spath 1993). Initially, process management techniques were applied to administrative functions, such as timeliness of laboratory results. Then, in response to pressure to adapt process management to the clinical realm, hospitals began to plot patient care with a tool called "critical (or clinical) pathways." It "defines the optimum sequencing and timing of the functions performed by physicians, nurses, and other staff for a particular diagnosis or procedure" (ibid. 49). Care plans and flow sheets were already part of nurses' repertoire. Critical paths enlarged upon these nursing strategies by being multidisciplinary, in keeping with the tenets of CQI and Joint Commission standards. This means getting *everyone* who contributes to a therapeutic or diagnostic process (physician, nurse, physical therapist, dietician, pharmacist, social worker) involved in developing consistent care plans for patient groups, recommending appropriate education and training for clinical staff, implementing the plan, monitoring and evaluating clinical outcomes, and then adding to the plan as necessary. Automating information from critical pathways on the care for various procedures and illnesses was expected to create a database for measuring outcomes. Typically, hospitals' earliest critical paths focused on the most manageable conditions, such as pneumonia, total hip replacement, and caesarian section without complications. These paths are essentially diagrams of the expected treatment for each day, with squares to be filled in acknowledging accountability as each task is completed.

Critical pathways are the application of Deming's teaching that the most effective way to improve quality is to reduce variation in the provision of a service or product. As advocated by two health care business consultants, "Naturally there will always be some unpredictable variations among patients and illnesses; and of course every physician has her or his own way of doing things. But by using critical pathways, a hospital can do things consistently to reduce the impact of common causes of variation" (Hart and Musfeldt 1992, 56). A number of states have already passed, or are considering, legislation requiring hospitals to implement critical pathways. Unfortunately, while some hospitals have successfully launched pathway programs, in practice they have run into problems with updating and relevance and, in a world of massive record-keeping, tend to get overlooked amid daily paperwork.

Practice Guidelines

While advocates carefully stipulated that critical pathways should be physician-directed, a radical confrontation with medical decision making has been proposed in the form of practice guidelines (Field and Lohr 1990). Traditionally, medical practice policy has evolved "through textbooks, journal articles, speeches, letters to the editor, pronouncements by department chairpersons, and conversations in hospital cafeterias" (Eddy 1990, 1265). Peer review of medical practice in hospitals is no less haphazard:

> Subjective evaluation tends to result in selective decision. An incident of mismanagement by a respected member of the medical staff might be interpreted by peers as "one of those things that can happen to anybody," while an identical incident involving a less prominent physician might be treated as a significant deficiency. One physician is excused, the other is penalized. Moreover, too often nothing is done about a physician's deficiencies until a serious incident occurs or the hazard to patients cannot be ignored. Because of the elaborate appeal process, reviewers do not recommend restriction of privileges unless deficiencies have been so well documented that the decision is certain to be upheld. Essential as the appeal process is for protection against capricious accusations and unwarranted penalties, it does tend to limit peer review proceedings against physicians to cases where the deficiencies are flagrant. Thus peer review is oriented more toward penalty than prevention or remedy. (Skillihorn 1980, 106–7)

The mythology of American medicine includes an idealized picture of medical peer review in hospitals—physicians on the medical staff meeting together to review carefully and objectively the professional performance of fellow medical staff members and willing to recommend education, surveillance and, on occasion, punitive interventions (Hershey 1992). PSROs and then PROs, discussed in Chapter Two, were required to review cases but they were not powerful enough to impose order on clinical decision making. Hope currently resides in practice guidelines, developed in the last two decades to replace clinical decision making based on "standard and accepted practice." Under this departure, practice policy may be developed by a task force of a specialty society, an advisory panel of a third-party payer, or a government-convened consensus panel. Many in the accountability arena are optimistic about this educational trend and its potential to reduce inappropriate treatment. A QA/I professional made the following comparison: "A good analogy is if you're going to make beef stew. There are not 35 ways to make beef stew and you can always do what is called 'exception management' to take care of the variation." A quality coordinator in another hospital was optimistic that a practice guideline on asthma would lead to consistency. She described the process:

> We have a group that's been meeting about a year that's part of a state-wide consortium of pediatric hospitals to put into place what you should do when you get an in-patient asthma child and try to track if we do what we say we should do. Then what are the variations and what does it cost and what's the length of stay, and then outcomes. The ones who are on the team like it because *they want the community physicians to conform to what these specialists think should be done* (emphasis added). Because a lot of community physicians don't always buy into the cutting edge, now use theophylline instead of beclomethasone or whatever the debates are about what should be done. For example, I know one of our leading admitters believes epinephrine should be what you do first, and that's not in the guidelines. So we're going to have a job convincing him to go along with this and to justify why his kids either cost less, get better fast, stay less, or whatever.

As part of drive to establish guidelines for the practice of medicine, Congress created the Agency for Health Care Policy and Research (AHCPR) in 1989 to determine, in the legislature's optimistic language, "how diseases, disorders and other health conditions can most effectively and appropriately be diagnosed and treated." (The new office was almost named the Agency for Health Care Research and Policy, "until senate aides noticed during a late-night drafting session that the acronym might sound undignified" Kosterlitz 1991, 576.) Agency guidelines, developed by multidisciplinary panels of health professionals *and consumers,* were to be based on reviews of relevant scientific evidence as well as professional judgment

(Agency for Health Care Policy and Research 1995). The assumption was that by combining the vast records that have been accumulated by hospitals, insurers, and government health programs, one could get a handle on which medical interventions worked best. When the National Academy of Science's Institute of Medicine was asked to advise the agency, its president, Samuel O. Thier, said, "One of the problems is that each of the different communities looks at the development of guidelines and sees something else. It's almost a Rorschach test" (Kosterlitz 1991, 574).

John Wennberg, Dartmouth University Medical School's expert on regional variations across geographic areas in the per-capita use rates of many medical and surgical procedures, was the inspiration for the AHCPR practice guideline program (Stano 1994; Wennberg and Fowler 1977; Wennberg and Gittelsohn 1973, 1982; McPherson et al. 1982). Much earlier, British researcher Archie Cochrane had postulated that the effectiveness of medical care was unproven, advocating well-designed randomized controlled trials and review of the knowledge base to remedy this situation (1972). Wennberg argued further that geographical variations arise from differences in physicians' clinical judgment about what constitutes appropriate treatment (1984, 1985). He and several others (Clark 1990; Escarce 1993; Folland and Stano 1990; McLaughlin et al. 1989; Stano 1991, 1993) promoted awareness of the limited information on which practitioners and patients often base their decisions. Many physicians, on the other hand, are wary of practice guidelines, calling them "cookbook medicine" prompting the observation, "Asking doctors to practice according to a formula, particularly ones promulgated by government functionaries, they felt, was akin to asking Julia Child to consult Betty Crocker" (Kosterlitz 1991, 574).

Testifying in 1995 before a congressional subcommittee, a Government Accounting Office (GAO) representative reported that physicians, nurses, health plans, insurers and regulators could now choose from more than 24,000 guidelines developed by more than 75 organizations. As to AHCPR's practice guidelines, the GAO found that during the agency's first five years it had received mixed reviews from potential users. The witness praised the AHCPR for "its use of a rigorous, evidence-based methodology, multidisciplinary panels, and emphasis on health care consumers." On the other hand, the guidelines were criticized for not being "user-friendly." Texts were too long, the GAO representative said: AHCPR's guideline for depression at that time weighed in at two volumes and 327 pages. Moreover, topics were too broad, prompting the Institute of Medicine to recommend that the agency develop a practice guideline on, for instance, the pharmacological management of a heart attack rather than a heart attack in general. In the end, it was a political fight, rather than any criticism of the form AHCPR's practice guidelines had taken, that almost brought the agency down (*see* Chapter Four). Under pressure from a new lobbying organization, the Center for Patient Advocacy, the House of Representatives passed a 1996 budget with zero funding for the AHCPR. Congress finally decided to preserve the agency, though with substantial cuts to its budget, bringing its guideline development work to an abrupt end (Deyo et al. 1997).

Nevertheless, a cottage industry is rapidly building around practice guidelines. One example is a 1996 seminar called "Implementing Practice Guidelines," sponsored by the Zitter Group, a provider of education programs on health-related issues. COR Healthcare Resources published the transcripts of the proceedings as *Changing Physician Behavior Through Practice Guidelines.* Issues covered include "achieving physician buy-in for practice guidelines; measuring and improving physician compliance; addressing patient preferences; creating feedback systems; using technology to support guideline implementation; measuring the impact of practice guidelines; tying guidelines to outcomes measurement and management." The book is offered for $247, and as a bonus, each order includes 12 issues of a new monthly newsletter, *Medical Management Network,* which contains "strategic tools for implementing evidence-based care."

Benchmarking

Another outgrowth of the CQI philosophy, "benchmarking," calls on a health care organization to examine like institutions in order to identify best practices; then to use that information to guide decisions that will enhance quality and reduce costs. A relatively new concept in health care, this tool is widely used in industry. A quick computer search gleaned 66 references, from air cargo to semiconductors to central heating. The acknowledged benchmarking guru is Robert Camp of Xerox Corporation, where the methodology originated. AT&T was another early proponent.

One "how-to" book devoted to applying this method to the health care arena (over 400 pages long with annual supplements) promises, for $249, a step-by-step guide through a sample benchmarking study, an exposition of the regulations that govern benchmarking, legal and ethical boundaries and a benchmarking code of conduct, and—perhaps most important— "government awards available for health care benchmarking . . . and how benchmarking fits into the Joint Commission certification" (Czarnecki 1994, promotional flyer). Another such guide, by two experts in health care management, opens with the eye-catcher, "'Re-create your self, or die' might be the dictum for health care organizations as they prepare for the 21st century." They continue:

This transformation requires changes of unprecedented scope and magnitude on the part of organizations to develop their capacity to assume responsibility for the health status of the communities they serve. Services must be provided faster, at less cost, and with better results. This means that organizational work processes must be improved and structures changed at near-blinding speed; then improved and changed again, with virtually no period of stability.

The roots of benchmarking in the CQI model are evident in its descriptive language. It is portrayed as an ongoing process, involving measuring, evaluating, and comparing both results and the process that produces them. . . . Conversion of the familiar noun "benchmark" to a participle is meant to denote the dynamic aspect of the goal. Indeed, the authors assert that experience with CQI principles, methods, and tools is a prerequisite to optimum use of this methodology (Gift and Mosel 1994; Leibfried and McNair 1992). Benchmarking may occur internally to locate best practices within a particular hospital but competitive benchmarking (learning from others in the health care field) and functional benchmarking (cross-industry comparison of the same or analogous process) "offer the greatest potential for breakthrough improvement" (Gift and Mosel 1994, 6). That an International Benchmarking Clearinghouse of the American Productivity and Quality Center exists is testimony to the rapid growth of this business. More important, in light of the emphasis on cost-control in health care, this organization has estimated that direct costs of an external benchmarking study—this was in 1994—can range from $30,000 to $60,000 (ibid. 13). Costs vary among institutions, but are concentrated in four areas: training of team members, leaders, and facilitators; project costs, such as data-collection studies, investment in improvements, and consultants; information systems for data gathering, analysis, and dissemination; and salaries.

Hospitals apply benchmarking very differently. Moreover, competitive benchmarking requires a large database which can be obtained only from an outside source. Enter a company such as HCIA (*not* an acronym but rather the firm name), which has developed benchmarking to a fine art. The firm is the brainchild of a small group of business management / computer experts who parlayed their consultancies into a large data analysis company, serving many health care institutions. Their sales pitch emphasizes that HCIA is "not a software company, not a decision-support vendor," but rather a "health care information content company." They claim to maintain the largest, most comprehensive health care database in the country (which they sell to other companies) and provide the software, developed elsewhere, to the hospital—plus the guidance on how to use it and the information they have compiled to facilitate cross-hospital comparison. HCIA, according to its promotional material, offers many modules which can be added to the package: Market Share, to demonstrate a competitive profile in terms of product lines, service areas, managed care penetration, and so forth; CARE, to obtain information on mortality rate, cesarian section rate, postoperative infection rate, and more; Physician Analysis, which provides a profile of individual physician practice history and outcomes performance with respect to severity-adjusted length of stay, severity-adjusted charges, mortality, and complications; and Comprehensive Operations Management Performance Service, from which the hospital can "uncover operational inefficiencies, identify opportunities for significant cost reduction, and improve competitive market position."

In addition, HCIA takes the data the hospital has collected for reporting to the state and/or data from DRG reporting on Medicare, and translates them into information on, for instance, severity-adjusted length of stay, severity-adjusted charges, severity-adjusted costs, and payer types, plus quality indicators such as risk-adjusted mortality and risk-adjusted complications. Using a computer program called SoleSource, which HCIA provides, a person can call up such records and assess them against those from comparable hospitals. HCIA's responsibility is to show the hospital where to find its own data, what to look for, and how to use them. In addition to using benchmarking to counter arguments from physicians who say, "My patient is sicker and requires a longer length of stay," HCIA sells its product as a means to satisfy Joint Commission requirements and to refine the data before they are published.

Patient-Focused Care

"Patient-focused care" is a model of care delivery that became popular in the 1990s, aiming to organize care around the patient instead of the hospital structure. Multidisciplinary teams bring as many services as possible to the patient, rather than taking the patient to a decentralized department. "Such tasks may include patient registration; insurance verification and financial arrangements; and medical record assembly, analysis, abstracting, and coding" (American Health Information Management Association 1993, 2). The model may include "simplification and redesign of work to eliminate steps and save time (e.g., providing care according to predetermined protocols and charting only exceptions to the protocol) and increased involvement of patients in their own care" (Vogel 1993, 2321).

Patients may wonder why focusing on them requires a new model. In 1987, Picker/Commonwealth established a program of "Patient-Centered Care," with financial support from The Commonwealth Fund of New York. The program set out "to explore patients' needs and concerns, as patients themselves define them, and to promote models of care that make the experience of illness and hospitalization more humane" (Gerteis et al.

1993, xii). Picker/Commonwealth continues to fund projects designed to enhance communication between patients and their health care providers (Beatrice et al. 1998). In addition, Picker Institute programs promote "improving health care quality through the patient's eyes" (1999) by, for example, engaging them in a discussion about diagnostic and treatment options, offering them their charts and visit notes to read and edit. The programs also stress staff education—for example, on the varied health beliefs, practices, and mores of ethnic and cultural groups.

Not to be confused with "centered" care, "patient-focused care" originated in projects of the health-care consulting industry in the mid-1980s. "Some of the independent initiatives in patient-focused care have involved experimentation with various nursing practice models and creation of a case management role for nursing through the use of 'critical pathways' or 'care maps' ('map' stands for 'multidisciplinary action plan'" (Vogel 1993, 2322). A three-year review of twelve institutions conducted by Booz-Allen Health Care Inc. was the chief catalyst for patient-focused care. Measuring the distribution of wage dollars in support of various tasks and functions in large hospitals, Booz-Allen found that only 16 percent of all personnel time was dedicated to direct care, such as giving medications, changing dressings, taking temperatures, or assisting with surgery or procedures. Forty-nine percent was dedicated to scheduling, transportation of patients and goods, and documentation of care. An additional 20 percent of wage dollars was spent for structural idle time, that is, time that staff members with narrowly assigned tasks spent waiting for the opportunity to carry out those tasks. Booz-Allen concluded that the excessive compartmenting within modern hospitals is the primary contributor to poor service and high cost (Lathrop 1991). The situation described by Vogel is all too familiar to patients:

> In most hospitals today, patients accommodate themselves to rules, procedures, and schedules designed for the convenience and efficiency of various departments or disciplines. It is not uncommon for patients to wait hours for tests, treatments, or medications. Patients suffer numerous inconveniences, such as the all-too-common 4 A.M. phlebotomy. Each day, patients interact with many different people, often without an introduction. Most of these hospital workers carry out narrowly defined functions for many patients, rather than focusing on the total care of a few patients. (1993, 2321–22)

Patient-focused care drew attention to these deficiencies. Advocates hoped that with a commitment to this model quality would become "a matter of providing excellent and efficient medical care and satisfying the demands of the larger patient experience" (Jirsch 1993, 27).

REORGANIZING THE HOSPITAL

Patient-focused care was tied to a general drive to reorganize hospitals under the value of efficiency—now efficiency writ large. Again, this movement had already taken hold in American industry. Management gurus such as Tom Peters and Peter Drucker and their colleagues had published and lectured in the 1970s and 1980s on the revolution in American management that would occur if only organizations would attend to the key areas of competence practiced by successful organizations (Peters and Waterman 1982; Peters and Austin 1985; Drucker 1973). The restructuring of business processes that became popular during this period is known as "re-engineering," which calls for radical rethinking of existing practices in order to decrease costs, increase customer satisfaction, quality, and market share.

In applying this concept to health care management, references to a "clean slate" appear repeatedly. "Comparisons are often made to Total Quality Management, which is said to make merely marginal improvements to existing processes while re-engineering discards and replaces them" (Arndt and Bigelow 1998, 59; *see* for example, Hammer and Champy 1993; Champy 1995; Carr and Johansson 1995; Hammer and Stanton 1995). Not only did corporations look to re-engineering, but government followed the trend: Vice President Gore took on the task of "reinventing government," to cut waste, downsize the workforce, and improve the "information flow" (Menand 1998).

Clearly, information-based technologies were transforming the manufacturing and service sectors of American society. In 1995, former senator Bill Bradley gave a thoughtful speech to the Commonwealth Club in San Francisco in which he called the transformation "unforgiving" in terms of job loss.

> If you're a manager, you want to increase productivity. If you can put a computer in to replace an entire credit department, instead of 300 you can have 12 work stations, you're going to put the 12 work stations in. And it happened in company after company. AT&T laid off 85,000 people; IMB 60,000; GE over 100,000.

Press reports were adding to workers' anxiety with statements such as: "Since 1989, about 3 million people have been laid off from their jobs" (Weiser 1996, 10). Understandably, by the time re-engineering and work redesign reached the hospitals in the mid-1990s, staff apprehensively translated these "re-words" into "layoffs."

Again, this became a boom period for business management consultants and generated another newsletter, *Re-engineering the Hospital,* a subscription to which would teach hospital administrators the requisite management strategies and assist them with such problems as comparison shopping for a re-engineering consultant, keeping employee morale high during reorganization, and "using techniques like brainstorming, and mind-mapping to get the creative juices flowing" (according to its advertising brochure). Publications such as *Streamlining Healthcare Delivery: The Comprehensive Guide for Operational Restructuring* appeared, offering strategies, practical tips, and case studies to help "restructure your organization to realign operations to meet the new requirements of managed care and capitation, cut unnecessary management layers, speed up gains achieved through quality improvement programs" (according to the advertising brochure of COR Healthcare Resources, Santa Barbara, California) and much more. A new monthly newsletter devoted exclusively to patient-focused care and bearing that title appeared. By the time one Bay Area hospital announced that it was rebuilding its service delivery structure using *"Patient-Focused* work redesign," it was able to distribute a bibliography containing sixty-two references to articles on the subject during the required training session.

One account estimates that 60 percent of all U.S. hospitals have been involved in re-engineering initiatives, and asserts that "literally billions of dollars are being spent" on this endeavor (Walston and Kimberly 1997, 143). Like CQI, re-engineering was sold to hospitals by business management consultants as an ideal way to increase patient satisfaction while reducing costs. In one of the hospitals observed during my research, management decided to hire a well-known consulting firm for re-engineering. In-house teams were formed for training. They met in all-day sessions, described by one member:

> It was the most intense experience I've ever had professionally. We were put in a room, the six of us with three consultants full time. The nine of us got to know our bathroom habits, for crying out loud. I mean, there were no breaks. We were told by what we called the time police—the guy who was heading our group had been a Marine, and he ran us like the Marines—he said: "If there are six of you in this room, if you take so much as ten minutes to chit chat over the water cooler, and you multiply that ten minutes times six of you, and you multiply that hour over five days a week, and you multiply five days a week over the course of this project, you are going to find yourself at the end of this project absolutely not able to meet your time lines simply because each of you wasted ten minutes a day." And we got so we didn't go to lunch because we had thirty minutes and you couldn't get from the room to the cafeteria and back up again without insulting ten people along the way who want to say how are you and how are things going and let me tell you about my life. So we supported Take-Out Taxi for about seven months.

According to another team member, the work included nights and weekends and work at home preparing summaries of current practices, "to-be process" vision and design goals, change recommendations, new role descriptions, and analysis of measurement and evaluation issues. The stacks of paper filled with bulleted lists, diagrams, and graphs would make environmentalists shudder. As they worked, the job-related anxiety level of hospital staff increased proportionately.

Consultants commonly choose hospital admission systems first because they are manageable problems. And so it was with this team. A dysfunctional system of hospital admission was pinpointed. Patients were required to register multiple times for surgery—in the doctor's office, at the registration desk, before pre-surgery work-ups, and worse, it was discovered that some departments registered their patients and some did not. The team discovered also that no one person was in charge of bed control. As described by a team member:

> It was a sort of negotiated thing between Admitting and the nursing supervisor. And on the day shift, there is no nursing supervisor, so it was sort of up in the air. If the staff didn't want any more patients, Admitting had no power to say, yes, you do have empty beds.

The team then did an analysis using the principle of activity-based costing, assessing the time spent (such as five minutes to fill out the form, ten minutes to do data entry into the computer), and calculated how much was spent admitting patients. Analysts used a manufacturing tool called "eye depth," by which each activity of a process, in this case admitting, is costed out. To quote another team member: "You may have ten people in the organization doing an activity in a different way, and you take their salaries and their percentage of time, and you roll it all together in this wonderful software package." The team found that it cost annually $376,000 to admit obstetric patients and $4,380,851 to do case managing (the process that was analyzed next as part of the re-engineering project).

The team ended up recommending bedside admitting. Asked some time later how things were going, the response was dispirited:

> I would say that it has been implemented to maybe 60, 70 percent. And I think it's a classic example of taking a product which I think was good and valid, and based on fact and data, and handing it to people and saying, 'Now, go do it,' and not giving them the support that they needed. It was also an instance of a lot of people did a lot of organization and then they were out of the organization. New people came in. It has not gone well for implementation.

What she did not mention is another condition that has emerged in all hospitals. Except in emergency admissions, bedside admitting is impossible because insurance information must be obtained and verified prior to admission if the hospital is not to lose money.

The consultants advising this hospital made a semantic distinction between re-engineering and redesign, the former applying to business practices (which included the admitting system) and the latter to what a team member characterized as "general visioning" over what patient care *could* be in the hospital. This led to the most problematic aspect of patient-centered care—work redesign and cross-training of personnel—especially since definitions of these terms vary with the setting. Under patient-focused care, "Work may be reassigned and concentrated with better qualified staff (e.g., by creating nurse care-manager positions). Work may also be reassigned to staff members with less training who can accomplish the work at a lower cost (e.g., by designating care technicians to take vital signs)" (Vogel 1993, 2324). As to cross-training of personnel, "Nurses might perform basic phlebotomies, record ECGs, and administer basic respiratory care; unit-based technicians might perform basic laboratory tests and roentgenographic procedures" (ibid.). The goal of cross-training is to reduce the amount of workers' idle time while simultaneously reducing the number of persons who come in contact with the patient—to enhance caregiver-patient relations and patient satisfaction (Lathrop 1991). But there's the rub. Although theoretically commendable, presenting some staff with termination notices, moving others around, changing tasks and role definitions, and all the while expecting employees to remain loyal and happy is a daunting proposition.

Following the patient-focused care precepts regarding skill mix and cross-training of workers, the redesign team in the hospital that I observed decided to replace the position of charge nurse or head nurse with a "team leader," assisted by clinical partner I's (the equivalent of a licensed vocational nurse LVN), clinical partner II's (equivalent of a nurse's attendant), and patient support technicians, who were to combine the duties of housekeeping, delivering food trays, ordering and replenishing supplies, and transport. Obviously, the patient support technicians were pleased with the change since it represented new opportunities and a better salary. The change also promised richer and more exciting work for the clinical partners. Many RNs, on the other hand were very angry about relinquishing patient care to those they considered less qualified. After reclassifying staff and hiring new workers, the hospital faced the task of retraining; they found, in the case of support technicians, that they needed additional classes in literacy. Those participating in the training sessions understood full well the problems inherent in skill-mix and cross-training as described by a training instructor:

We would do skits about role conflict among the RN, clinical Partner I, clinical partner II, and the patient support technician. And they had to come up with a problem of role confusion and role conflict in a ten minute skit. So this one group, I'll never forget it. He was an Indian guy, not Native American, an India Indian who's a Patient Support Technician and he's mopping the patient's room. And the patient is, "Uhhh, my hip hurts and now I've got to go to the bathroom. And my hip really hurts. I've just had surgery and could you tell the nurse I want some Demorol?" She was on the potty and "I've been like this for an hour and a half." At first he says, "well, it's, uh, ok." Like he didn't get it, it's someone else's job. And then the patient says, "Can you tell the nurse?" And he continues mopping. He keeps mopping because he doesn't want to get yelled at for not finishing. And by now everyone's laughing because it's real clear. So he goes down to the nurse's desk, and he says, "Uh, that hip in whatever it is, 101, she's been on the potty. And she wants to get off. And she also wants some Demi Moore."

Lest it appear that "team training" in this hospital was all fun and games, it should be emphasized that the sessions were marked by serious discussion and evoked the full panoply of reactions from stoic silence to expressive anger. Most evident during the two-day session I attended was a general expression of disengagement from an institution to which staff felt they had been loyal—as well as a pervasive resentment over no longer feeling valued.

A number of articles appeared at this time claiming that savings would come from collapsed job categories or replacement of RNs with lower-skill workers. Thus, despite the quality improvement element implied in the term "patient-focused care," all leaders interviewed in this study were clear about cost reduction being the primary motivation behind it. As a nursing administrator reported:

> The reason this was done is because this hospital was losing millions of dollars and basically it wouldn't have survived. Last year we lost seven million dollars from operations. This year we're going into a budget year with a 3.8 million dollar loss. We are four million dollars more in personnel costs last year than we will be in this budget season because of skill mix.

Some proponents of re-engineering are quick to emphasize that it is not synonymous with layoffs. "Yet most employees or people in the community served by a hospital are unlikely to read the re-engineering literature, and may see claims to re-engineering as window dressing for staff reduction" (Arndt and Bigelow 1998, 64). So it was in this hospital:

> I have never worked with this consulting group, but their reputation precedes them and if a hospital hears them coming, the nursing staff becomes hysterical—their slashing, not being medically oriented, not wanting quali-

ty of care. They have not a clue what nurses do, they have not a clue of quality of care. They wouldn't want their father in one of the hospitals they've re-
designed. That's the perception out there.

Researchers who have studied the effect of restructuring on the nursing
profession reinforce the comments made by nurses interviewed in my
study. "Nurses are expected to move flexibly from one specialty unit to another, or take 'call off' time, according to variations in census. Hospitals
have fewer permanent staff and save benefits costs by using part-time and
per diem nurses" (Olesen and Bone 1998, 319). As working conditions for
staff nurses deteriorate, better-educated and more experienced nurses
move away from direct patient care into case manager or supervisory roles.
Furthermore, for those remaining as staff nurses, time spent on direct patient care has decreased while responsibility for patient outcome has increased. Consequently, "nurses' responses to organizational restructuring
have included feelings of uncertainty, impotence, anger, grief, frustration,
resentment and insecurity" (ibid. 320; *see also* Gordon 1997; DeMoro 1996;
Johannes 1997; Droppleman and Thomas 1996).

In 1994, the American Nurses Association (ANA) conducted a survey of
1,835 RNs who asserted that staff cuts in their hospitals were causing dan-
gerous changes in patient care and massive increases in the work load of
those who remained (American Nurses Association 1994). In the same
year, the California Nurses Association (CNA) filed a lawsuit on behalf of
the nurses at Alta Bates Medical Center in Berkeley, charging the hospital
with consumer fraud for its announced reduction of RN staff by 50 percent
coupled with its assertion, under the rubric of patient-focused care, that
this change would be good for the public. (At this writing, in 1999, the lawsuit is still pending.) A series of one-day strikes by Kaiser Permanente
northern California nurses was launched in 1997 in order to draw attention to reduced staffing. Regarding the delegating of tasks to less-skilled
workers, one respondent captured the essence of the problem from a nursing perspective:

> I think that some staff nurses like this because they don't have to do the less
> desirable nursing. Emptying bed pans and commodes and things like
> that. . . . But I've always been committed to patient care and you know in this
> day when you have shorter hospital stays and you have more complex,
> chronically ill patients in the hospital, it's necessary for me to see how some-
> one, you know, when I get them to the commode I can judge their balance,
> judge their movement, how short of breath they get, as well as observing
> their skin. And it tells me a lot about . . . I use that time to really get to know
> the patient. I mean, you can establish a nurse-patient relationship because
> they depend on you.

For the most part, however, hospital management remains unmoved by the protests of nurses. When, for example, RNs in one hospital talked to their unit manager about the additional burden of work on the wards, they were told "to improve their organizational skills, that *'professional* nurses should be able to get all their work done'" (Brannon 1994, 143). This is echoed by a nurse in my study: "If we say the work load is too heavy, they answer, 'It's because you're disorganized, or you're not capable of managing your time. You have to set priorities, you don't know how to delegate to the nurses' aides.'" Suffice it to say that to improve quality of care amid the demoralization caused by job redesign requires superhuman effort.

EXPERIMENTING WITH PERFORMANCE MEASUREMENT

If hospitals are to be held accountable using business methods, then what is the product of the hospital and how do you measure it? One of the many new publications designed to answer this question warned in its marketing letter, "Your organization's future now hinges on how well you can *prove* you're delivering high-quality, cost effective care. . . . Those who don't will be swimming against a tide that may wash away much of their market share" (emphasis added). During the entire period of my research, QA/I personnel who looked to the experts for help found a wealth of information—filled with a variety of systems for measuring performance. Dealing with the myriad requirements of the Joint Commission, the PRO, the state medical association, and the state health department, QA/I personnel felt they were swimming in a turbulent sea—and too many of the lifeboats had leaks.

It is an axiom in business that every regulation and law turns into an opportunity, a potential market. For example, QA/I has spawned a wealth of subscription newsletters that is growing exponentially. In my experience, acceptance of a free copy of a newsletter led to mail advertisements for twenty others. An extensive literature on methods for QA/I data collection and dissemination has burst forth, including academic journals such as the *American Journal of Medical Quality,* the *International Journal for Quality in Health Care,* and the *Journal of the American Medical Informatics Association.* Recommendations that appear in publications cover a wide range.

Some authors propose integrating all aspects of quality management by incorporating the concerns of quality assurance, risk management, utilization review, and infection control into a single system (Creps et al. 1992; Lord and Ciccone 1992; Longo et al. 1989; Weissman et al. 1990). Advocates promise that an integrated model "reduces redundancy of chart review;

identifies relevant issues while the patient is still hospitalized or under treatment; coordinates concurrent review with retrospective review; and assists hospitals in reappraisal and reassessment of physicians' credential" (from an advertisement for Longo et al. 1997). Many publications describe a variety of models for quality management and improvement, detailing success factors for such quality tools as CQI and benchmarking or combining them with educational handouts for staff (Harris 1994; Gaucher and Coffey 1993; Joint Commission on Accreditation in Healthcare Organizations 1993; Melum and Sinioris 1992). Other publications are devoted to clinical performance—for example, medical staff peer review, addressing such issues as corrective actions, legal considerations, motivation, and medical accountability (Lang 1991; Ramsey et al. 1996; Feldman and Roblin 1992). In addition, numerous software companies hawk the "best" computer program to accomplish a variety of QA/I goals. (The exhibit hall of the 1997 International Congress on Performance Measurement and Improvement in Health Care housed thirty-seven exhibits, predominantly representing health-care information management and performance monitoring systems.) Whether hospitals are indeed industries may still be in question, but that an accountability industry has been born is without dispute.

As part of the original mandate given to AHCPR (in addition to the aborted effort to convene panels that would develop practice guidelines), the agency awards numerous grants and contracts for research on health-care costs, quality, and access. By 1994, nearly $200 million had been spent on the enterprise known collectively as "outcomes research," but critics were claiming that this research had yielded little that clinicians and policy makers could use to make rational decisions about health care (Anderson 1994). "Physicians themselves, let alone government bureaucrats, often don't know which medical interventions work best. And even a relatively straightforward comparison—between a 10-cent aspirin and a $1000 shot of a genetically engineered anti-clotting drug, for example—requires a clinical trial costing tens of millions of dollars and lasting upward of a decade." Hospital personnel Anderson interviewed admitted readily that retrospective analysis of clinical records and tracking of clinical practice are fatally flawed by hidden biases in the data—that researchers simply cannot correct for the subtle reasons doctors choose one treatment over another for a particular patient. Arguing that AHCPR could not point to a single case in which its database studies have changed general clinical practice, Anderson observed, "Just this month, its most definitive result—that 'watchful waiting' is often a better option than surgery for benign prostate disease—was issued as a guideline to physicians. Even then, the researchers recommended a clinical trial to confirm their findings." And Oxford University epidemiologist Richard Peto charged, "Investing in a lots of outcomes research is worse than just destroying the money because it gives the illusion of information" (ibid. 1080).

In 1997, ACHPR took another tack, awarding five-year contracts to twelve institutions in the United States and Canada to serve as "evidence-based practice centers." They were charged with gathering and reviewing all scientific literature on assigned medical topics, conducting additional analysis when appropriate, and doing relative cost analyses, to serve as the foundation for health care providers when developing guidelines. Thus, AHCPR's charge was no longer to generate guidelines but rather to help centers do so. Then, in a classic example of the fluctuating fate of government agencies, AHPR was reauthorized and renamed the Agency for Healthcare Research and Quality (AHRQ, pronounced "arc") in December 1999—with a widened range of authority to conduct *and* support outcomes research.

Quantifying Outcomes

The main emphasis in QA/I has shifted to a quest for the means to quantify outcomes, in keeping with the American assumption that only in numbers will we gain insight. Taylor's scientific management theories, discussed at the beginning of this chapter, had spread to the education arena early on, leading to the "mania for measurement that has enmeshed contemporary students, from kindergarten to college in a self-contained maze of quantitative testing" (Lears 1997, 32).

This mindset arrived rather late in health care. Very few of his colleagues were interested when physician Vergil Slee advocated, in the 1960s, using computers to find out which hospitals presented better care (1966).[2] Prior to that, physician Ernest A. Codman (now remembered as the "father of outcomes measurement" through an award the Joint Commission has established in his name) was in his own time dishonored. In the early 1900s, following the Flexner report's recommendation to standardize medical education, Codman had proposed standardizing the way that medicine is practiced. A numerologist who, when he went hunting, counted and recorded in a diary the number of birds shot and shells used, Codman had proposed an "End Results System," based on the common-sense notion that every hospital should follow every patient to see if s/he got the best care, in the interest of beginning a "True Clinical Science" (1915, 4). To say that his colleagues did not embrace his utopian view—everyone in the hospital working together to achieve this end, resources assigned according to their importance, physicians welcoming the exposure of their errors—would be an understatement. Nevertheless, Codman's Puritan conscience drove him to preach his doctrine. In the two books he published describing the precomputer card system he had devised and found to be efficient (ibid.; Codman 1918), he recommended that at a certain hour, the chief of surgical service or a member of the hospital's efficiency commit-tee—or, in a large hospital, the chief of each service—would be handed the end-result cards of all his cases that had been discharged the previous week. Asserting that a service of sixty beds can thus be easily reviewed in one hour a week, Codman proposed that the physician would then mark with symbols those cases that lacked perfection, those where there was no flaw, and "graciously star the cases which he considers creditable" (Cod-man 1915, 5). All along, he would be asking: what was the matter; did they find it out beforehand; did the patient get entirely well; if not, why not; was it the fault of the surgeon, the disease, or the patient; what can we do to prevent similar failures in the future? Codman reasoned that if he could present a report for 337 cases, the 100 doctors of Massachusetts General Hospital could do the same for 33,700 cases, even though they then treat-ed about 6,000 ward patients a year. Use of the end-result system in all hos-pitals "in matters that are tolerably certain . . . will prevent my telling fish stories, and my friends at hospitals telling fish stories, and eventually lead to Statistics (capitalized in the original) which will help everybody in the world" (Codman 1918, 97). Codman's 1918 book contains a poignant but telling insert that reads,

> This report will be sent gratis to any member of the American College of Sur-geons or to any member of the Massachusetts Medical Society. To others the price will be one dollar. When you are through with this copy, kindly hand to some other persons—preferably to a Hospital Trustee.

For all his good intentions, Codman remained a small footnote to Ameri-can medical history until 1997, when the Joint Commission presented the first Codman Award.

The obsession with statistical micromanagement reached its apogee during the Kennedy administration, personified in the 1960s by Kennedy's defense secretary, Robert McNamara.[3] The impact of his approach was per-vasive:

> This led to the computerization of *everything*. Contracts all asked for chi-square, as if that were all that was needed. It fit with government statisti-cians' requirements—never mind anything else. (Wiener 1981, 183)

Certainly, it is reasonable for a funding source to seek evidence of a re-turn on its investment. Furthermore, statistical outcomes echo Deming's emphasis on quantifying the production process so that managers would make decisions based on data rather than anecdotes. Regarding the zeal to develop statistical outcome measures, however, a comment made on the occasion of Daniel Patrick Moynihan's announced retirement from the U.S. Senate should be heeded: "He insisted upon ideas and he insisted upon numbers; and he did not mistake the one for the other" ("Notebook" 1998). Unfortunately, this has not always been in the case in the accountability movement in hospitals. The search for the best numerical indicators of quality of care in hospitals has been costly, chaotic, inconsistent—and confusing to those asked to produce the figures.

Obtaining the Data

Expectations about the feasibility of quantifying outcomes have been abetted by the mushrooming development and marketing of health-care information technology. When first asked to produce statistics on outcomes, hospitals discovered that databases set up for billing are not suitable for assessing clinical practice. The growing field of medical "informatics"[4] has promised improved computer capability, the results of which are expected eventually to help the public, providers, and employers' groups assess the relationship between price and quality for a specific physician, procedure, laboratory, treatment outcome, or hospital. Proponents of this approach warn that if assessment of quality is to survive in the increasingly competitive realm of health care, it must remain "data driven," i.e., direct its course on the basis of hard data (Reerink 1992, 1–2). Some computer-assisted patient care is already in place—in hospital pharmacies, for example, where, used properly, it can prevent harmful drug interactions and dosage errors. Further, the electronic patient record is a necessity in this age of complicated care. (At the Mayo Clinic in Florida, for example, results of tests done in the morning are available in the examining room the same afternoon.) Visionaries foresee a link between practice guidelines and information technology: "New developments in computer technology and information sciences can make it easier to provide information to physicians in a user-friendly way at the time they need it. The physician of the future will most assuredly have on his or her desk a computer that will provide access to these guidelines with their appropriateness ratings" (Brook 1989, 3029).

Others have linked critical paths and outcomes-based quality measurements to cost, predicting that this information will become the primary method for describing a unit of health care to which a price can be assigned (Kidder, Peabody & Co. 1994). Columbia/HCA, before its legal problems, was well on its way to pursuing this dream. Then CEO Richard Scott, apparently the supreme gourmand of cookbook medicine, was determined to build an efficient system of "disease management" that would standardize treatment:

Instead of individual physicians planning each patient's care on an ad hoc basis, drawing on a blend of their experience, medical education, reading of medical journals and so forth, disease management would offer a predetermined set of possible medical steps to take, depending on a patient's symptoms, health history, and numerous other variables. Proponents envision a day when a doctor could punch in specifics about a patient and get back a treatment plan showing everything from length of hospital stay to drug regimen and exercise recommendations. (Sharpe and Jaffe 1997, A1)

A flyer advertising a new program, the 1999 Disease Management CD-ROM, promises "a veritable library's worth of coverage on one convenient disk." and offers "extensive information on 20 chronic conditions which—if managed improperly—are most likely to result in costly and catastrophic consequences " (Faulkner and Gray 1999). A caveat often overlooked by health-care practitioners, and least understood by the physician absorbed in his or her own practice of medicine, is the extent to which information-processing technology permits greater oversight of health care by lay managers: "Once it is possible to describe the quality of physician practices in terms that lay managers can apply or algorithms that computers can manipulate, the genie is out of the bottle and physician dominance of quality of oversight has been broken" (Jost 1995, 838).

Columbia/HCA, one of the first if not *the* first, to refer to patients as "customers," was also among the first to class its services into "product lines": cancer, cardiology, diabetes, behavioral health, workers' compensation, women's services, senior care, and emergency services. Columbia/HCA had to get information on past patients out of individual manila folders and into a vast information system—a capability that would have been enhanced by the anticipated acquisition of Value Health Inc., a pharmacy-benefits and disease-management company. The pending takeover was aborted when Columbia/HCA ran into legal problems (*see* Chapter One). Kaiser Permanente has spent more than $80 million on a disease-management center and database (Sharpe and Jaffe 1997, A8). Hospital chains are following a similar course.

As the organizations that set and enforce hospital quality standards have raced to determine which one can devise the best quality-measurement system, a few voices have questioned the impact of this endeavor on the rising health care dollar. Serious problems in the Joint Commission's Indicator Measurement System (IMSystem) were revealed in a cover story in *Modern Healthcare* (Burda 1994. *See also* Stano 1994). Despite eight years of research and development at a cost of millions of dollars—and hospitals were required to pay for the privilege of serving as pilot sites!—the American Hospital Association concluded that the IMSystem was inferior to existing internal informational systems. Over half of the hospitals that had agreed to be test sites had dropped out, claiming the project was too complicated, labor intensive, and costly to justify what little benefit they received.

Finally, after ten years of effort, the Joint Commission dropped it. According to the commission's president, Dennis O'Leary, the accrediting body had learned a valuable lesson: "the shortest distance between two points is not always direct."[5] O'Leary explained that the commission had embarked on its program believing, incorrectly, that researchers would find performance measures in the clinical literature. Moreover, when they put together their own measures and tried to test them in the field they found that data from the hospitals were not available. Worse still, by the time they got the IMSystem ready, they discovered that there were many measurement systems already developed and "rather than being praised, we were castigated." Indeed, when what the Joint Commission called the "new art" (Loeb and O'Leary 1995, 1405) of performance measurement was introduced, a growing army of measurement experts, health services researchers, and database developers was already on the scene.

In the spirit of American federalism, some states had already taken the initiative to develop their own systems. Pennsylvania is a case in point. In the late 1980s, the state, through its Health Care Cost Containment Council, mandated the use of MedisGroups, an abstracting system that required the hospital to submit on a quarterly basis certain demographic, financial, and clinical information, as well as the identity of physicians involved in the patient's care. The comparative data on hospitals and physicians were expected to permit purchasers of health care to make more informed decisions, even though the data were far from comprehensive. MedisGroups did not develop sets for psychiatry, rehabilitation medicine, or transplants, and no data on these expensive categories have ever been submitted. The council also collects only minimal data on ophthalmology, ear-nose-and-throat, obstetrics, and newborn care. Furthermore, the first data, by hospital, were two years old when they were published in 1988. While some have questioned what this information has done to contain costs, there is no question that it has been expensive for hospitals. A representative of a 500-bed teaching hospital in Pennsylvania told me,

> Each year, my hospital must pay a software fee. This year it is over $45,000. In addition, there are now six additional employees to perform this function—annually about $300,000 in salaries and benefits. Very expensive computers had to be purchased. While I do not know how much, the support from the Information System Department must be a big line item. Also, the business office has an on-going cost for their generation of computer tapes to provide the financial data to the Council. I can attest to the hours spent clarifying reporting formats, abstracting definitions, installing annual up-

dates to the criteria, running back-ups of data and validating that what we sent them was what they got. It would be conservative to guess it costs us over $250,000 a year. Multiply this by every acute care hospital in the state!

Once the Joint Commission accepted that it had to drop its plan, a request for measurement systems was sent out. In its call for collaboration, Joint Commission spokespersons referred to the widespread production of individual indicators and performance measurement systems as a "potpourri" (ibid.). And what better body to identify criteria for evaluating performance measurement systems than a new council on performance measurement?

After issuing invitations to more than 250 organizations, the Joint Commission appointed a council of "nationally recognized experts with backgrounds in outcomes measurement, clinical practice, evaluation methodology, health care informatics, and public policy" (ibid.). The targeted date for mandatory compliance was extended to 1997. Someone (or more likely, some committee) with a sense of humor had renamed the information system "ORYX," for once not an acronym but rather named after an African antelope, whose primary trait is its speed. One wag suggested wryly that the initials really stand for: "Our Requirement, Your Xpense" ("Outliers: Asides and insides" 1998, 40.)

Hospitals could now select from some two hundred software vendors (one of which was the Joint Commission's IMSystem) and were required for the first year to choose one accepted system and two to five clinical performance improvement measures that represented at least 20 percent of the hospital's patient population. (Examples of indicators are "foot exams for diabetic patients in managed care," "prevalence of inappropriate medication prescriptions,"and "ACE inhibitors for congestive heart failure patients.") Amid protests from the field, deadlines for compliance were extended—and finally established as March 1998. Moreover, the original goal of covering 100 percent of a hospital's patient population in four years was modified. Identification of two more measures, representing 25 percent of patients (or a total of eight measures if four do not cover 25 percent) was required by December 31, 1998, followed by identification of six to ten measures representing 30 percent of their patient population by the end of 1999; and, by the end of 2000, eight to twelve measures representing 35 percent of their patient population. A QA / I coordinator who had followed the protracted evolution of the IMSystem felt justified regarding her initial reaction to it: "My suggestion to everybody that ever talked to me about this was to rush into it as slowly as they could!"

But with a deadline facing them, hospitals could move only so slowly. On the one hand, indicators had been reduced to a reasonable minimum. On the other, hospitals had a wide choice of vendors and their different costing systems. Implementation was likely to require at least a half-time employee—or, in most cases, an additional load for already-overburdened QA/I staff. The large number of software options added to the tension: correcting a bad choice and changing vendors later would obviously increase the cost. Said a QA/I coordinator,

> They've gone from one extreme to the other. When the Joint Commission had one system, they were criticized for being autocratic. Now they've gone the other way. Of the 200 vendors, how many are going to survive? And if the one you've chosen fails, then where are you? I've decided we need a selection team to designate criteria. *This is loaded—when you choose your indicators, you have to decide ahead what do you want to publicize?* (Emphasis added.) What information do you want going out there? If the data blows up in your face, you need committee responsibility.

A representative of the hospital association described the situation to me as "insanity," adding that the Joint Commission "should have maintained strict criteria rather than agreeing to 200 systems that met the loosest criteria." Her advice to hospitals was to take into account individual variables—for instance, what information they want to share, what data are available. Zeroing in on the best indicators and the best vendor became a chicken-and-egg proposition. (By 1999, many vendors had gone bankrupt.)

At one vendor presentation I observed, it was clear that the objective was not so much to learn more about problematic delivery of care but rather to find the most accessible data, in this case mortality data that were already being submitted to the California Office of Statewide Health Planning and Development and California Medical Review Incorporated (CMRI) for Medicare review. The vendor-salesperson urged her audience not to make "too big a deal" of their choice since "the Joint Commission, when they come in, only want to see that you're improving, that you have a system in place." A far cry from O'Leary's characterization of the purpose of this exercise: "What do you want to know about whom?" (ibid.).

A *Wall Street Journal* article characterized the system as leaving enough wiggle room for an elephant, adding,

> Got a shining record for prostate-cancer screenings? Measure that. Got bad pneumonia-complication rates? Choose a different measure. Not only do hospitals have ample opportunity to gloss over their problems, but the current system also makes it impossible to compare the country's hospitals across the board on the quality of care they provide. (Jeffrey 1998)

The Joint Commission says this is just a first step toward getting hospitals into the habit of measuring quality; it promises its coddling approach will eventually nudge hospitals into a single yardstick (ibid.). At the end of 1998, the Joint Commission announced that it had approved twelve acute-care "focus areas" for identifying "core performance measures." The focus areas were adverse drug reactions, acute myocardial infarction, antibiotic use, breast cancer, congestive heart failure, depression, diabetes, equipment failure, maternal/newborn, medication errors, pain management, and pneumonia. In a press release, the commission announced that "the accreditation process of the future will evaluate not only a health care organization's ability to do the right things (as assessed through standards compliance) but the outcomes of these efforts as well" (Joint Commission on Accreditation of Hospitals 1998, 2). Although the final word on this endeavor has yet to be written, the following can be said. One of the aims of the International Society for Quality in Health Care is to develop and maintain an internationally accepted terminology of quality improvement. Similarly, the original IMSystem goal was to develop a common set of measures that would shed light on practices across hospitals. Both goals remain elusive. Furthermore, the purchase price of a performance measurement system remains formidable. For instance, Abbott Laboratories' Total Quality Pain Management Program, with twenty performance measures approved by the Joint Commission, is operated with a hand-held personal computer and sells for $20,000.

Issuing Report Cards

The search for the perfect reporting system, which will contain cross-hospital comparative data, goes on. When President Clinton, as part of his health plan, proposed a national "report card" that would allow healthcare purchasers to compare plans on the basis of quality and consumer satisfaction, he was echoing the desire of business coalitions to use such information to select preferred providers, in keeping with the business dictum "It doesn't count unless you can count it."

Acknowledging that the state-of-the-art is "a crazy-quilt of information that lacks the uniformity required for meaningful comparisons" and that "comparative data are scattered and incomplete" (Blackwood 1994, 6a). employers and providers have high hopes for the Health Plan/Employer Data Information Set (HEDIS) performance criteria for *health plans* (not hospitals), developed by the National Committee on Quality Assurance (NCQA), described in Chapter Two. HEDIS covers quality, access to care, enrollee satisfaction, enrollment and utilization, and financial stability—with breast cancer, for example, NCQA distinguishes between performance measures (mammography screening rate) and outcome measures (five-year mortality rate for the disease) in hopes of eventually being able to say which patients get better, what is their quality of life, who lives, who dies, and at what stage did the HMO diagnose cancer. NCQA will update HEDIS as more extensive quality measures are developed.

The notion of report cards, presumably to facilitate consumer choice, has become very popular. Kaiser Permanente, California's pioneer HMO, for instance, issues its own report card, using HEDIS data plus "external benchmarks" from the California Department of Health Services and the U.S. Department of Health and Human Services. According to one reckoning, health plans and employer groups issued nearly 50 different report cards between 1994 and 1996, based on patient-satisfaction surveys, other indicators, or both (Anders 1996).

Reinforcing the characterization of the United States as a nation of competitors, *U.S. News and World Report, Newsweek,* and *Consumer Reports* all produce their own "Super Bowls" on America's best hospitals. In 1995, *U.S. News and World Report* offered their findings in book form, advertising it as "the ultimate family guide to choosing the best care." Another twist is the report card compiled by a number of managed-care companies for internal use. Rather than release them to patients, the companies use them as a basis for reimbursing physicians. Some companies give points based on, for example, number of referrals, number of tests ordered, and number of prescriptions written inside and outside the formulary (the company-endorsed list of drugs). Too many undesirable points, and the physician's reimbursement is reduced.

Governments also rate hospitals' track records. In 1987, HCFA published a multivolume edition of *Medicare Hospital Mortality Information,* a compilation of data on death rates of Medicare beneficiaries at about 6,000 U.S. hospitals. The rates were calculated on the percentage of patients who died within 30 days of admission, and were broken down for 16 different causes of death. They were then compared to a predicted death rate, using a formula that considered the hospital's mix of patients and location. Mortality data, however, met with an outcry from hospital representatives, who protested that the statistics were skewed. Researchers backed them up, pointing out that what appeared as "outlier status" (deviations from expected deaths) was due to chance and insufficient adjustment for severity (Park et al. 1990. *See also* Berwick and Wald 1990). HCFA then gave up on its plan to issue an annual volume using this reporting system, and started to work with NCQA to design report cards specific to Medicare and Medicaid programs.

The data collected through Pennsylvania's hospital outcomes reporting system were for the purpose of issuing report cards to guide consumers. By 1994, quality managers were complaining that the reports were so complex they were of little use to consumers "who at any rate have less choice all the time in which hospital they go to" (American Health Consultants 1994, 17). After the states of Colorado and Iowa joined Pennsylvania in mandating outcomes and cost reporting by providers, a business newsletter reported, "Providers have criticized every program, saying the data are oversimplified misleading and incomplete" (Kidder, Peabody & Co. 1994, 33). State governments and researchers have since tried to avoid problems by focusing on a narrowly defined group of patients, such as reports on coronary-artery bypass grafting or acute myocardial infarction (*see*, for example, Luft and Romano 1993). A reporter's comment after reviewing the health of California HMOs strikes a responsive chord: "You could make yourself sick sorting out the results while trying to find the best health plan for you and your family" (Hall 1996).

Nurses—following their own path, as always—have developed their own report cards. In the 1990s, the American Nurses Association contracted with a private consulting firm to develop an acute-care nursing report card that could be used to educate consumers about what constitutes safe, quality nursing care. Their goal was to get nursing indicators included as part of hospital report cards. Twenty-one indicators were isolated, ten of which were considered core: (1) mix of registered nurses (RNs), licensed practical nurses (LPNs), licensed vocational nurses (LVNs), and unlicensed staff; (2) ratio of nursing staff to patients; (3) RN education and qualifications; (4) nurse staff turnover; (5) use of agency nurses; (6) nosocomial infections related to hospitalization; (7) decubitus ulcers (bed sores); (8) medication errors; (9) patient injury rate; and (10) patient satisfaction (American Nurses Association 1995). A press release announcing this move protested that "report cards typically rely on claims and administrative data, supplemented with medical record review. Nursing is virtually absent from current hospital report cards, even though nurses are critical in protecting the safety and quality of a patient's care while hospitalized. In a statement included in the press release, ANA President Virginia Trotter Betts made argued, "Hospitals are not required to disclose their current level of nursing personnel or most data relevant to patient outcomes. It makes no sense to us that research suggesting good nursing care has positive effects on mortality, length of stay, readmission rates, and, ultimately, costs is being ignored in hospital executive suites."*U.S. News and World Report*, in its annual ranking of "America's best hospitals," commendably uses data on the number of full-time registered nurses on staff relative to each hospital's patient population, but this component is minimal compared to the other crucial factors the ANA suggested.

Obviously, the reliability of hospital data depends on personnel welltrained in documentation and coding aspects, skilled at excerpting data and getting them into the database—at a time when hospitals are laying people off and cutting back on service, and when no consensus exists on a standard methodology or on the most rigorous, valid approach for adjusting outcomes data for risk. Indeed, there is such diversity of content, format, and level of detail in health-plan and hospital report cards (Nerenz 1998, 463), that there is a risk that report cards will do to hospitals what Neilsen scores have done to television: place too much emphasis on the numbers to the neglect of quality.

ENLARGING THE ARENA

Clearly, the cow paths have merged into a superhighway with multiple off-ramps. The QA/I industry of consultants, measurement experts, health services researchers, database developers, external review agencies, journals, newsletters, conferences, and seminars continues to proliferate and the number of people with an interest in building an arena around accountability balloons exponentially. A relative newcomer, the Foundation for Accountability (FACCT), for example, has drawn together a board of directors comprising consumer groups (e.g., the American Association for Retired People); union representatives (AFL-CIO); public purchasers (HCFA, Federal Employees Health Benefits Program, U.S. Department of Defense); private purchasers (American Express, American Telephone & Telegraph, General Motors); and at-large members (Access Health, the Jackson Hole Group). To its credit, the organization is striving for a means to portray the complexity of health care rather than simplify it for the sake of an easy-to-use measurement scheme (Lansky 1996). Quality measures focus on the experiences of people who receive health care services and the end results of that care, such as functional status, quality of life, and patient satisfaction—for which an elaborate structure has been established. First, experts and consumers help select clinical conditions to measure based on criteria such as prevalence in the population, cost of care, opportunity for improving care, etc. Then, a "nationally renowned expert" is commissioned to prepare a review of the scientific literature on a chosen condition and measurement options. The paper is peer reviewed by a smaller panel of physicians, researchers, consumers, and patient advocates before it forms the basis for FACCT's proposed measurement set. After drafting a measurement proposal, FACCT convenes a meeting to consider its approach and each of the measures suggested. These meetings, attended by clinicians, researchers, and purchaser and consumer representatives, often result in revisions to the proposal. When FACCT has prepared a final draft of a proposed measurement set, it is brought before the Measures Council (a group of health services data specialists, physicians, nurses, purchasers, consumers, and methodologists) for review, comment, and final revision if necessary. Final endorsement of FACCT measures lies with its board of trustees. Even after approval, FACCT solicits ongoing input from experts about many issues related to the measures, such as specification of the sample size, survey implementation, and data collection (ibid).

On yet another front, three health care quality oversight organizations—the Joint Commission, the National Committee for Quality Assurance, and the American Medical Accreditation Program—have joined together in a Performance Measurement Coordinating Council charged with "making performance measurement more efficient and coherent across all levels of the health care system" ("AMAP, JCAHO, NCQA announce plans to merge performance measure development efforts" 1999). The council's initial aim is to develop common criteria and common processes for prioritizing and evaluating areas for the creation of new measurement sets in the near future. However, the three organizations plan to merge expert panels in selected areas (e.g., cancer care)" (ibid). And so the arena grows.

In the 1950s, medical audit looked like the yellow brick road to hospital accountability. In the 1970s, hope resided in peer review through PSROs. In the 1990s, the promise shifted to CQI, critical pathways, practice guidelines, and outcome measures. Which of the latter is a fad and which will have lasting power is still unclear. In assessing them we would do well to heed the observations of the Editor-in-Chief Emeritus of the *New England Journal of Medicine* in his "medical-industrial complex" article published almost two decades ago (Relman 1980). His main point—that health care is different from most of the commodities bought and sold in the marketplace and that most people consider it, to some degree at least, a basic right of all citizens—is even more credible today when the complex health-care system (or nonsystem, depending on one's point of view) is even more market-driven than it was in the 1980s. During a phone call to one of my informants, she suddenly said:

> The other day I was thinking that if this were just a nice, normal little business where we made widgets it would be fine but we're really, you know, we have an unspoken contract to people to take care of them when they're vulnerable. And, we're not doing a good job. The industry isn't, hasn't stabilized enough to be able to provide good medicine. We don't have stable providers because nobody's staying. None of our, of our system has worked because it's just kind of out of kilter. It's like a bicycle wheel that's off its chain.

David Lansky, president of FAACT, has called for a national health care advisory board along the lines of the Financial Accounting Standards Board (which recommends changes in accounting methods based on input from practitioners in the field), coupled with a regulatory body similar to the Securities and Exchange Commission. Lansky has suggested that the board could recommend changes in insurance regulation, adopt standards for measuring and reporting quality, and coordinate and conduct outcomes research (Larkin 1998, 1–2). Before one more layer of oversight is established, it is important to confront some of the basic deficiencies in the accountability enterprise—the assumptions and organizational barriers that will continue to make the work of defining and standardizing quality elusive.

NOTES

1. Claire Crawford-Mason, in a discussion of Deming, following his death, on "Forum," National Public Radio, December 22, 1993. See also Dobyns and Mason (1994); Walton (1990); and Walton (1986).
2. Slee (1966). Millenson (1997) correctly recalls Florence Nightingale as an earlier advocate of "information-based medicine," describing her gathering of statistics to buttress her case before Parliament regarding the high mortality rate in military hospitals, following her nursing experience during the Crimean War. *See also* Huxley (1975).
3. In a small but elucidative book on national defense, James Fallows characterizes McNamara as desiring to make defense a more straightforward and efficient business by applying the disciplines of economics and management to military plans. Distinguishing between efficiency, in the economic and technological sense, and effectiveness on the battlefield, Fallows provides a lesson that resonates in the quest for accountability in hospitals: "The real problem is the use of an oversimplified, one-dimensional form of analysis, often based on simulations and hypotheses, in place of more complicated judgments, based on data from combat or realistic tests, that take into account the eight or ten qualities that must be combined to make a weapon effective" (1981, 19). Regarding the eagerness to compute the relative advantage of the United States over its adversaries—for example, the enemy body count diligently reported by the press—Fallows quotes an army officer:

> It has always been natural for one side in an armed conflict to estimate the number of casualties it has inflicted upon the other side. Not until Vietnam, however, did "estimated enemy casualties" become an all-encompassing obsession of the army. . . . Officially it was the U.S. policy to claim as enemy dead only those bodies that had actually fallen on the battleground and had been physically counted by an American commander. Any man who has ever been to war, particularly anyone who ever fought in Vietnam, knows that such a policy was impossible to implement or enforce and consequently was conducive to "estimates" which could easily be falsified. Yet once entered on a report form, such estimates took on a reality of their own, transcending anything that might have actually happened. No matter how arrived at, the figures themselves became real "Cincinnatus" (pseudonym) 1981, 84.

4. Medical informatics is the scientific field that deals with the storage, retrieval, sharing and optimal use of biomedical information, data and knowledge for problem solving and decision making (*see* Shortliffe and Perrealt 1990). There now is an American College of Medical Informatics (ACMI), comprised of elected fellows who have made significant and sustained contributions to the field.

5. The Ernest A. Codman Address, International Congress on Performance Measurement and Improvement in Health Care, Chicago, Illinois, November 12–15, 1997.

4

Implementing the Accountability Endeavor
Overcoming Assumptions and Surmounting Obstacles

The greatest obstacle to discovery is not ignorance—it is the illusion of knowledge
—*Daniel J. Boorstin*

Many people (both internal and external to the hospital) are working on QA/I standards, investigating and testing new systems, grappling with coordination. Quality personnel, caught in the throes of this, do not question the need for regulation, surveillance, or improved information management. A number of those interviewed for this study alluded to standards, such as those of the Joint Commission, as useful tools, since, as one said, "every program needs a measure against which it can either self-evaluate or be externally evaluated."

Neither does anyone deny that money spent by payers, government and private, should be spent wisely. Differences arise, however, over such terms as "meaningful standards," "valid outcome measures," "consistent reporting," and "wise fiscal policy." By whose definition of these terms are we operating? That those who advocate measuring and comparing performance improvement are aware of current limitations is clear from my interviews, public discussions, and most of the literature, but the actors continue to argue that what is being done is "better than nothing." Is it?

Measuring performance is seen as a means to improve efficiency and standardize care. Too often, however, clear distinction is not made between medical accountability data and clinical outcomes data. The implications are serious:

Medical accountability data are collected to describe two things: first, how often each specific disease category is encountered, diagnosed, and treated; second, what specific services or treatments are delivered. This information is listed by patient and by disease. The data give providers a "scientific-legal" legitimacy to justify their rationing of treatments of procedures in the name of cost efficiency while simultaneously telling them what categories of customers are the most profitable. For example, such data tell medical managers that "coronary bypasses" are more profitable than "strokes," while they simultaneously describe a statistical norm of practice and highlight physicians and hospitals that fall outside the range. Clinical outcomes data, on the other hand, describe the impact that the treatment or service had, on the disease, on the patient's health, and on our national morbidity and mortality statistics. Although these are very different kinds of concerns, in discussions of outcomes research the lines between them are often ignored or crossed. Both health care analysts and management experts tend either to use them interchangeably or to claim that manipulating medical services through statistical processes will result in desirable clinical outcomes, an ideological leap that is not always supported by the data. (Leyerle 1994, 133–34)

The debate over the present state of data collection and dissemination raises doubts as to whether the desired goal is feasible, leaving those who must perform these tasks with serious questions to confront. They must first deal with the assumptions on which measuring performance is based and then maneuver around the obstacles that present themselves in the hospital setting.

EXAMINING THE ASSUMPTIONS

Assumptions about a Simple Cause and Effect Relationship

The assumption that performance can be measured in a linear, cause- and-effect equation is exemplified in two commonly used indicators: number of falls and infection rate. By focusing on whether a patient fell or developed an infection while in the hospital, however, quality professionals are not assessing quality of care but rather whether the patient escaped harm based on these simple measures.

Similarly, using hospital-readmission rates as a measure of the number of patients who were discharged too soon assumes that those patients who were not readmitted got better. This measure does not capture the patient who is not in a managed care program and, dissatisfied with the physical outcome of her knee surgery, changes doctors and/or chooses to be admitted to another hospital. Nor does it reflect patients who are coping with unnecessary suffering brought on by an untimely discharge from the hospital. Much less does it reflect quality of life. As a chief administrator interviewed in my research quipped, "We're looking at patients who were resuscitated to see how many were readmitted. A better outcome measure would be who's back on the golf course."

Sensing the deficiencies of cause/effect thinking, some researchers emphasize the need to make distinctions among structure, process, and outcome when evaluating quality of care. Based on the "Donabedian typology" (Donabedian 1980; *see also* Brook et al. 1996) of quality assessment, structure refers to the basic resources that are prerequisites to quality care: professionals, equipment, educational attainments, the ownership of a hospital, etc. Process data are the components of the encounter between a physician or another health-care professional and a patient (e.g., tests ordered), and the manner in which care is provided. Outcome refers to the results of the process, such as the patient's subsequent health status (e.g., an improvement in symptoms or mobility) (Donabedian 1980). It is, however, much easier to quantify a process (the rate of mammography or childhood immunizations in a large population) than to determine the success of, say, efforts to palliate congestive heart failure in a few individual patients.

> We do not mean to deny the importance of mammography and childhood immunization, only to point out that their use can be measured by a simple yes/no question in a group large enough to give the answer some significance. And it is simple enough for plans to ensure that their doctors perform such procedures, so that plans can score well on quality reports. In contrast, treating congestive heart failure or urosepsis in a patient with diabetes mellitus, who may have other medical problems as well, involves not only a complex series of decisions and interactions, but also the nearly imponderable element of individual variation. (Angell and Kassirer 1996, 884)

Moreover, within a particular hospital, deciding on what is an outcome and how it should be measured requires extensive negotiation among hospital workers. "The cloned team might well find themselves tied up in Donabedian knots: structures dissolve and one researcher's process is another one's outcome" (Carr-Hill 1995, 1467).

An illustration of the pitfalls of linear thinking emerged in the course of my research. During a discussion of a potential study of "overuse" of laboratory services, the laboratory director gave an example of deceptive statistics: An increase in laboratory orders may reflect *more* rather than *less* efficiency by leading to earlier discharge from the hospital, and such figures reveal nothing about the consequences of early discharge. Reliability of data depends on the context—without additional data, the term "overuse" remains meaningless.

Assumptions About Reliability of Data

To accept statistics with confidence, one must believe they are reliable and consistent. The truth is, however, that a number of approaches to measuring performance in this arena are conceptually flawed or based on inaccurate data. An example is the Health Care Financing Administration's program for measuring and publishing hospital mortality rates among Medicare patients. "After many years of publishing such statistics, the agency came to the conclusion that without a better method to adjust for the severity of illness, the data were too inaccurate to be useful, and the program was abandoned" (Blumenthal 1996, 893; *see also* Berwick and Wald 1990; Chassin et al. 1989). In the words of a Medicare specialist I interviewed, "Who's to say that the hospital care had anything to do with the patient dying? Even physician-specific mortality rates don't necessarily mean anything—oncologists have a really high number of deaths!"

Nevertheless, mortality rates, largely because they are easy to obtain from those hospitals that lack more sophisticated information, continue to be used in many studies. Mortality rates can be useful if they reveal enough of a discrepancy to indicate that they are the tip of the medical-error iceberg. For the most part, however, such statistics say little about the quality of health care. For example, a study published in 1996 (based on 1994 clinical and financial data) declared that Northern California has some of the most "cost-effective" hospitals in the country. The survey did not address who benefited from the savings achieved by for-profit HMOs—patients, employers, or shareholders. Nor did it address to what extent patients were denied services. Rather, managed care was adjudged cost-effective because it had not resulted in higher mortality or complication rates (KPMG Peat Marwick 1996).

Another study, by the California Office of Statewide Health Planning and Development, examined 68,012 heart attack cases that occurred from 1990 through 1992 at 398 hospitals and then published the comparative death rates. Although the rates were "risk-adjusted" (to make allowances for hospitals that treat an abundance of patients with severe illnesses), those who fared badly quickly cried "foul." The administrator of a small, community hospital at which 16 heart attack patients had died among 87 admitted, protested that five patients arrived at the hospital brain-dead and two others were undergoing cardiovascular resuscitation by paramedics when they arrived. The administrators's comment, "They're trying to quantify everything, but the fact is these kinds of things can't be quantified," was echoed by hospital industry officials who agreed that "the science of assessing health care quality is still in the dark ages" (Hall 1996).

A lesson might have been learned from the so-called Caper incident is a case in point. In a *New England Journal of Medicine* editorial, Philip Caper, a physician and president of the Codman Research Group, charged that physicians at the Scripps Memorial Hospital–La Jolla (SMH-LJ) overused coronary-artery bypass surgery. Based on data the hospital had submitted to the California Office of Statewide Health Planning and Development, Dr. Caper claimed that residents of La Jolla were three times more likely to undergo this procedure than residents of Palo Alto—where the surgery was done at Stanford Hospital, "a world renowned cardiovascular-surgery center" (Caper 1988, 1536).

Physicians from SMH-LJ cried "foul" in a letter to the editor, pointing out that their hospital had contracted to do all the open-heart surgery for Kaiser Permanente of San Diego, which at that time insured 300,000 people. "Regardless of the Kaiser patients' actual residence, the SMH-LJ billing office recorded a LaJolla zip code. When the data are corrected, there is no difference between La Jolla and the state average." The aggrieved physicians charged in turn that "the extent of damage from the editorial is indeterminable, but it has already been cited in the San Diego newspapers and in a reply from a private foundation to a grant request" (Cherry et al. 1988, 800).

Caper then expressed regret and attempted to turn the incident into an learning opportunity. He called for greater accuracy in coding and reporting, interpretation of data by clinicians at the local level, and involvement of physicians and hospitals in the government's interpretation of data. One of Caper's conclusions must have struck the Scripps physicians as ironic. In the spirit of Polyanna, he found a virtue in the experience: the quality of data does not improve until they are used. "The systematic reporting error at Scripps had been occurring since at least 1983. It was detected only when the results of this analysis commanded the attention of the medical staff, who then pursued the source of the apparently high rates and discovered the error" (Caper 1998a, 801).

Quality personnel interviewed in my research told similar tales of harm done by disseminating erroneous data. One of the most dramatic involved a firefighter, badly burned, who was being flown by helicopter to the hospital with the most up-to-date burn unit the Bay Area. Having read an "outcomes report" that was published in a magazine devoted to consumer awareness, he remembered that this hospital had shown a high complication and mortality rate. Unbeknownst to him, the figures had not been adjusted to reflect the hospital's higher volume of seriously burned patients. The firefighter begged to be re-directed but the hospital he selected refused to receive him, citing inadequate facilities. As the QA/I director described it, "The poor patient was screaming, 'I don't want to go there. They're going to kill me'—all based on this inaccurate data."

Quality personnel interviewed in this study do not have much faith in published data. Even as seemingly simple a statistic as the number of patient falls can be deceiving. One professional bemoaned the lack of consistency in reporting, not only on a national basis, but even among hospitals within the same corporate management:

> The data are all over the place. Stuff like falls, you know, what's a fall? Some people say a fall is when you see the patient fall down, others say when you find them on the floor.

In some instances, the realities of competition intrude upon obtaining consistent data within a corporate structure (e.g., Catholic Healthcare West, Kaiser, or Sutter Health). A quality analyst explained: "What's happening is that hospitals are turning in data or making data collectible in a way that will reflect favorably upon themselves."

Examining data from 31 Midwestern rural, rural referral, and urban acute care hospitals, researchers found similar inconsistencies. Much of the variation in the reported infections in these hospitals was due to different surveillance practices. Addressing the issue of report cards, the researchers warned, "Failing to assess the comparability of the data collection methods used by providers may result in incorrect conclusions about differences in quality and potentially reward providers which appear to have 'good results' when in fact they have 'bad data'" (Wakefield et al. 1994).

In the current market, with many hospitals struggling to stay afloat, high stakes tempt hospital administrators to manipulate the data. During the 1980s, when Medicare changed from fee-for-service to prospective payment based on DRGs, the term "DRG creep" was coined for the deliberate and systematic shift in hospitals' reporting (opting to report higher-income DRGs) to improve reimbursement (Simborg 1981). Similarly, there is a risk of "death code creep"—increased coding of catastrophic events for dying patients—to boost hospitals' outcome-based report cards (Iezzoni 1997a, 1606). One observer pinpoints the essence of the problem of reporting manipulation:

> Some states want a list of all the people who are doing heart bypass surgery, by name, and what their scores are. And they want it made public. Well, imagine what that does to a person who's going to be more interested in what their score is and how to hook (influence) the numbers—a lot of energy is spent defending the number instead of improving the process. ("Hospitals must decide" 1994)

Although the New York reporting system must be recognized for having achieved a 41 percent decline in risk-adjusted mortality associated with coronary-artery bypass grafting (Blumenthal and Epstein 1996), there is also a downside. Researchers discovered a dramatic increase in coexisting conditions, which they attributed to changes in coding practices by physicians and hospitals wishing to improve their risk-adjusted statistics (Green and Winfeld 1995).

Given the improved efficiency often credited to managed-care organizations (MCOs), it is important to note that their data also have inherent deficiencies. In a candid address before the 1999 National Managed Care Health Care Congress, industry expert Matthew Rosen pointed out that the data from which MCOs are building "these great epidemiological databases" are essentially financial transactions—leading him to conclude, "We really are trying to make silk purses out of a sow's ear here." The reporter who covered his speech observed,

> The environment is rife with opportunities for data errors, particularly because claims approvers typically are paid based on how many claims they process. This has set the stage for the prolific use of "dump codes"—where claims approvers are unable to readily assign the correct code for a certain symptom, and so instead of taking the time to find the right code, they simply type in any numbers that will allow them to progress to the next screen. (Newman 1999)

Rosen was no less damning in his appraisal of how the data are flawed at the provider level.

> Faced with constantly changing fee schedules and utilization management programs, along with several thousand fee codes, many of which can be applied to the same thing, "it's not surprising that physicians will try and find the code that will maximize their reimbursement," Rosen said. Specialists often issue "superbills," in which they have a sampling of codes for their most common procedures. "Is that the most accurate code? Probably not, but it suits the purpose. It creates a more efficient process," he noted. . . . "We focus a great deal on computer systems, software, algorithms, but I suspect we underestimate the importance of the human component," he says. "When you get down to it, that still is what's driving the train." (ibid.; *see also* Yao et al. 1999; Smith 1989; Lloyd and Rising 1985)

Assumptions about Timeliness of Data

Obviously, for data to be valuable they must be timely. Yet quality personnel I interviewed constantly bemoaned the lack of timeliness.

> All hospitals report to the California Office of Statewide Health Planning. They publish reports but they're always so far behind. They're just now (1994) reviewing the data for July through December, 1992. It isn't valuable at all to us when they finally send the report. . . . We can look at it but we've already got that data internally and have moved on.

The four-volume *Report on Heart Attacks* (CMIs), released as part of the California Outcomes Project and covering over 400 hospitals, was issued in

December 1997 but was based on data covering 1991–93. Similarly, quality managers criticized the four report cards the Pennsylvania Health Care Cost Containment Council issued for being out of date: 1991 data were issued in 1993, and 1992 data were not due to come out until most of 1994 was over (American Health Care Consultants 1994, 17).

Also, regarding research findings, lag time between completion of a medical study and publication results can be two or three years. For example, the highly respected study by Luft and Romano on coronary-artery-bypass-graft patients contains data covering 1983 to 1989, but was not published until 1993. Add to this the dynamism of the research process. Increasingly, the general public is learning to be cynical about the latest findings on cholesterol, hormone replacement therapy, or treatment of prostate disease—hoping that, as Woody Allen proposed in the movie *Sleepers*, future researchers will find that steak, cream pies, and hot fudge are actually healthful foods. Research is *supposed* to stimulate subsequent research. That is how science works. Medical knowledge and medical technology are emergent and unpredictable—a discovery in some laboratory or through some population study can abruptly reverse previous understanding. Under these circumstances, it is unrealistic to expect reseach to be useful as a foundation for practice guidelines (Stano 1994).

Assumptions about the Usefulness of Patient Surveys

Interest in providing information to payers, health plans, clinicians, and the public in order to boost quality has led hospitals to consumer ratings, obtained through patient satisfaction surveys. As important and attractive as patient input is, however, surveys make unrealistic assumptions of public expertise regarding both precise knowledge of what happened to them as hospital patients and adequate understanding of the publicized results of what happened to others. A recent comprehensive review of the literature showed that measures of patient satisfaction are not evaluations of the quality of care from the perspective of either the provider or the patient and "are only weakly related to the criterion of quality care that providers specify" (Cleary and McNeil 1988, 31; *see also* Cleary et al. 1991, 1992, 1993; Gerteis et al. 1993; Edgman-Levitan and Cleary 1996). Subsequent research yielded some useful lessons:

First, amenities (e.g., food, parking, cleanliness) that are so prominent in many satisfaction questionnaires are seen as very distinct from quality of care by most patients. Second, these studies suggest that the very concept of "satisfaction" is not adequate. Satisfaction implies only that expectations have been met. Patients can be satisfied with care that is not high quality and can be dissatisfied with quality care. Third, certain issues, such as being treated with respect and being involved in treatment decisions, aspects of care not included in many satisfaction surveys, are paramount issues for patients. (Cleary and Edgman-Levitan 1997, 1608)

In addition to these weaknesses, the phrase, "patients can be satisfied with care that is not high quality" needs to be examined. Considering the intricacies of hospital care, why should we assume that patients who complete a survey regarding their hospital experience understand what constitutes technical quality? Then there is the issue of underuse of technology: If a physician neglected to order the CT scan that would have aided diagnosis (increasingly possible in light of pressure from management to contain costs), would the patient necessarily know?

In California, which has one of the highest rates of coronary artery bypass surgery in the world, fully 25% of people with serious coronary artery disease, regardless of whether they are enrolled in a managed care plan, are still not offered coronary artery bypass graft surgery because the system has failed, i.e., somehow the results of the coronary angiography never resulted in a conversation between the patient and the physician about the need for cardiac revascularization. (Brook 1997, 1614; Laouri et al. 1997)

Any close observer of everyday hospital care is struck by how unaware patients or their family members are of technical near-misses, let alone downright error. The complexity of health care makes it easier to hide mistakes. Discussion of adverse events remains within the cloistered walls of the medical peer review committee—if it gets that far. Nor do malpractice suits serve as an adequate barometer of patient awareness of error. Very little research has been done on the incidence and scope of adverse hospital events; even less on patient awareness of them. One study that stands out in this regard replaced the conventional reliance on review of medical records with a prospective, observational design. Ethnographers trained in qualitative observational research attended day-shift, weekday, regularly scheduled conferences and other scheduled meetings in three hospital units as well as various departmental and section meetings. They recorded all adverse events discussed at these meetings, and thus based their analysis on health-care providers' own assessments about the appropriateness of the care that patients received. This study revealed that although 17.7 percent of patients experienced serious events that led to longer hospital stays and increased costs to them, only 1.2 percent (13 of the 1,047 patients) filed claims for compensation (Andrews et al. 1997).

One problem with surveys is their distortion of the social-psychological reality of patients' experiences. What sociologist Neil Smelser has said of public opinion polls is equally true of patient satisfaction surveys. By offering forced-choice alternatives, most surveys minimize and delegitimize both ambiguity and ambivalence, universal attributes of human behavior (Smelser 1995). Moreover, there is the shaky methodology and inconsistency of satisfaction surveys. The importance of dimensions of care most frequently measured—the social-psychological aspects of the physician-patient interaction, the technical quality of care, continuity of care, patient convenience, physical setting, financial considerations, and efficacy—are often viewed differently by different hospitals. Some hospitals observed in my study distributed surveys that covered a wide range of questions from courtesy to food service to emotional aspects, e.g., "Were your spiritual needs adequately met?" Others used global measures of satisfaction: "Looking back on your experience at X Hospital, how would you rate the overall care you received?" and "Was the care you received so good that you would brag about it to family and friends?"

If results from these surveys were used internally to pinpoint and correct deficiencies, the exercise would seem worthwhile. In fact, they rarely get back to caregivers. The worrisome aspect of using these surveys, considering the inconsistency of methods and the absence of standards, lies in their increasing use in reports cards and their absolutely unknown impact on consumer choice. Despite widespread agreement about the complexity of decision making, very little is known about how people use the report cards—how they interpret the information or how such information influences their decisions. "Many have noted that information needs vary dramatically among different population groups and that the way people receive and respond to information is a complex process that is influenced by a wide array of social factors"; further, "information that seems intuitively obvious to researchers in this area borders on incomprehensible for many people, even those with a lot of education and interest in health care issues" (Cleary and Edgman-Levitan 1997, 1610).

Researchers have discovered that many indicators of quality are not well understood at either basic or more abstract levels of comprehension (Jewett and Hibbard 1996). Comprehension problems include not understanding terms, whether high or low rates of an indicator show good performance, and what an indicator is supposed to tell about quality of care. "Aggregations and quantitative concepts are particularly difficult to understand" More significant, "if consumers do not understand information, they are more likely to dismiss it as unimportant" (Hibbard and Jewett 1997, 220, 226).

Last, we have to ask how the public can be expected to understand either the complexities or the subtleties of "satisfaction," when, as is common practice, hospitals selectively excerpt the information from surveys and then use it as a marketing tool. We do not expect the public to judge airline safety by how clean the plane is, but all too often hospitals use methodologically unsound surveys that lump together disparate categories and turn them into advertisements. And if they need guidance, a how-to book is at the ready for $189. Called *Collecting Information From Health Care Consumers*, this resource manual (with annual updates to be added to the loose leaf binder), according to its cover letter, is designed to provide "meaningful and actionable information" for today's competitive market and inform users on "how to use the survey results to document quality and boost your health and business outcomes."[1] The danger is, of course, that the zeal to use this information for marketing purposes will confuse the public even further.

CONFRONTING PREVAILING CONDITIONS

Underlying all the ramifications of these assumptions is a significant problem: Care delivery is too large and too varied and human physiology and disease experiences too complex to be squeezed into the narrow concept of using gross numbers to measure performance. Good care cannot be completely standardized: "If critical illnesses were less variable and more predictable, a manual of performance standards might be developed as a guide to professionals for making decisions. But there is no such thing as a standard illness or standard patient" (Skillihorn 1980, 32). The language of the Deming model of continuous quality improvement adds emphasis:

> A health facility . . . deals with an infinitesimal number of "products" and the outcome will vary, not only according problems with the system of care or with the people providing the care, but also with "raw materials" provided. These will vary according to the state of the patients at presentation, their age, anatomy, physiology and particularly their psychology, in other words their case-mix and illness severity. (Collopy 1993, 3)

Equally important, and frequently overlooked, are two important elements: the "case-mix" of the people providing care and the circumstances under which care is provided. Not only does each patient come to the hospital with a personal biography and unique "raw materials," but the caregivers, the unit to which the patient is assigned, the medical specialty, the hospital itself—all of these have their own histories and characteristics which intertwine in unpredictable ways and produce unique consequences (Wiener et al. 1979).

It is useful here to look at the distinction drawn by Strauss et al. (1997) between a course of illness and an illness trajectory. *Course of illness* is both a commonsense and professional term, indicating that each kind of illness has its characteristic phases and symptoms, and often only skilled intervention will reverse, halt, or at least slow the progress of the disease. In contrast, *trajectory* refers not only to the physiological unfolding of a patient's disease but to the *total organization of work* done over that course, plus the *impact* on those involved with the work and its organization. ("Workers" include the patient and kin.) This concept is particularly useful now that patients are likely to have multiple chronic illnesses—may be hospitalized for an acute episode of heart disease, with an underlying condition of diabetes, or hospitalized for a stroke while on medication for Parkinson's disease. Patients may not be sociologists, using a term like "trajectory" to convey the larger scope and context of their illness, but they are more likely than health workers to describe their illnesses in larger terms of episodes of care rather than single visits to the doctor's office or hospitalizations.

> Heart-attack patients, for example, might refer to care received in the emergency department, the medical service of one hospital, the surgical service of another hospital, the office of a cardiologist, the office of their general physician, and a rehabilitation setting all in a single story about the quality of care received. (Cleary and Edgman-Levitan 1997, 1609)

When the fast pace of change in medical technology is added to the mix, a truer picture of modern health care emerges. Obviously, today's practice is radically different from that of a century ago when "everything physicians needed was found between their own two ears or in a small black bag" (Blumenthal 1996, 1148). Medical discoveries are reported almost daily in professional journals and—significantly—on the business pages of newspapers and magazines. Pacemakers were news when they first appeared in the 1980s. Now they, as well as the ability to service them over the telephone wires, are taken for granted. Cataract surgery, which formerly required a long hospital stay during which sandbags held the head motionless, has been replaced with a technique that uses ultrasonic energy and allows the patient to go home the same day. Similarly done as day surgery is gallbladder removal (known as laparoscopic cholecystectomy or "lap chole") through a technique using a minute camera and instruments that surgeons manipulate through tiny incisions. This surgery formerly required as much as a six-day hospital stay and a painful recovery. Fetal and newborn surgery for treatment of birth defects, several generations of rate-control devices that allow safer infusion of drugs and solutions, imaging techniques that map the brain, direct-bloodstream feeding that bypasses the digestive system through "total parenteral nutrition"—all are evidence of evolving technology improving treatment while at the same time creating new contingencies.

Conversely, as discussed previously, new discoveries can suddenly reverse thinking on established procedures. For example, after right-heart catheterization had been used for 25 years, researchers studying 5,735 intensive-care unit patients at five U.S. medical centers discovered a clear association between the use of this heart-monitoring procedure and a higher death rate (Connors et al. 1996). Two doctors found the data sufficiently alarming to warrant either immediate clinical trials by the National Heart, Lung and Blood Institute of the National Institutes of Health or a government moratorium on the procedure (Dalen and Bone 1996).

Intricate technology requires expert knowledge, specialists who deal not only with the uncertainty of each person's course of illness (often illness*es*), but with the risks attached to use of technology—hence, specialties such as pediatric oncology and neonatal cardiology. Hence also, all the balancing and juggling of options and the use of consultations. "Often debates are going on among physicians regarding what is the right option, or about the appropriate sequence of options. Each decision about options can be crucial, with multiple factors being weighed and balanced, often by a multitude of people who may have different perspectives and different stakes in the decision making" (Wiener et al. 1982, 23). This fact of hospital life supports the argument that the underlying population characteristics—patient and provider—present formidable obstacles to meaningful measurement of outcomes. Indeed, one of the most ardent proponents of practice guidelines acknowledges the role of clinical judgment:

> Even when medicine was simple (20 years ago), much was written about observer variability, and virtually every time this subject was examined startling results were obtained. Two cardiologists who listen to a patient's heart will often hear different murmurs. If a patient's blood is divided, placed in two test tubes, and sent to different laboratories, the resultant cholesterol measurements may differ widely. . . . A roentgenographic study of the stomach is performed and the resulting films are read by two radiologists; one may conclude that an ulcer is present, the other that the results are normal. (Brook 1989, 3028)

Admittedly, in other fields where total quality improvement has been used—engineering, computer science, some manufacturing—the technical activity is complex and difficult to monitor and control. But much of health care involves art as much as it does science. "Until we successfully develop an ability to understand, monitor, and control art, we will not have an ability to assess that aspect of medical and health care" (Ziegenfuss 1991, 117). One commentator wryly suggests that physicians who continue to claim that medicine is an art should be asked to seek payment not from Medicare but from the National Endowment for the Arts (Sager 1997). But there is no denying that medical performance contains intangibles:

"How closely the physician, or any health professional, approaches the limits of available knowledge and of skill, judgment, and application in his care of the patient is not handily reducible to quantitative terms. Much less the patient, the physician himself or even his dispassionate peers has some difficulty in assessing by how much he achieved or fell short of doing the very best anyone knew how to do" (Porterfield 1970).

Work in the contemporary hospital is fueled by the interplay among patient biography, provider and setting biography, complex illness trajectories, increased medical research, rapidly evolving technology, and the need for specialized clinical expertise. Indeed, these conditions and their incalculable effect on the process of care are the Achilles heel of the entire outcomes enterprise, as demonstrated in the debate surrounding even the best efforts to rank "America's Best Hospitals." Despite the claim of *U.S. News and World Report* that its annual rankings "remain the sole source of relevant, rigorously conceived information" (Comarow 1997, 74) and are "the only effort that subjects all 6,400 hospitals in the United States to scrutiny in this way" (Comarow 1998, 65), this ranking (in its ninth year in 1998) still stumbles over measuring the process of care. With due credit to its strong conceptual design and its attempt to incorporate Donabedian's widely respected theoretical paradigm—of structure, process, and outcome—into its framework, the newsmagazine's annual evaluation is still weak because the national data sources for all three components are severely limited. More important, the magazine's decision to compensate for a lack of valid national data by using a *reputation* survey to measure the process-of-care is seriously flawed. "One consequence of reliance on reputation is that a small group of prominent hospitals in each specialty receives such high scores that they automatically rise to the top of the rankings, regardless of structure or outcome score" (Green et al. 1997, 1152). Then, in a suprising conclusion, the researchers propose that the way to deal with the paucity of process-of-care data is to throw more money into research on the variation in quality of care across the nation's hospitals. While admitting that the money involved would be several orders of magnitude greater than that currently being spent, they refuse to accept that the goal is unattainable. If health-policy experts continue to sidestep the prevailing conditions underlying health-care delivery, research on quality variation will just be more money down the drain.

EXAMINING ORGANIZATIONAL BARRIERS

Other obstacles to a true measure of performance arise from what is called within the arena "the changing culture of health care," another way of saying "the way we've always done things."

Turf Protection

Those who assume that the tools of continuous quality improvement necessarily "promote collaboration and minimize interdisciplinary battles" (Ziengenfuss 1991, 119) forget that turf protection dies hard. A QA/I director described a scene familiar to all organizations:

> They tend to want to point fingers. If there's a medication problem—is it the way the doctor ordered, or he wrote his order, or is it the way the nurses gave it, or what happened there. Or they might look at infection problems and say, "was it the way the doctor did surgery, or was it the way the nurses took care of the wound afterwards?" And they're not real willing to do a lot of give and take there.

Quality improvement meetings can be adversarial; they may call for extraordinary patience as controversial issues arise, such as which department will pay for a procedural change. Certainly, evidence exists to support the claim that interdisciplinary CQI has produced instances of organizational improvement, but hospitals will always have to deal with competition among professions and battles over turf.

Nurses, for example, get caught in the whipsaw of cooperating on projects while also retaining a valued professional identity. Quality analysts who were nurses and were interviewed for this study enthusiastically greeted the shift to interdisciplinary decision making. They decried what they characterized as "silo" thinking—that is, the previous practice of separate and often conflicting decision making by administration, medicine, and nursing. In the meantime, nurses specializing in the new field of medical informatics are developing their own theories of outcome measurement. Concerned that "measurement of patient outcomes has been sporadic, often discipline specific, and frequently focused on medical practice" (Maas et al. 1996, 295), this segment of the nursing world calls for a means to identify and measure the effects of nursing interventions so that nurses will become full participants in the developing discipline of evaluation science (Jennings 1991; Marek 1989). To develop a comprehensive classification of nursing-sensitive patient outcomes, these nursing-information specialists have used as their source 4,500 outcome statements in nursing textbooks, published care-planning guides, nursing diagnosis manuals, critical paths, etc. Their initial outcome labels range from broad statements such as prevention of complications to mid-level statements such as knowledge of proper dressing care to very specific statements such as cardiac index 2.5 to 4.0 liters per minute. A nurse remarked that if she and her colleagues relied on physician-centered information only, "the impact of nursing care would remain largely unmeasured and therefore invisible" (Mallison 1990, 7). The same can be said for nursing-sensitive

patient outcomes: "If outcomes are identified only for the composite of interdisciplinary interventions, each discipline will be unable to judge the effects of specific interventions and, further *no one discipline can be held
accountable*" (Maas et al. 1996, 300, emphasis added).

Organizational Power Structure

In some instances, turf issues are related to the traditional hospital power
structure, says the chief operating officer of one hospital:

> There are lots of problems with CQI. I can see the positives: empowerment,
> exposure to other peoples' perspectives. But it's time-intensive and ex-
> tremely costly. *It's supposed to work on the stakeholders but they're not coming
> from an equal place.* (emphasis added)

Accordingly, turf disputes may stem from the traditional medical committee structure of hospital organization. An illustration emerged during observation of quality improvement meetings as part of this study. Although
in most hospitals, the medical record department is responsible for the
timeliness of medical charts (completion of notes on patient care), in this
particular hospital the physician-chair of the medical records committee
was charged with reviewing charts for "clinical pertinence," a Joint Commission requirement. If, for instance, a chart shows elevated potassium in
the lab values, standards related to clinical pertinence require a note to that
effect and another note describing corrective steps taken. The chair's job
also included reviewing the quality of medical charts to determine inclusion of all necessary items: patient history and physical, signed face sheet,
document of surgery, discharge summary, etc.

A more delicate part of her job was to report physicians who do not keep
these records current, since chart timeliness is clearly defined in the standards that affect physician licensure and hospital accreditation. Repeated
meetings to address the accuracy and timeliness of charting never resolved
this problem since the physician-chair, loathe to confront her colleagues,
kept minimizing its seriousness and, as explained to me by a meeting participant, the medical records department manager had, for years, deferred
to the chair's greater power within the hospital structure. While most medical records managers would find this an affront to their professional integrity, the fact remains that similar problems arise—idiosyncratic as to
place and players—in relation to the traditional power imbalance within
the hospital.

In addition, there is often a push-pull phenomenon regarding compliance with the CQI philosophy. The hospital administrator may be a proponent of CQI tools but middle managers can sabotage this intent by
continuing to make top-down decisions. Middle managers may pull the

same trick on staff. After a while, a manager will ask: Is a team necessary? What will be gained? How will we measure our gains? Inevitably, managers become more interested in concrete results than in fostering good feelings among employees. As *some* managers and *some* hospital personnel become disenchanted with the "business flavor of the month," those who bought the CQI philosophy may become more cynical, deciding, like employees elsewhere, "If we wait until Monday, this too shall pass" (Nohria and Berkeley 1994, 130, 131).

Clinical Style and Values

After E. A. Codman failed to convince his colleagues of the value of a serious end-results examination, it took a few decades for his successors to champion the cause of medical accountability (Donabedian 1980, 1982, 1985; Williamson 1978; Brook et al. 1977; Brook 1979). Their attempts to impose some order on medical decision making have met the same lukewarm response afforded Codman. Resistance often stems from the very values that attracted physicians to medicine in the first place and have become ingrained in the course of practicing medicine. Physicians seem to have difficulty seeing themselves as participants in processes, rather than as lone agents of success or failure. A QA/I director interviewed in this study described the obstacles to initiating critical pathways:

> If a physician can't get something done, he or she circumvents the system and they create their own system for getting it done. It happens a lot. It happens when you order medicine and it doesn't come the way you want it. When you can't get the lab test you want. You create other systems for getting all this information which, again, increases the workload of the people who are trying to do the work because they have the regular system, which doesn't work, and they have your system to meet your needs. And then they've got four other systems to meet five other doctor's needs.

For physicians to be data collectors they must be interested in process flow and cause-and-effect diagrams, which most are not. Most are not only lone wolves, but are among the busiest people in the hospital—busy with their practices and hospital politics. Physician resistance is most evident when it comes to critical pathways and practice guidelines (terms that are often merged by doctors into one threatening concept). The medical director of one hospital found that the tepid response to critical pathways from some physicians was related to medical specialty:

> There is a small, but very vocal, group of internists who are highly resistant. Basically, the physician practices in a reactive way—encounters an illness and then decides that he's going to have to do something about it. They don't

like what they call "cookbook medicine." Surgeons, who are used to filling out standard orders, are less resistant.

Another QA/I coordinator added,

> We find the least resistance from surgeons. Surgeons really don't like taking care of their patients; they just want to cut them. So when they get done with them, and you have a pathway, they're tickled. It's like wonderful standing orders that they get to check off. And guess what—they get to check them off once and they're done.

Quality analysts also noted that they had always to adjust to the medical specialty they were working with; one added, "It's like working in the tower of Babel sometimes." Another analyst made the same comment about nurses during a discussion of quality improvement projects that require prolonged meetings to identify problems, negotiate roles, and define aims: "It is important to understand that people who work in intensive care units (ICUs) have different values that don't always lend themselves to a slow process. They like immediate results." This was confirmed in another hospital, where the ICU nurses refused to participate in the CQI format but insisted that they were fully capable of making any changes they deemed necessary.

Threat to Medical Autonomy

It is a truism in health care that medical judgment was inviolable in the past. Nurses, when they scoff at physicians' "cowboy mentality," are alluding to the fact that collaboration has never been part of medical training. Rather, physicians have felt that they themselves would ensure that patients received quality care. "In ordinary day to day life . . . the physician answered to no one but himself. His practice was largely invisible to his peers, incomprehensible to his patients, and unconstrained by external institutions" (Jost 1995, 831). Few cases of questionable treatment or behavior resulted in discipline of the offending doctor. Medicine as a profession managed to maintain the mythology of self-regulation. For the most part, observations by physicians about their colleagues were kept under wraps: "There is a reluctance among physicians to exert active influence over another's performance—a reluctance that results in avoiding him rather than in seeking to change his practices. . . . Since bits of information were scattered piecemeal through the colleague group, no really organized control of performance could be initiated unless a man behaved so outrageously as to personally offend everyone" (Friedson 1970, 94). Another observer commented, "It was the physicians who oversaw the quality of hospitals rather than the hospitals that supervised the quality of physicians" (Jost 1995, 830).

External review of medical performance is, in a word, anathema to many physicians. Moreover, unless it is backed by medical peer support, pressure from quality personnel for a change in medical practice often goes for naught. In my research, entreaties from a quality analyst that a surgeon alter his pre-AIDS practice of using nonautologous blood for transfusions (blood obtained from a donor other than the patient) was dismissed by the chief of surgery, who saw no reason to break with tradition.

It is thus hardly surprising that doctors find the prospect of "physician profiling" a threat to their autonomy. Quality and utilization review data in most hospitals are now sorted for each physician, giving the department chair a profile to review every two years when reappointment to medical staff rolls around. Although hospitals are legally enjoined from engaging in "economic credentialing" (using utilization rates as criteria), physicians understandably are skeptical regarding one more encroachment on their practice.

Even more threatening is the trend to hire businesses that collect data from diverse sources, develop schemes to judge the performance of individual practitioners, and sell the profiles to third-party payers and employers. Much is drawn from reimbursement claims which may be grossly incorrect, since they fail to disclose baseline functional status or important coexisting illnesses, contain nothing about patients' compliance, their desire for care, or their socioeconomic status, and little information about medications, preventive services, postoperative care, or laboratory results (Kassirer 1994). Another limitation is that a physician who is mainly a consultant may have outcomes that are a result of an attending physician's decisions (and vice versa).

Evidence that physicians are losing ground on this issue under the highly competitive managed-care market can be found in the announcement of a workshop that makes no bones about linking physician performance and compensation. The blurb heralding this event proclaims, "Profiling the practice habits of physicians may be the most effective way to realize your organization's goals for clinical performance, cost containment, and utilization."[2]

Reluctance to Disclose Data

Just as physicians are concerned about public disclosure of profiling data so too are hospitals—historically protective settings that have always valued performance privacy—leery of sharing data. Competition among facilities, which as noted earlier affects the reliability of data, also keeps useful information from people who would benefit from it. A QA/I coordinator remarked:

I see benchmarking and report cards as a competitive thing. We're comparing hospitals that, like us, are all owned by X Corporation and I suppose in
a political arena that's all we really can do because we don't want to let everybody else know what we're doing. Unfortunately, that means that we don't
know what anybody else is doing.

One of the more important issues facing hospitals as they confront the
demand for outcomes information is how much data to release to the public, and in what form. Physicians and hospitals object to sharing with the
outside world internal data that may put them in a bad light or expose
them to liability problems. Physicians are also concerned about liability
if, in their judgment, it is necessary to deviate from a critical pathway.
Lawyers tell them, "If a provider wants to depart from map guidelines because the provider disagrees with the map, the provider should include a
written explanation of the variation. Although there is a risk that the map
will be used against the provider by a plaintiff, a good explanation that appears in the record can act as a significant deterrent to a suit" (Nolin and
Clougherty 1994, 4). Nevertheless, busy physicians, with the specter of
malpractice always looming, are not likely to find much solace in this legal prescription—or in the prospect of more paperwork.

Some observers have suggested that data disclosure *may* introduce a bar-
rier to the care of severely ill patients. Since 1992, Pennsylvania has published
the *Consumer Guide to Coronary Artery Bypass Graft Surgery*, which lists annual risk-adjusted mortality rates for all hospitals and surgeons providing such
surgery in the state. In 1995, researchers surveyed a randomly selected sample of 50 percent of Pennsylvania cardiologists and cardiac surgeons to determine the guide's usefulness, limitations, and influence on providers.
Fifty-nine percent of the cardiologists reported increased difficulty in finding
surgeons willing to perform this surgery in severely ill patients who required
it, and 63 percent of the cardiac surgeons reported that they were less willing
to operate on such patients (Schneider and Epstein 1996).

The reluctance to disclose data usually arises from a sense that comparison is unfair, expressed typically as, "But our patients are sicker." Enter
"risk adjustment"—the noble effort to control outcome figures so that they
will account for severity of illness in a particular hospital and in particular
disease categories. Inevitably, the search for appropriate ways to adjust the
figures so that risk is taken into account has swelled the ranks of accountability marketers. Sales to hospitals and government agencies of risk-adjustment software have increased, supported by a tidal wave of articles by
their developers (Freeman et al. 1995; *All Patient Refined Diagnosis Related
Groups. Definition Manual* 1993). Refining the clinical accuracy of a risk-adjustment software program is a tricky business, as described by a QA/I
professional:

These programs are incredibly expensive and the labor requirements just don't stop. Say you want to identify all the different variables that go into a pre-term mother. You'd want to look at what point the woman first got pregnant, what were the pre-delivery symptoms, is this a first baby, what ethnicity is the woman (for example, our black population tends to be hypertensive), did the woman get medical consultation early in her pregnancy, is she English-speaking (does she understand the language that the physician is speaking), is she literate in her own language (you can't give Spanish instructions to a Hispanic woman who doesn't read Spanish). Also the definition of a low-birth baby has to be adjusted. Obviously a low-birth baby of a Tongan mom is going to be something under eight pounds; the low-birth baby of an Asian mom is going to be under four pounds.

Finding that "choices of severity measures are often idiosyncratic, sometimes based on the vendor's marketing approach" (Iezzoni et al. 1996, 1379), one group of researchers set out to evaluate ten "off-the-shelf" severity measures that were representative of approaches used in comparing hospital mortality rates around the country. They asked: Does choice of severity measure affect which hospitals are seen as having lower- or higher-than-expected death rates? It is hardly surprising that the researchers found a very complicated picture, leaving them to conclude that "use of discharge abstract data to judge quality—as in hospital report cards—raises serious concerns."

> Discharge diagnoses include all conditions treated during the hospitalization, even events occurring late in the stay possibly due specifically to substandard care. To draw conclusions about quality based on severity-adjusted outcomes, it is essential to adjust only for preexisting conditions, not those arising after hospitalization. If, for example, cardiac arrest appears on the discharge abstract, it is impossible to determine whether the patient had cardiac arrest late in the stay due to poor monitoring and care. (ibid. 1384)

The researchers go on to say that discharge abstracts are used despite their shortcomings because they are the only data readily available across institutions, and are inexpensive and computer-readable. Moreover, hospitals or groups often purchase a single severity measure, often at considerable expense, and then use it for multiple activities, which makes it impossible to draw comparisons among hospitals.

This is hardly a recent phenomenon. In London in 1864, William Farr of the Registrar General's office released comparisons of death rates across English hospitals. Farr was accused of not only using questionable statistical methods but also failing to account for differences in patient characteristics. "As one critic asserted: 'Any comparison which ignores the difference between the apple-cheeked farm-laborers who see relief at Stoke Pogis (probably for rheumatism and sore legs), and the wizzened [sic], red-herring-like mechanics of Soho or Southward, who come from a London Hospital, is fallacious'" (Iezzoni 1997a, 1600).

Analysts are no more confident today about making meaningful comparisons across institutions, nor does the immediate future look much more promising (ibid. 1606). Which prompts the question, Why risk adjust? Two reasons present themselves: to avoid penalizing providers who treat high-risk patients, and to begin a productive dialogue with physicians and other clinicians about using outcomes information to motivate quality improvement.

The Quandary of Professional Consensus

Clinical epidemiology, developed in the 1970s, raised expectations that there could be a science of quality measurement and improvement. As noted in Chapter Three, pioneers in this discipline discovered the wide variation in the processes and outcomes of care among patients who received routine treatment for the same health care problems in different places and health care settings (Wennberg and Gittelsohn 1973; Vayda 1973; Detsky 1995; Blumenthal 1994). Their work contributed to the establishment of the Agency for Health Care Policy and Research (AHCPR).

The impact of their research, however, has been much greater than the establishment of a government agency. It has had a profound impact on the health care debate. "Politically, it has created the impression that much medical practice lacks scientific foundation, and it has emboldened purchasers and policy makers to challenge physicians' claims that they know authoritatively what constitutes optimal health care" (Blumenthal 1996, 1146–47). Further undermining respect for medical decision making were public reports that a sizable proportion of medical services are marginally beneficial, even unnecessary. When the RAND Corporation's Robert Brook claimed, "our best guess is that one-quarter of the things we do to people— not only surgery but all medical procedures—we could get rid of without having any impact on health," his statement was picked up by the *AARP Bulletin* and widely disseminated (Henig 1992, 2). *Consumer Reports* seconded this assessment, proclaiming that 20 percent of the estimated $650 billion spent on procedures in 1992 was clearly unnecessary ("Wasted health care dollars" 1992).

That may explain the persistent belief that variation can be reduced if expert panels establish practice guidelines. But consensus is often elusive due to network of conditions affecting care—patient biography, provider and setting biography, complex trajectories, rapidly evolving medical research and resultant technology, and specialized clinical expertise—to which another human element must be added: the different perspectives of panel members *and* the professional community. In medicine as elsewhere, there are honest differences of opinion.

A case in point is the experience of an expert panel convened by the National Institutes of Health (NIH) in 1996 to evaluate the value of mammography for breast cancer screening for women in their forties. Although NIH followed the same procedure it had used in more than 100 consensus-development panels, one witness characterized the response to this one as more akin to the Queen's order in *Alice's Adventures in Wonderland*: "Off with her head!" (Fletcher 1997, 1180). After two days of presentations, the conference panel presented its draft report, listened to comments from the audience, met in executive session, and then held a news conference to announce its conclusions: "The data currently available do not warrant a universal recommendation for mammography for all women in their forties." Lacking consensus, panelists recommended that women weigh the risks and benefits and decide for themselves. Lost in the fervor that followed was an additional recommendation: "Given both the importance and complexity of the issues involved in assessing the evidence, a woman should have access to the best possible relevant information regarding both benefits and risks, presented in an understandable and usable form" (National Institutes of Health 1997).

Given the long and heated debate that has dogged this subject, it is not surprising that the panel's announcement was controversial (even the head of the National Cancer Institute (NCI) said he disagreed with the conclusion) and met with outrage in the press. One journalist described the report as "fraudulent" (Kolata 1997, C1), while another coined the phrase "expert deflation." She compared it to the inconclusive report of the experts gathered to investigate Gulf War Syndrome and to the panel convened to study Social Security who told the public, "Here are three ideas— you decide." She further likened the panel to a hung jury, quoting ethicist George Annas: "A hung jury is irresponsible. Experts owe us an opinion if they are going to speak to the public. Otherwise what are they good for?" (Goodman 1997, A23)

Sadly, the attacks did not capture the intricacies of obtaining professional consensus. First, there is the test itself. Many tumors too small to be detected by examination can be seen in the visual image of mammography. The area is then tested further, usually with surgical biopsy. Mammography, however, fails to detect some tumors, and radiologists sometimes find normal breast tissue suspicious, requiring an "unnecessary" biopsy (in a climate of cost consciousness). So at issue, and difficult to resolve, was whether mammography is effective enough to justify the expense and medical risk of both the test itself and the procedures that women with abnormal findings may undergo. Three months later, faced with political pressure from Congress, the press, and the public, NCI reversed the recommendations of the panel, recommending that women in their forties undergo routine mammography screening. (In the same week, the American Cancer

Society reversed its position that women in their forties have the procedure every two years, recommending they have the procedure annually.)

The NCI's track record on the subject had already undermined its recommendations. In the mid-1980s, the NCI touted mammography as the only effective weapon against breast cancer. Then, in December 1993, it recommended that only women aged 50 and over should have the procedure. Questions arose, especially since the Clinton administration quickly endorsed the NCI announcement, and it was "hailed by health economists as an example of how medicine can learn to hold the line against unnecessary health care" (Gladwell 1994, 24). The implication that the guidelines were evidence of the new age of cost-conscious medicine—"when medical advances are celebrated as much for saving money as for saving lives" (ibid.)—were hard to ignore. Now the 1997 consensus-development conference, "held to update the scientific information, with the hope that it would get the NCI off the political hot seat it had occupied ever since it changed its recommendation" (Fletcher 1997, 1181) had spiked the temperature even more.

Early on, some had questioned how a consensus could be developed (even with some preliminary reading) in areas where there are so many disparate opinions, given the brief time allowed for presentation of evidence. Oliver (1985), for instance, discussing two meetings—one on the need for increasing coronary artery bypass surgery in Britain and the other on the practicability and value of lowering blood cholesterol in the general population in the United States—expressed concern about the time constraints: "The construction of a consensus statement by a panel working for 12–14 hours into the early hours of the morning (4 am in the case of the UK meeting) for presentation that day is bound to lead to hurried conclusions" (ibid. 1088). Political pressure is another impediment to consensus. Following the 1997 mammography panel's news conference, its chairman, Dr. Leon Gordis, was called before the Senate Subcommittee on Labor, Health and Human Services, and Education Appropriations, where Senator Kay Bailey Hutchison charged that the panel's statement contained factual errors. Presumably agreeing with Senator Hutchinson's opinion that women in their forties should have mammographic screening, the Senate voted 98 to 0 in favor of a nonbinding resolution supporting this position, leading Fletcher to ask,

> Should scientific controversies be approached by examining facts deliberately and carefully with the aid of unbiased, independent scientific experts representing multiple disciplines? Or should these controversies be settled in the halls of Congress and on the front page of *The New York Times* or as the lead story on *ABC World News Tonight*? If NIH directors disagree with the conclusions reached by scientific groups they have convened, how should

they handle such a situation? How should congressional committees and other legitimately interested parties deal with scientific reports that are not politically popular? Indeed, how should scientific colleagues deal with disagreements among themselves? (Fletcher 1997, 1181)

In many cases, moreover, there are powerful financial interests involved—in the case of mammographic screening, billions of dollars in equipment and professional incomes. Early in the 1990s, a group of researchers published several studies indicating that spinal-fusion surgery has few scientifically validated indications and is associated with higher costs and more complications than other back operations (Deyo et al. 1992, 1993; Turner et al. 1992). According to their own report, two members of the research team participated in a multidisciplinary panel, sponsored by the Agency for Health Care Planning and Research (AHCPR) that conducted an exhaustive literature search, identified the highest-quality studies, and developed guidelines for managing acute back problems. Nonsurgical approaches were recommended in most circumstances. What followed was stunning:

> The research and guidelines inspired a letter-writing campaign to members of Congress by the North American Spine Society (NASS), which protested the research team's alleged bias and ineptitude and criticized guidelines it regarded as biased against its preferred form of therapy. This campaign culminated in the founding of a lobbying organization called the Center for Patient Advocacy by an orthopedic surgeon on the NASS board.

The Center for Patient Advocacy called for the AHCPR's elimination and the House of Representatives passed a 1996 budget with zero funding for the agency. "Only after great efforts in the Senate to expose the reasons for the attacks was it possible to preserve the AHCPR, though with substantial cuts to its budget" (Deyo et al. 1997, 1176). As discussed in Chapter Three, this episode was the nail in the coffin for AHCPR's guideline-development work.

A similar controversy erupted over the safety of silicone-gel-filled breast implants, a quarrel that has raged in the United States for nearly a decade. It illustrates, said a commentator, "better than almost any other event in recent times how litigation, fear, bias, and greed can interfere with scientific efforts to answer an important public health question" (Angell 1996, 1513). The researchers on guidelines to manage severe back pain encountered similar reactions to studies on chemical sensitivity syndrome and on the association between myocardial infarction and anti-hypertensive drugs. In each case, an attack was marshaled—through marketing, professional, media, legal, administrative, or political channels—on scientific results that ran counter to financial interests and strong beliefs.

The interested parties had financial stakes in maintaining their market share or the legitimacy of a model of illness or a particular treatment. Their responses, which by-passed peer-reviewed scientific debate and further research, were nonscientific and aimed at discrediting the findings, investigators, or funding agencies. In each case, the attacks intimidated investigators, discouraged others from taking up the same lines of investigation, and took up the time of investigators and staff with legal, professional, and media responses. (Deyo et al. 1997, 1178)

Rounding out the political picture, all too many investigators have a vested interest in the results of their research: "Their careers may depend on the results, their funding may come from those who benefit from the results, or they may supplement their incomes by serving as consultants and expert advocates" (ibid. 1179). Professional groups that represent a single medical discipline often blur the lines between research and self-interest: "No one should be surprised, for example, that the American College of Radiology supports breast-cancer screening for women in their forties" (Fletcher 1997, 1182).

All these ramifications affect the credibility and utility of practice guidelines. Physicians in clinical practice are dealing with the uncertainties inherent in an incremental, evolving science—leading to conflicting reports on the benefits of angioplasty over so-called clot-busting drugs, total versus type-of-fat intake, acupuncture as an effective therapy, and so on. Most physicians are aware of the political components inherent in "consensus." In addition, a number of federal agencies sponsor expert advisory groups that issue clinical practice guidelines. "These guidelines activities are uncoordinated, however, and different agencies sometimes issue different guidelines on the same topic. Occasionally, their recommendations conflict" (Power 1995, 205). Since physicians have been schooled in scientific thinking, "including an understanding of the nature of evidence, the concepts of chance and error, and the value of skepticism" (Angell 1996, 1517), they are not surprised that so many research and consensus panel reports end along the lines of: "More research is needed to determine . . . " That some physicians question the validity of practice guidelines should not be surprising.

A Climate of Distrust and Demoralization

If indeed hospital culture has changed, it is not to one of grand cooperation and harmony, bringing together as equals all levels of hospital personnel. Rather, the massive changes brought about by cost-containment measures (especially the downsizing of staff) have undercut organizational loyalty and created a climate of distrust and demoralization. Once re-engineering of hospitals came into full swing, comments from my respondents were markedly critical. One said, "they've taken the title away from my office; my co-worker refuses to answer the phone, saying she doesn't know what to answer with." Another remembered, "I grew with this organization and good performance was rewarded—loyalty carried you through. The present situation is undermining that." And yet another, "It's hard to get people excited about projects. You hear Deloite & Touche are coming in for consultation and you say, 'uh, oh.'" Urged by the speaker at a professional meeting to look to the organization's human resources people for support, a QA/I director said, "the human resources people are going through the same thing."

> The problem is larger than us. I feel cosmically depressed. There are too many people and not enough jobs. I like technology but every time I use the ATM I think of the jobs it's displaced. For the first time in my life, I've advised young women not to go to nursing school. All America is interested in is business.

Another told of a dream she had:

> There's a fire and I go to rescue a patient, who clings to me and whom I try to comfort as I carry her out. But when I escape the fire and put the patient down I discover there's nothing there. That's how I feel about what I'm doing. I keep working, putting out fires and I fear I'm going to find that there's nothing there—no job!

Fearful survivors of two, sometimes three, employee layoffs are not eager to participate in a critical pathway task force that they suspect will make further reductions in patients' length of stay—and their own!

Moreover, it is harder for physicians to be QA/I believers when they share this cynicism: "Much of what passes for quality improvement can justifiably be viewed as thinly veiled cost containment or marketing. When hospital teams charged with achieving 'continuous quality improvement' focus on reducing stays and try to engage physicians in such exercises, the physicians may understandably feel that quality of care is made to play second fiddle to the imperative to reduce expenditures" (Chassin 1996, 1060). As critical pathways have become more obviously a means to reduce length of stay, hospital personnel who thought the goal of this tool was to improve patient care justifiably ask who is benefitting, the patient or the HMO shareholders? A nurse-respondent, disheartened at seeing elderly patients discharged from the hospital to cope at home with tubes, dressings, all manner of equipment, and "how-to" instructions, derided her hospital's marketing newsletter for calling reduced length of stay the "successful recovery of patients in the comfort of their own home."

Resistance to Behavior Change

Serious examination of quality improvement reinforces the observation that it is "a painstaking and time-consuming business that depends for its success at least as much on our ability to modify the behavior of patients, purchasers, and providers of care as it does on the collection of good data about performance" (Blumenthal and Epstein 1996, 1330). Behavior modification is the stumbling block. For example, in a hospital where hip-replacement was chosen as the first critical pathway (because such cases were expected to be the most manageable and predictable), the strength of the path relied on presurgery classes. The classes were well-prepared and hospital personnel praised them as a means to shorten length of stay and ease home care. A chance remark by the manager of the physical therapy department, however, revealed an unexpected problem: "Only 39 percent of the patients are coming to the class. Their hip hurts, they don't want to go out."

Providers are just as stubborn about modifying their behavior.

We had a patient who was colonized with Vancomycin resistant enterococcus (VRE)—a fulminating gut bacteria that basically is incurable. There is no antibiotic that will kill it. It's treated with Vancomycin but it's also caused by Vancomycin. It's got this unusual capacity to change its DNA. It will respond to the drug and then build up its own resistance to the drug. So once you've used Vancomycin frequently it will increase your likelihood of acquiring the enterococcus. We had the director of microbiology at ____ University give a medical education session and she said the cardiac surgeons there no longer use the drug. Well, doctors love it because it kills everything in its path, and it's cheap as hell. It's been the drug of choice for the past 15 years. Doesn't have a lot of side effects so everybody used it. The hospital epidemiologist went to the cardiac surgeons and said, "We want you to stop using Vancomycin on the pre-op cardiac patients," and they said, "No, we really don't want to do that. We'll limit its use to one dose." They just don't want anybody calling anybody on their practice. They say, "What's worse? What's the likelihood of my patient getting VRE as compared to getting a sternal wound infection and having to stay in the hospital for six weeks?" So we had to accept that—and then today at the meeting we learned that the pain treatment people are using it with the implantable devices, again because it's cheap. So there we are again. The university epidemiologist will go talk to them.

Of course, by no means all physician resistance to practice changes stems from sheer obstinacy. Even when physicians can agree on a particular practice guideline, other obstacles may block implementation. For example, a team of researchers who introduced a guideline in Kaiser Permanente Northwest Division for the management of low back pain subsequently discovered that neither the guideline alone, nor the guideline plus feedback of imaging test ordering, had any impact on the total number of tests or the variation from physician to physician in test usage. Most of the difference arose from such nonclinical factors as patient age and work status, time constraints, and access problems. "Especially relevant, however, were tensions and conflicts the physicians faced as they attempted to meet conflicting role obligations" (Shye et al. 1998, 83). Physicians often felt obliged to satisfy patients' demands for tests, even when they recognized them as medically inappropriate. "They explained this in the context of their need to foster and continually reinforce their patients' trust and confidence in them. They regarded this trust and confidence as essential to their ability to enlist the patient's adherence to their recommendations and advice, not merely in a current episode of low back pain but in their ongoing relationship with the patient" (ibid. 86, 87). Significantly, these physicians recognized that the pressure they felt was directly related to the public suspicion that HMOs are increasingly skimping on their care.

> What is also new is that there is so much concern among the general public about the incentive structure of managed care that even physicians who have practiced for a long time in managed care organizations and have hitherto enjoyed a trusting and trusted relationship with their patients find those relationships strained. . . . Most physicians practicing today were not trained to have conversations with patients about why they are not writing a prescription or ordering a test. Some, probably many, physicians simply find it easier to order a test or treatment than to have a "difficult" discussion with the patient. . . . What the paper by Shye et al. should bring into our minds is how little we know about the factors that lead to this individual variation and what we can do to manage those factors. (Schoenbaum 1998, 81–82)

Given the sheer number of these factors and the dilemma over how to manage them, it is instructive to find a managed care company—in this case the nation's largest, United HealthCare Corporation—facing the flip side of the coin, undertreatment. United was reported to have used its vast computerized medical-billing and pharmacy records to evaluate "only 1,600 cardiologists and internists in four states, Colorado, North Carolina, Ohio and Texas—just a fraction of the 200,000 doctors in its nationwide network" (Burton 1998, A1). The survey found a failure to prescribe widely recommended drugs such as beta blockers for heart-attack survivors, ACE inhibitors for chronic heart-failure patients, and glucose-monitoring tests for diabetics. Despite the managed-care industry's reputation for withholding care, the newspaper reported that United plans to continue and expand this research to change adherence to recommended norms—not, it must be noted, out of pure altruism. "I can buy a lot of beta block-

ers by avoiding the cost of treating a second heart attack," Dr. Lee Newcomer, United's medical director, was quoted as saying (ibid.)—a more
constructive cost-conscious assessment than has been evident in the past.

WORKING WITHIN THE LIMITATIONS

The erroneous assumptions and organizational obstacles described above
are the conditions under which hospital quality measures are being introduced, implemented, and managed. If QA/I professionals and hospital
staff are going to bring about change, these conditions will have to be faced
and overcome. To make matters worse, the assumptions and obstacles are
sometimes interrelated. In certain instances, for example, the reluctance to
disclose data is related to lack of confidence in their reliability. Knowing
that the statistics do not reflect reality—that hospital care is more complex
than what is represented in mortality figures—does not create a zeal to report them!

As to quality improvement techniques, the paramount point is that they
do not descend on the hospital like a DNA imprint. Rather, they arrive to
be worked out amid all the conditions already described, there to be negotiated.

Often committees collect too much information. Then, as they sift
through it, debates ensue over what is important, what is reliable, what is
the cost/benefit ratio, what is the risk/benefit equation, etc. It is hardly
surprising that QA/I personnel find their jobs stressful, often frustrating.
Although well-meaning and conscientious, they grapple with external
standards that lack uniformity and are constantly changing, physician
skepticism and resistance, and the gnawing sense that to hospital administration QA/I is a euphemism for cost-cutting. As described in Chapter
Three, implementing each quality-improvement technique entails lengthy
meetings, where roles and responsibilities are negotiated, egos must be
massaged, and staff members convinced and sometimes brought along re-
luctantly. As the theories are tested in the hospital setting, more adjustment
is required to mold these strategies to the practical needs of each hospital.
There is, of course, a learning curve for some participants in the process—
one QA/I analyst said she estimated that changing physicians' attitudes
can take two to three years.

Throughout, actors (internal and external to the hospital) are shaping
the action, the direction of which remains emergent, contingent, and uncertain. In the end, hospital personnel involved with QA/I have to tease
out the benefits of the tools available to them and negotiate within the obstacles they confront—finding that they are dealing with a mixed array of
options that are effective under some conditions but not under others.

Nevertheless, monitoring can serve a useful purpose. One analyst said, "When we're monitoring caesarian sections they go down and when we stop they go up again." Another, mindful of the weaknesses of report cards, found an advantage: "They turned up the heat in Medical Records on improving coding and documentation." Similarly, although it is important not to exaggerate the link, consumer reports have been found to influence provider behavior in unpredictable ways. For example, although the purpose of a consumer report in Missouri was to help consumers make informed health-care choices, one year after its release, increased services were being offered in 50 percent of the hospitals rated in the report.

Despite the vast differences this chapter addresses, production processes in hospitals do bear some similarities to those in other industries. Hospital personnel and machines are organized around tasks, controlled by protocols and policies that lay out how situations are to be handled. Indeed, much of the exchange among QA/I professionals on the online network consists of sharing information on how best to phrase these protocols and policies. But it must also be remembered that protocols in hospitals are often idiosyncratic to a particular unit and based on the experience of the head of the unit. Also, especially in this era of reduced resources where part-time nurses and aides float from hospital to hospital and from unit to unit, knowledge of policies and protocols remains problematic.

That said, production processes in hospitals *can* be identified. Patients are admitted, fed, cleaned, toileted, moved for a variety of procedures (e.g., X-rays, echocardiography, surgery), connected to and disconnected from machines, medicated, monitored, and discharged. Machines are purchased, calibrated and maintained; records are created, filed, and retrieved; drug orders are received, filled and delivered; tests are ordered, analyzed, and their results transmitted (Strauss et al. 1997). Identifying defects in these production processes and designing strategies for curing those defects is a laudable goal that is "generally an easier task for management than is the task of rationalizing professional judgment" (Jost 1995, 848). There is no question that an emphasis on locating systems problems as opposed to singling out individual culprits is a tremendous advance. For example, a study of errors in drug dosages confirmed that, not surprisingly in a setting with a multitude of actors, errors were not attributable to a single physician or pharmacist but were distributed among many physicians, order transcribers, pharmacists, and nurses (Leape et al. 1995; Bates et al. 1995).

With great tenacity, some projects effectively break through the obstacles. One such concerns a project that began in a climate of outright hostility among team members. The problem addressed by a CQI team was the dramatic growth in demand for patient-specific blood products. Prior to the AIDS crisis, volunteer blood could be given to any suitable patient sub-

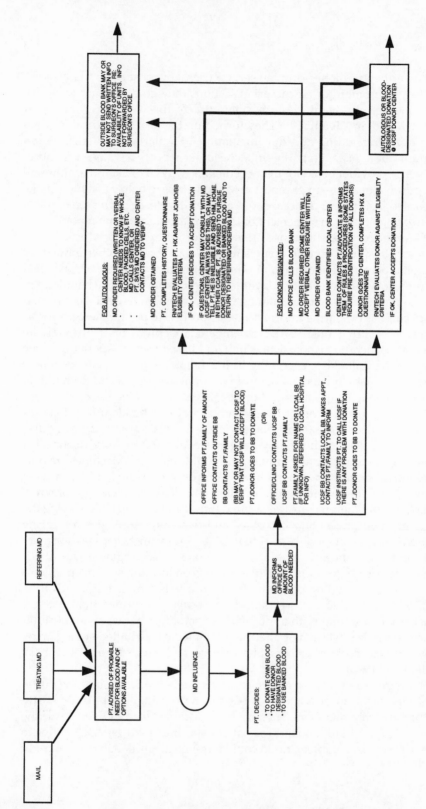

Figure 2. Allison, M. and Toy, P. (1996). Quality improvement team on autologous and directed-donor blood availability. *Joint Commission Journal on Quality Improvement, 22, 801–810.* Reprinted with permission.

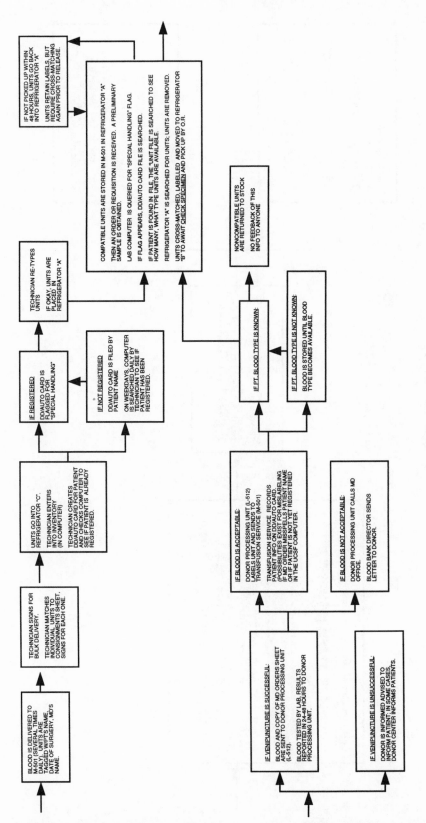

Figure 2. (*Continued*)

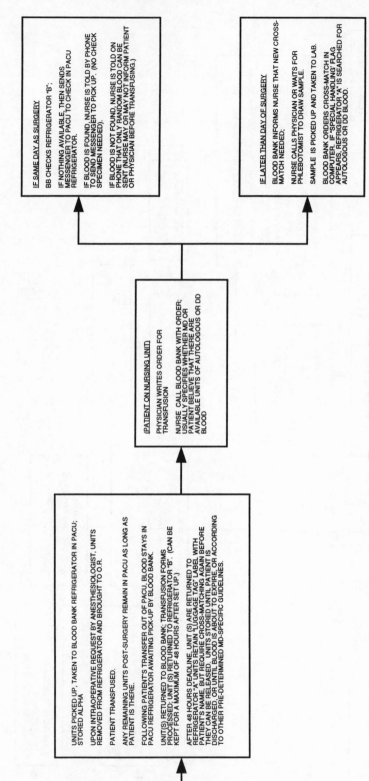

IF SAME DAY AS SURGERY

BB CHECKS REFRIGERATOR "B";

IF NOTHING AVAILABLE, THEN SENDS MESSENGER TO PACU TO CHECK IN PACU REFRIGERATOR.

IF BLOOD IS FOUND, NURSE IS TOLD BY PHONE TO SEND MESSENGER TO PICK UP. (NO CHECK SPECIMEN NEEDED).

IF BLOOD IS NOT FOUND, NURSE IS TOLD ON PHONE THAT ONLY RANDOM BLOOD CAN BE SENT. (NURSE MAY OR MAY NOT INFORM PATIENT OR PHYSICIAN BEFORE TRANSFUSING.)

IF LATER THAN DAY OF SURGERY

BLOOD BANK INFORMS NURSE THAT NEW CROSS-MATCH NEEDED;

NURSE CALLS PHYSICIAN OR WAITS FOR PHLEBOTOMIST TO DRAW SAMPLE.

SAMPLE IS PICKED UP AND TAKEN TO LAB.

BLOOD BANK ORDERS CROSS-MATCH IN COMPUTER. IF "SPECIAL HANDLING" FLAG APPEARS, REFRIGERATOR "A" IS SEARCHED FOR AUTOLOGOUS OR DD BLOOD.

(PATIENT ON NURSING UNIT)

PHYSICIAN WRITES ORDER FOR TRANSFUSION

NURSE CALL BLOOD BANK WITH ORDER; USUALLY SPECIFIES WHETHER MD OR PATIENT BELIEVE THAT THERE ARE AVAILABLE UNITS OF AUTOLOGOUS OR DD BLOOD

UNITS PICKED UP, TAKEN TO BLOOD BANK REFRIGERATOR IN PACU; STORED ALPHA

UPON INTRAOPERATIVE REQUEST BY ANESTHESIOLOGIST, UNITS REMOVED FROM REFRIGERATOR AND BROUGHT TO O.R.

PATIENT TRANSFUSED.

ANY REMAINING UNITS POST-SURGERY REMAIN IN PACU AS LONG AS PATIENT IS THERE.

FOLLOWING PATIENTS TRANSFER OUT OF PACU, BLOOD STAYS IN PACU REFRIGERATOR AWAITING PICK-UP BY BLOOD BANK.

UNIT(S) RETURNED TO BLOOD BANK; TRANSFUSION FORMS PROCESSED; UNIT (S) RETURNED TO REFRIGERATOR "B". (CAN BE KEPT FOR A MAXIMUM OF 48 HOURS AFTER SET UP.)

AFTER 48 HOURS DEADLINE, UNIT (S) ARE RETURNED TO REFRIGERATOR "A"; UNITS RETAIN "LUGGAGE TAG" LABEL WITH PATIENT'S NAME, BUT REQUIRE CROSS-MATCHING AGAIN BEFORE THEY CAN BE RELEASED. UNITS STORED UNTIL PATIENT IS DISCHARGED, OR UNTIL BLOOD IS ABOUT TO EXPIRE, OR ACCORDING TO OTHER PRE-DETERMINED MD-SPECIFIC GUIDELINES.

Figure 2. (Continued)

sequent to required compatibility testing. In the late 1980s, autologous blood (the patient's own blood) and designated-donor blood (blood donated by a specific patient's family or friends) became the options of choice. By 1991, the surge in demand for these options had surpassed the capacity of existing systems to respond effectively. Although incalculably resource- and time-intensive, a CQI tool called "process flow analysis" (*see* Figure 2) was used to convince non-blood bank team members of the complexity of the processes involved and the need for information, supports, and monitoring systems that would ensure reliability (Allison and Toy 1996). Seven years after the CQI team's launch, a follow-up call to one of the leaders affirmed that the revised system was still in place, although it required constant vigilance.

> We meet twice a year to make sure we are maintaining the gain. It's like being married—you have to constantly work on it. Things are forgotten, new people come in and there have to be reminders.

Another project started with a committee convened to write a critical pathway for treatment of congestive heart failure (CHF). Their work took on added momentum when a nurse-educator and her nursing colleagues became aware of the deficiencies in the pathway and took on leadership roles in converting it to a CQI project. Since this was done in a research hospital, team members had the advantage of financial support, clinical expertise, a cooperative house staff, and student research assistants. The project remained multidisciplinary, including dieticians, physical therapists, and social workers as well as medical and nursing representatives.

Such a broad approach brought about improved documentation of severity of condition, enhanced patient education, reduced length of stay, and increased and timely referral for ancillary services such as physical therapy and nutrition counseling. Perhaps even more important, investigating the poor response to a patient satisfaction survey, team members discovered that a large percentage of patients were cognitively impaired— a condition previously masked by intact social behaviors that became evident only during complex conversation.

The project then led to a significant question: "Many of these patients live alone so how are they supposed to be able to manage these complex pharmacologic protocols?" Also discovered was that a large percentage of the CHF patients spoke Russian only, leading to another endeavor: translating patient education materials. The project also unearthed a major coding problem, national in scope, in medical records tied to the inadequacy physician documentation—which has serious implications for reimsement and is still unresolved. More important from the standpoint of patient care, the project led to further research on the inadequacies of home care for CHF patients under the restrictions of managed care.

Another project, on creating a critical pathway for ventilator-dependent patients, also suffered through a lengthy evolution but its effect has been sustained and its procedures copied by nearby hospitals. Under the old procedures,

> We lost millions of dollars prior to recognizing our ventilator-dependent patient population as a problem. And families weren't satisfied. Patients weren't satisfied. You know, they would stay in the ICU for weeks to months and, you know, after several weeks we would think, "oh, okay it's time to trach them (perform a tracheotomy)" because they can't be intubated for that long. Communication was fragmented with the families. When patients were in the ICU for that long, normally you have a group of consulting physicians. Their dynamics are extremely dysfunctional. They don't talk to one another. It's hard to know who's the chief. I mean, it's just incredible.

Based on the findings of a ventilator-dependent task force, the procedure was changed. When a patient's dependence on the ventilator exceeds four days, the family is approached by a case manager to discuss alternative options such as transfer to long-term board-and-care facilities or to a nursing home, or to cessation of life-sustaining equipment. Thereafter, for as long as the patient remains on the ventilator, multidisciplinary conferences are held with the family to review prognosis and treatment options.

Success of such projects depends on a number of factors, primarily strong leadership and a physician champion. Also necessary are a common-sense understanding of negotiating skills and an inherent diplomacy on the part of leaders—plus a creative approach that enables one to seize the moment when the door opens to another serendipitous opportunity. Although some teams find that religiously following a CQI procedure such as process-flow analysis is essential in bringing a team together, many have had greater success when they use a pragmatic approach, flexibly adapting what they have learned from the CQI philosophy.

One of the most disheartening aspects of the current state of affairs is the growing mountain of unexamined data that never gets turned into information.

> It's a real deficit. We do not use our data to make change. What we do is we collect data and don't cull it. We haven't said, "Here's the data, what are we going to do with it, let's do it and then let's go back and look at it again."

The California Association for Healthcare Quality called its 1997 spring conference "The Ruby Slippers Syndrome: You've Had the Power All

Along—Transforming Data Into Useful Information." The association's advertising brochure proclaimed, "How do we make sense out of highly aggregated data like unplanned re-admissions, customer satisfaction rates, or HMO panel usage of emergency services? How do we figure out how to make anything better from this data?" Meanwhile, the field of medical informatics balloons and analytic models for identifying performance indicators grow more intricate (Normand et al. 1998).

Meanwhile as well, journalistic excess fans the flames of misunderstanding regarding the public disclosure of aggregate data, especially mortality statistics. In an otherwise responsible article in the *Wall Street Journal*, the reporter concluded that as a result of the federal government's decision to stop publishing a list of death rates at U.S. hospitals, "patients often know less about the hospitals and doctors to whom they entrust their lives than about the cars and toasters they buy" (Burton 1998, A8). A comment made by a financial advisor about hedge funds offers a useful insight into QA/I. After analyzing the number crunching of financial experts and the subsequent crumbling fortunes of two leading hedge funds, he concluded, "Once more, the lesson is that the brilliant manipulation of numbers can be wonderfully helpful, but only if accompanied by an evaluation of their honesty, relevance and underlying assumptions" (Peterson 1998, A23).

There is unquestionably a symbiotic relationship among those who are involved in the accountability enterprise—regulators, the QA/I industry of publications and software, consultants, producers of management information systems, and hospital QA/I personnel alike. Whether the arena continues to grow depends on their interests and needs, which show no sign of abating. Accordingly, one more factor—lucrative to some but costly to health care sector—has been added to the medical-industrial complex of pharmaceutical corporations, diagnostic equipment and medical supply companies, managed care and other insurance corporations, and hospital chains. When an arena is in its growth period, new careers are being forged. As it takes on added momentum and more people have stakes in its survival, fewer questions are asked about the paths taken. But the problematic issues do not go away. The ultimate question is, How close is the accountability enterprise to being a reliable yardstick of quality of hospital care and, more to the point, is "close" good enough or merely deceiving?

NOTES

1. Aspen Publishers, Inc.
2. AIC Conferences, Innovative Strategies for Linking Physician Performance and Compensation, Philadelphia, Pennsylvania, April 1–2, 1998.

5

Demonstrating the Accountability Endeavor
The Art of Show and Tell

The sublime and the ridiculous are often so nearly related that it is difficult to class them separately. One step above the sublime makes the ridiculous, and one step above the ridiculous makes the sublime again.

—Thomas Paine

How critical is JCAHO accreditation to a hospital?

There's so much effort that we make at hospitals because we want to improve performance. And always with performance improvement there is one eye to the Joint Commission standards. I mean you're always eyeballing it as you do it, and thinking, "How am I going to make this *fit* into the Joint Commission and have time for the Joint Commission survey?" Sometimes you just kind of go off and improve something because financially (or whatever) you have to do it. But when the Joint Commission rolls around every three years, you take your piece of art work, no matter how it's shaped, and you beat it into shape. You say, "Well, I don't think this is going to quite fit through the Joint Commission keyhole, but if I just beat on it a little bit I can *make* it fit." That's where . . . when I look back over the time I've put in on the Joint Commission survey those last few weeks—the eighty-hour weeks— you're taking all your stuff and you say, "Here I have sort of the art work. I have the clay here. Our institution molded it to do a certain thing and now what I'm going to spend my last four weeks here doing is, *on paper* (emphasis added). I'm beating it into a shape that I can put into a Joint Commission binder and say, 'See how we're doing everything you want us to do?'" But it would have to word it *their* way and include their verbiage and take all the little idiosyncrasies that they're looking for and kind of pull your piece of art work apart and say, "Yeah, I've got this ingredient; I've got this ingredient;

161

I can pull this out and shape it a little differently and so that I can make the Joint Commission buy it."

While much of QA/I work (for example, establishing critical paths, refining outcome measures, feeding data into report cards, etc.) is geared toward show-and-tell to satisfy oversight agencies and to compete in the market place, Joint Commission surveys take the presentation to the point of dramaturgy, with back stage backstage preparation, rehearsals, script rewriting—all in the name of demonstrating accountability.

The Joint Commission's website defines accreditation as "the determination that an eligible organization meets applicable Joint Commission standards in all performance areas." Accreditation is voluntarily sought and achieved through on-site surveys. There are seven possible results. Accredited with commendation is the highest level, followed by accredited without recommendations for improvement, accredited with recommendations for improvement, conditional accreditation, provisional accreditation, preliminary nonaccreditation, and adverse decision, in appeal. Based on a scale of 1 to 100, an overall evaluation score and an evaluation score for each performance area reviewed during the survey are determined.

According to the commission, most hospitals—approximately 80 percent—fall into the category of "accreditation with recommendations for improvement," which means they must rectify specific problems within a specified time. If the verdict is "conditional accreditation," not only must a hospital correct the problem areas within a time limit, they must undergo another on-site survey.

"Provisional accreditation" denotes an early partial survey used for hospitals seeking accreditation for the first time. It reflects general compliance with selected standards. Once the hospital has implemented its new systems, policies, and procedures, a full accreditation survey is conducted, approximately six months after the first. Surveys are conducted every three years by teams that usually include a physician, a nurse, a hospital administrator, and, sometimes, an additional specialist. They spend several days at the hospital reviewing documents, observing activities, interviewing staff, and interviewing patients.

In California's accreditation and licensure surveys (CALS), nursing and technical surveyors from the California Department of Health Services (DHS) and physician surveyors from the California Medical Association (CMA) accompany the commission surveyors. The CMA physicians spend only one day surveying not only for compliance with Joint Commission standards and state licensing regulations but they also use CALS Criteria, a set of their own standards. Not only does this expand the scope of the scrutiny but QA/I professionals interviewed in this study agreed that the CMA surveyors were even harder to please than those from the Joint Commission.

To understand the molding, beating, and shaping described by the co-ordinator quoted above, one has to go back a bit. As mentioned in Chapter Two, the American College of Surgeons' original one-page set of five standards has grown to 564 Joint Commission standards for the year 2000. A nurse who became a hospital QA/I coordinator in the mid-1980s looked back:

> My first real awareness of the QA section of the Joint Commission manual was that it was relatively small. You needed to have a program; you needed to have peer review and to tie it into credentialing. . . . The first year I was really aware of it was, you could sit there with the Joint Commission manual on your left and a piece of paper on the right. And you could write a plan that would follow all of the various requirements. And you wrote the plan and then you could pass Joint Commission because you had a plan that addressed this, and they were less interested in how you'd actually process that plan. And then we had a survey that first year and that was the first time that it became extremely obvious to me how driven we were by regulations. . . . That was really the first time I truly understood how we had to have all our paperwork—minutes and followthrough and CRAE (Conclusions, Recommendations, Actions and Evaluations). All that had to be put together so that when the surveyors came in you shoved all this paper work in front of them . . . and that's what it was, it was a paperwork trail. We spent that whole eight months making sure we had the appropriate paper work.

When I first began this study, QA/I professionals were complaining that the Joint Commission "keeps changing its 'little' book and making us jump to adapt." As one observed, "There's a lot of sledge-hammering effect. Kill it because it's all bad, and then we realize that some of it's good." As has been said about accountability in the education arena, "For every rule there is a reason. Somebody thought it would be good, so we pile one rule on another" (Schorr 1997). When the commission's Agenda for Change started to filter down to the hospital level, QA/I professionals were heartened because, as one put it, "the 'gotcha' philosophy has been replaced by coming in as educators."

In 1994 the Joint Commission implemented a new survey process, moving from evaluation of specific departments and services to "assessing, across an organization, performance of important patient-focused and organizational functions that support quality of patient care, *rather than evaluating activities that may have been conducted primarily to pass the survey*" (Joint Commission 1995, emphasis added). The former strategy of handing each department director a manual chapter and expecting him or her to implement the standards would work no longer.

These "functions," the new designation, are very broad. Patient care, for example, includes "assessment of patients": whether physicians and nurses take an appropriate medical history, perform an appropriate physical exam, and assess how well the patient is functioning; whether the hospital has a system in place to evaluate if patients receive the appropriate diagnostic tests, and whether those tests are carried out by trained and qualified staff. Other patient-care functions are medication use, operative procedures, patient/family education, and patient rights, all broken down into specific components. To detail each function would require almost as many pages as the accreditation manual itself. In abbreviated form, suffice it to say that the other functions pertain to such matters as medical staff (competence, rules and regulations or bylaws, etc.); nursing (qualifications and competence); staff training (orientation for new employees, continuing education requirements); and physical environment (infection control, safety)—this is but a partial list of components.

Additional functions pertain to leadership and management. They cover such items as having a hospital mission and vision and a strategic plan for carrying them out, whether there is a functioning governing body and records of its proceedings, and whether the hospital prohibits discrimination and establishes a process for receiving and responding to complaints. Yet more standards pertain to whether the hospital ensures the accuracy of its information and whether the access provided to information is balanced with appropriate security and confidentiality safeguards, and the degree to which ongoing processes are in place to improve patient care. Regarding the latter category, known in the arena as "performance improvement," surveyors are expected to assess how effectively the hospital measures performance in relation to patient-care outcomes; whether the collected data and information are used to identify opportunities for improvement; whether the hospital takes action to implement improvements and then determines the effectiveness of these improvements. In addition, there are standards to ensure that each department provides services that are appropriate to the hospital's population, and that they are delivered in a timely, proper, safe, and effective manner. As part of the big change in 1994, the commission committed itself to surveys that are more individualized, consistent, and helpful in improving performance. It also promised to tailor the survey process to a specific organization's characteristics and to use a more "interactive" approach.

SETTING THE SCENE

A Joint Commission administrator told me that hospitals do not have to scramble to prepare for a survey if they are doing the right thing. She then gave me a commission publication entitled *Doing the Right Things Right: Case Studies on Strategies for Maintaining Survey Readiness.* Nevertheless,

QA/I professionals know that survey preparation is like painting one's house. Every corner is cleaned in anticipation of the painters but then there is a gradual accumulation of life's artifacts and dust returns to the hard-to-reach places. QA/I coordinators can have spent the three-year interim putting systems in place but much backstage preparation is still necessary and must be orchestrated well in advance. The big change in 1994 and 1995 required a new orientation:

> The old standards, where everything was departmentalized, as bad a system as that was, it was something that people could hang on to. All you had to do was take the chapter with the department name on it, take it back to your department and say, "If I worry about these ten pages here, I'm home free." But the new system is really more of a team approach. It forced hospital departments to talk to each other, to share with each other, to say, "Do you have this?" We had to use nurses, and pharmacists, and respiration therapists, because the standards were so global that the chief pharmacist realized, "Hey! I can't fix this by myself. To make this work I've got to get a team of people together who will go back to their unit and help me to pull information and straighten it out."

Thus the Joint Commission has accomplished one of its purposes—to promote greater collaboration within a previously compartmentalized environment. That apart, the intricate detail of the standards and guidelines for the survey means that a frenzy that precedes the arrival of the surveyors. Take, for instance, the requirements for performance improvement projects (shown in Figure 3), or the fourteen pages in the guidelines for organization of documents. These require clearly marked three-ring binders—often as many as five—including an index of standards issues, tabs to identify the material in the referenced document, and, if thoroughly done, the number of the standard number addressed. For the Document Review Session, held on the first day of the survey, there should be, *inter alia*, an itemized list in the guidelines covering each function and its components: the policies and procedures, protocols, reports, and, where relevant, minutes of the past 12 months of committees addressing the item. "There are hoops you have to jump through for Joint Commission, such as making sure that your blood review has five certain components and your invasive procedure has five certain components. So we're doing studies and always trying to create extra boxes on the data sheet because Joint Commission says we have to have these." Some hospitals find it necessary to hire extra staff to help arrange and label documents (Higgins et al. 1996).

Hiring extra staff is only part of the cost. The fee hospitals pay for the survey is based on the size of the hospital and the number of surveyors involved, and includes such essential elements as the accreditation manual, scoring guidelines, survey planning package, etc. In addition, many hos-

---

Improving Organizational Performance (PI)

1. Any descriptions of the organization's approach to designing, measuring, assessing, and improving performance (e.g., performance improvement plan, other planning documents, reports of activities that reflect a planned, systematic organization-wide approach) (PI.1)

2. Plans for the design of a new process (e.g., the planning process for the development of a new service) (PI.2)

3. Description(s) of the organization's approach to measurement, to include the following:
   a. what existing processes are measured to assess the stability of its performance
   b. what data relating to priority issues that have been chosen for improvement are being collected (PI.3.3.2)
   c. needs and expectations of patients and others (PI.3.3.1)
   d. staff members' views regarding current performance and opportunities for improvement (PI.3.3.2)
   e. measurement related to the priority monitoring activities, as outlined in the standards, including processes
      i. that affect a large percentage of patients (PI.3.4.1.1)
      ii. that place patients at risk (PI.3.4.1.2)
      iii. that have been or are likely to be problem-prone (PI.3.4.1.3)
      iv. that are related to the use of operative and other invasive procedures (PI.3.4.2.1)

Figure 3. Joint Commission on Accreditation of Healthcare Organizations. 1999. *Hospital Accreditation Services Guidelines for Survey*, Appendix C., pp. 124–125. Chicago, IL. Reprinted with permission.

pitals purchase newsletters specifically geared toward survey preparation. According to a QA/I coordinator:

> Many people order these out of sheer desperation so they can glean where the glaring hole is. For a couple of hundred dollars they now will give you profiles on the surveyors after you know who's been assigned to you. Things like: OK, here's Surveyor A, in the hospitals he has surveyed, 20 percent of these hospitals have had deficiencies in the use of restraints. And then, of course, you don't know . . . you get a profile on A, then on B and C, but what

you don't know is how are A, B, and C going to work together. I'm telling you, we had information overload this time. I had more information in front of me than really I cared to have.

Inside the Joint Commission, a publication that is independent of the commission, has a website and a hotline for ordering surveyor profiles. The online professional network often requests information on specific surveyors: "Has anyone had any experience with Dr. X?" The hospital network itself is a rich source of ad hoc profiles: "Our biomed technician, who serves different hospitals in the area, told us that the lead surveyor, the administrator, was going to be very picky." More and more hospitals are trying to estimate the cost of surveys. One estimate to which I was privy was for a seventy-bed hospital, which was to be assessed in 1998 by four representatives from the Joint Commission, two from the California Department of Health Services, and two from the California Medical Association (CMA):

Joint Commission Survey Fees	$35,243.00
CMA Survey Fees	3,500.00
Survey Preparation Materials (manuals, training tools, storyboards, etc.)	11,940.00
Additional Training and Preparation (seminars, consultants, etc.)	42,700.00
Personnel Costs to Prepare for and Conduct the Survey	87,465.00
Other Costs	14,920.00
Total Estimated Cost of Survey	195,768.00

"Other costs" refers to a miscellany estimated by department directors, such items as dinner for medical staff "prep night," installation of cupboards to meet commission specifications, and contracting for extra typing and cleaning help. "Additional Training and Preparation" includes $20,000 for outside consultants, who conducted a mock survey. Many hospitals hire consultants at a hefty $1,000–1,500 per day plus expenses. Many send their quality professionals to commission seminars. The commission also has a nonprofit subsidiary that hospitals can hire to prepare them for survey and offers a software program called "Score 100" (a mechanism for checking adherence to regulations) at $1,295 for use on a single computer and $2,495.00 for use on multiple computers.

The California Healthcare Association has attempted to pinpoint the actual cost of surveys through questionnaires to hospitals. The 1999 estimates from forty-one hospitals ranged from $20,450 to $768,500, but "this is not clean data since different people interpret the costs differently and include (or do not) many different things in this answer" (personal communication with the author).

Arranging the Scenery

Throughout the country, QA/I coordinators draw on their peer network to learn about any surveys preceding their own. Web sites help quality professionals share policies, procedures, forms, and other documents, as well as appraisal of "hot issues." Coordinators try to anticipate the current emphasis. Even with longstanding issues, there is frequently a new twist. Among the recent hot issues are:

• *Use of Restraints.* Discussion concerns whether protocols can be nurse-generated or require a specific physician order, whether an individual order must be issued every time a patient is restrained, how often patients should be monitored and the observation documented, and the time frame of a "restraint episode."

• *Confidentiality.* Discussion ranges from whether calling out a patient's name in admitting, emergency, or outpatient departments is a breach of confidentiality and should be replaced by a color coding or numbering system to whether patients' charts should be secured in locked cabinets. Even though the commission does not bar sign-in sheets so long as they do not include a reason for the visit or diagnosis, coordinators struggle over such issues as using such a list for parents who are picking up monthly prescriptions for their children's Ritalin, thereby revealing who has Attention Deficit Disorder or Attention Deficit Hyperactive Disorder.

• *Adverse Drug Reactions.* Discussion concerns how to set up a mechanism, such as a reward system, to improve self-reporting on the part of physicians and nurses.

• *Post-operative Notes.* Since a dictated operative report is often delayed by the physician or the transcriber, a 1999 standard states that when a report is not placed in the medical record immediately after surgery, a progress note must be entered immediately. Discussion has centered on the definition of "immediately" and the content of the progress note.

• *Patient Satisfaction Surveys.* Discussion concerns how to obtain scientific results, how to improve response rate, whether phone surveys are more productive than mailed surveys, and how to simplify the form.

• *Physician Involvement.* Discussion concerns frequency of physician departmental meetings, minutes kept, participation in performance improvement programs, and motivating physicians who refuse to participate.

• *Blood Transfusions.* Discussion focuses on informed consent, evidence of explanation to patients of risks, benefits, and (sometimes neglected) alternatives to blood transfusion. Also considered are criteria for administration of blood, systems for tracking blood usage, and plan for monitoring nursing adherence to blood protocols.

• *Competence Assessment.* This refers to documentation of on-going evaluation of personnel based on proficiency in executing specific tasks. Although this has been a requirement for nursing for a while, since 1995 it has been required for other departments (laboratory, x-ray, physical therapy, respiratory care, etc.) Discussion concerns establishing a systematic method for assessing staff education, licensure, and evaluations. Also problematic is specifying qualifications for personnel treating age-specific groups, such as pediatric, adolescent, or geriatric patients.

As quality coordinators contemplate these hot issues, the importance of explicit and practicable policies and procedures (P&P) and by-laws is abundantly clear. Clear statements of staff to patient ratio, size of rooms, number of electrical and oxygen outlets—these are long-standing elements of internal documents, and are legal requirements in any hospital. But the wording of the P&P can be a land mine since a hospital will be held to one of its own making. As a surveyor explained, "If the P&P says, 'Nursing records shall make observations of significant psychological and physical manifestation and relevant nursing interpretation,' you could drive a truck through that. If the nurse says, as I saw yesterday, that the leg is cool and dusky, and does nothing to interpret it and doesn't do anything about it, that immediately gets a deficiency—there was no relevant nursing interpretation." It may indeed represent an absence of interpretation but it may as well be a lack of documentation, and there's the rub. In any accountability consideration, and certainly with accreditation, documentation remains the biggest problem that QA/I professionals must confront.

Tightening the Script

The importance of documentation cannot be overstated:

> Although arduous, a thorough and precise effort in gathering material for the document review is critically important to a successful survey. In all three surveys described in this article, the Joint Commission and Department of Health Services surveyors devoted the entire first morning of the visit to a meticulous examination of those documents and based their explorations for the remainder of the visit on any deficiencies or weaknesses they had identified in the documentation. On their arrival on the last day of the survey, the California Medical Association reviewed those document portions relating to the medical staff.
>
> It is during the document review part of the survey that decisions are made regarding the structure and intensity of review for the remainder of the survey. If necessary documentation is lacking or if existing documentation raises questions, surveyors will pursue those points throughout the rest of the visit. (Higgins et al. 1996, 16)

In addition, the surveyors conduct what is called a "clinical pertinence review" or Closed Medical Record Review (CMRR), checking medical records for timeliness of chart completion in a sequence that is appropriate to medical care. Clinical pertinence is dictated by a combination of Joint Commission standards, Title 22 regulations from the state of California, and the individual facility's medical staff by-laws; it pertains to the turn-around and completeness of history and physical forms, patient care summaries, and documentation of physician's visits to patients. Furthermore, during the CMRR, the quality of the charting is assessed and evaluated. For instance, if a laboratory test reveals high potassium, a note must also appear describing what action was taken. Or, if a patient is worked up for an appendectomy, there must be evidence of related history, data on physical findings, laboratory data and evidence that the test was reviewed, and how the findings were related. Preparing for a survey has aspects of a charade:

> For a good year before the Joint Commission would come, we would begin reviewing charts—so many charts—and identify those charts that we said were looking good. And we would get those all listed down by a medical record number and DRG on a piece of paper. And knowing that probably out of the percentage of things, they could, in fact, be able to collect one of those charts. Or if we knew that there was one that was especially bad, we would say, "When the time comes to pull, don't pull this one." They give you about an hour and they're just saying we need 10 from there, 10 from that, 10 from here. Medical staff was doing the same thing. They'd be reviewing all of theirs for medical documentation and for the DRGs. Well, their charts may be good for the medical piece, and stinking for the nursing piece, and vice versa. One year we were fighting over the same chart because the nursing surveyor only looked at nursing when they did the chart reviews and the CMA only looked at the physicians. We had a basket of charts and we said these are the ones we want. And the medical staff had half of those that they wanted, so they took half of them.

When I observed surveys in 1995, this particular hospital changed its preparation, finding that pre-examining overall documentation was too time consuming since it took an hour to peruse each chart. Instead, a task force was formed under an assistant nurse manager, whose team practiced going through the charts, using the tally sheet the commission would utilize in the actual survey. The tally sheet contains 54 possible forms that should be in the chart, depending on the type of case. The QA/I coordinator of the hospital was satisfied with this approach:

> On the first day, the surveyors gave Jane a list of types of charts they wanted, like three cerebral vascular accidents and two of this and a specific one like a dying patient, restrained patients and what not—a list of 30 records.

And Jane and her group went to another room and filled out a page on each one of these records and then collated the information. And then when they got together with the surveyors it was to validate all the "no" answers. They looked for charts where the person who reviewed the chart missed something that would bring the score up higher. But, you know, it was curious. It wasn't a real validation because I know the records I looked at, the person who did the original review had marked things off that weren't there. *So the surveyors really give hospitals the benefit of the doubt with this* (emphasis added). The state surveyor and the CMA were looking at nitpicky stuff but the Joint Commission claimed they're looking at process and they really are. I found the survey a very collaborative process, rather than their acting like auditors and bean counting.

A happy consequence of this shift is the motivation it provided for genuine performance improvement. Following the survey, the multidisciplinary task force in all three hospitals in which I observed survey preparation decided to meet periodically to continue monitoring charts.

Engaging the Players

With documentation so crucial to surveys, it is small wonder that so much of the preliminary work has to do with identifying "delinquent" records. It is a constant struggle in hospitals to maintain records in a timely fashion.

In one hospital I observed, a study ordered by the physician-chairman of the "Survey-Readiness Committee" revealed that more than 50 percent of the charts had deficiencies. Commonly, the biggest gap in the records is the absence of discharge summaries, although it can just as well be progress notes, operative reports, or affixing a signature after giving verbal orders, all of which are the responsibility of the physician. In this hospital, the by-laws specified that physicians who had not completed discharge summaries within four days were to be suspended. It was never enforced. The committee endlessly discussed incentives to improve physician compliance. A physician-member of the team suggested copying the practice of a nearby hospital, providing a room where medical records personnel pile the incomplete records in front of residents and entice them with early morning donuts. Another recommended paying interns to do it, rejected by the chief of staff as too costly. One team member reported that some hospitals deny attending surgical privileges until they complete their charts. Some hospitals fine physicians who not complete charts on time. At a professional meeting, a QA/I coordinator said her hospital set up an "amnesty table," where people could return delinquent medical records, prompting another to retort, "That doesn't cover the ones that are in the trunk of a car." Yet another strategy was to send a certified letter listing incomplete records to the offending physician's office. No response led to suspension—a far cry from the practice in a rural hospital: "We used to drive around to physicians' offices and collect the records."

REHEARSING THE CAST

Although some QA/I professionals referred to survey preparation as a "facelift" or compared it to mobilizing for war—or, as one said, "cleaning house and dressing-up for the in-laws"—dramaturgy is usually the metaphor of choice. Coordinators tend to think of the survey as "a performance" based on "who knows the script, who can teach the physicians what to say." The surveyors will be roaming around the hospital, albeit escorted, examining charts and asking questions of all levels of staff. How can interest be created among busy professionals who say, "Just let me do my work"?

Prompting the Lines

"In the old days, the Chief Executive Officer would close his door and hope the surveyors would go away," said a coordinator. Those days are definitely over. Coaching the leadership so that they can answer questions regarding how they track and prioritize performance improvement projects, what they know about the overall business plan of the hospital, how they improve employee satisfaction—all of these and more are part and parcel of preparation for the survey. Answers are expected to pertain to policies and procedures, critical paths, committee structure, etc. If, as happened in one hospital during surgical review, quality professionals discover that the Chief of Surgery does not care to change his form of documentation to comply with the standards and, what is more, he intends to so inform the surveyors, they must make sure he is disabused.

Staff work may be of the highest quality, but if it cannot be presented effectively it is useless to a survey.

> One of my strongest philosophies is that the only good surveyor is a happy surveyor. And apart from feeding them, watering them well, making them comfortable, you try to speak in their language, you use the terminology that they're familiar with, so you don't have to keep translating and saying, well, we still use "quality assurance" even though we mean "performance improvement." Or we're doing thus and so and we call it something else, but we mean, uh, operative and other procedure review. I strongly believe in using their terminology because it's their standards that you're trying to demonstrate that you're complying with.

Quizzes, contests, handouts, information cards to be inserted into employee identification badges and pulled out when needed—these are some of the strategies used to focus the staff's attention. Often newsletters are distributed on a regular basis during the preceding months, each devoted to a specific subject. One newsletter on safety asked, "Who do you report all occupational injuries and illness to? When? Who do you report hazards or unsafe working conditions or concerns to? When? What would you do if you spilled a chemical?"—and a string of similar questions. Another told employees, "As a general rule, if an employee doesn't know the answer to a particular question, it is better to respond, 'I will ask my supervisor,' than to say, 'I don't know.'" Discussing the new environment of care standards, employees were told to consult their new safety manual and that "knowing where to find answers when surveyors ask questions is not considered cheating."

Some of the subtleties are transmitted in talks to employee groups. An administrator who had been designated coordinator of the survey preparation emphasized that "nonverbals" are important. She had observed another survey where one interdisciplinary team member said of another, "He's great for the team," only to have a third member roll her eyes. Such responses are to be avoided! Mock surveys are conducted, sometimes by consultants, sometimes by QA/I staff. One hospital had a Quality Fair, the purpose of which was to demonstrate ongoing improvement projects to the physicians and to give staff a chance to be more comfortable about describing their projects. Practice interviews with physicians are conducted, not only to get the language straight but also to promote confidence. (In the past, participation in the survey was not required of physicians and QA/I was something other people did.) Now that physicians are assembled for their own session in the survey, this has become more important: "They are trained to look for the weak answer. And that's the person they go after in the questions." All of the months of planning and coaching take their toll. By the end of the survey preparation I observed in one hospital, the physician-chair of the survey-readiness committee was coming to work at 5 A.M. His anxiety was palpable and contagious. When he asked, after endless discussion, "Anything else about conscious sedation?" someone answered, "I'd like some."

In the 1995–96 surveys much of the anxiety and an inordinate amount of time stemmed from the requirement that every hospital have clear mission and vision statements. All staff, moreover, were to be proficient not only in the language of these statements but know how their own departmental or unit specifics fit with the generalized expressions of the hospital's goals. This standard mirrored the popularity of such statements in other industries at the time.

Drafting a mission statement for a hospital proved to be hard sledding. Hours of discussion were devoted to composing what often ended up as I-believe-in-motherhood-type statements. But how to ingrain these statements into staff consciousness? In one hospital, California Pacific Medical Center (not a site in my research), a reduction of work force and financial stress had diverted the QA/I coordinator from putting her extensive CQI training into practice. Finally, at two in the morning, she devised an acronym that would be simple for hospital staff to remember (personal communication):

Commit   the right people to solve an important problem or improve an important process.
Plan   and implement a solution or design of a new process.
Measure   and evaluate the results.
Continue   to look for new and better ways to improve.

Another hospital distributed CARE buttons, an acronym for its combined mission and vision, with the full statement printed on the reverse side: Cost structure improvements, Access to services and quality improvements, Relationships with the community, and Employee satisfaction. In addition, the statement was posted outside elevators and in nurses' restrooms. The latter did evoke humor, a survey-readiness team member suggesting they add to the restroom sign, "For a good time, call . . ."

Sharpening the Performance

Preparation for the final performance peaks with a quality improvement technique called "storyboarding," officially defined as "a shorthand method to streamline reporting of statistical analyses and process mapping" (QI/TQM 1992, 4) and described by one physician as "jumbo cue cards." Proponents see them as "an organized way of relating quality improvement progress made by a group of people who are working together in a disciplined fashion" (ibid.). Typically, they are used to demonstrate quality-improvement projects. They are about four feet square, of posterboard or foam material, usually with a problem or statement at the top followed by a process flow diagram, table, or text boxes with arrows. Ideally, a storyboard shows the way the process *was* working, the root cause of the problem addressed, potential solutions, perhaps the restraining forces, the major recommendation for improvement, and the action plan for implementation. Storyboards developed for a survey may be enormously colorful and impressive, revealing hidden creativity. While their preparation was very labor-intensive, in the surveys I observed they were prominently displayed in the room assigned for the opening session and were judged to be clear assets. Some hospitals choose to displayed storyboards in the units or lobby. One coordinator, however, sounded a cautionary note:

There are some real problems with that in a hospital. Where do you hang a storyboard that says, "You know what? We found all these problems with conscious sedation." Can you imagine the public looking and saying, "They were doing WHAT????"

Also prepared for the first session are slides and overhead projections that highlight the outline of the opening presentation. The general, retrospective consensus among QA/I coordinators is that highlighting improvement in performance in this way sets the tone for the entire survey. Certainly, television has encouraged Americans to think in sound bites and visuals that will not tax our attention spans. Furthermore, computer capability to produce colorful graphs has inspired a noticeable tendency to combine visuals with lectures, sometimes making the spoken word superfluous. Thus, by attempting to enhance the first impression in the drama that is about to unfold, hospitals are simply following a general trend.

PRESENTING THE MAIN PERFORMANCE

After months of preparation, the first day of the survey eventually arrives and commences with a brief private session where the surveyors determine strategies. Then the hospital presents its accomplishments, supported by all the bells and whistles it can muster.

Each subsequent morning the surveyors meet privately, and then with the hospital leaders. As they review the previous day's findings, hospital representatives attempt to rebut findings, provide additional evidence of compliance, or immediately correct a deficiency. An important component of the survey is the surveyors' judgment as to whether the board, the medical staff, and hospital management work together or in isolation.

Following the leadership interview, the surveyors and accompanying staff members undertake an extensive building tour. All aspects of safety are examined—from emergency equipment to exit signs to the control and security of anesthesia carts and all medications. There are also visits to departments and questions to staff on the scope of service, procedures, systems; also, visits to the nursing units with questions regarding care as well as examination of charts for such items as informed consent forms and restraint documentation. During visits to the units, surveyors do a review of medical records. They may look at twenty charts searching for any delinquencies in the record, such as a delayed history and physical form. Informal interviews with patients may be included. An interview with human resources personnel is conducted at some point in the survey, focused mainly on staffing—for example, on handling of peaks and valleys, competencies of employees (especially those that are cross-trained), the tracking system for delinquent performance evaluations, and priorities for training and education.

The Critics' Response

Tension mounts during these days of close scrutiny, culminating at last in a ritual akin to Broadway actors waiting for the first reviews. At the end of the survey's last day, the medical staff summation is held. In California, this must occur at a special medical executive committee meeting, in order to provide statutory confidentiality protection. This summation incorporates the CMA's findings with those of the Joint Commission physician surveyor. Then the leadership exit conference takes place, bringing together all the surveyors from the Joint Commission, DHS, and CMA. Each surveyor summarizes his or her findings and points out inadequacies, which are categorized by the Joint Commission as "Type I recommendations" and by DHS as "deficiencies."

Obviously, considering the comprehensiveness of the standards, inadequacies cover a wide range: absence of follow-up signatures on verbal orders; poor protection of confidentiality by having too little space between cubicles in Admitting; failure to secure the lock on crash carts; inadequate reports to the hospital boards.

> One Type I we got had to do with a little refrigerator in our recovery room area. The recovery room had just been remodeled and they had moved in the week before. The little refrigerator didn't fit the cabinet. A work order had been put in for the alternation but things being crazy right before Joint Commission, a decision was made, "Gee let's not worry about getting locked cabinets. This is a really secure area; there's no public back here. We'll just take care of the refrigerator after." Well, the gal walked through and said, "You know this is not a secure refrigerator." Her interpretation was, "This is unsafe medicine. The public's not walking through here, but what if you had a respiratory therapist walk through." She was referring to a respiratory therapist in a California hospital who had decided to put thirty patients out of their misery. So what the hospital had interpreted as a secure area, she interpreted as unsecured.

Obviously, a hospital can be tripped up by things easily overlooked in the frenzy to get everything shipshape. A classic example arose from the requirement to post a notice that the survey has been scheduled. The commission stipulates that such a notice must be posted in the hospital at least thirty days ahead of time so that anyone can schedule an interview with the surveyors. Notice must be posted in the local newspaper, although no time frame is specified. The hospital had published the notice twenty days earlier, and the surveyor insisted to one of the hospital administrators that it should have been printed earlier. The QA/I coordinator recalled, "They hadn't even gone to document review. It was a bad way to start."

Among the reasons to avoid "Type I's" and "deficiencies" are investment in the survey preparation and pride in one's work. Two rather frivolous Type I's sent a hospital's medical staff coordinator into a depression:

> She felt she was a failure. One concerned the letter that is sent to physicians who are requesting staff privileges, asking "have you ever had your privileges relinquished?" It should have said "voluntarily or involuntarily relinquished." Also the medical staff by-laws did not say there had to be a physician representative on any boards that made decisions on medical matters. In fact, there is a physician on every such board, but they said it should be reflected in the by-laws.

Another QA/I coordinator, disappointed with what she felt was petty criticism, said:

> You know, we worked hard. And some of it is, yes, we're working to please the Joint Commission. But you're also really proud of so much, as I tally it up and get to those final hours and I look at what's in front of me and I tell fellow employees, "You cannot believe when you finally take tally how many good things we have done." And in the end, I thought, "How did this survey help validate that we really are doing a good job?" And that's what was so sad. People really don't come to work to do a crummy job. And they take pride in this place where they spend forty hours a week. And if somebody comes through and slaps them around. . . . I mean, you have to have a real strong interior.

Another compelling reason to avoid inadequacies is the cost of correcting them. Infractions may require documented evidence that appropriate changes have been made or may lead to a "focused review"—a revisit. Some managed-care corporations have begun to ask hospitals to show them their Type I recommendations. Some refuse, arguing that it is not public information; others provide it with someone to explain the issues. For many QA/I coordinators, HMOs overreact to deficiencies: "In an arena of fiercely competitive bidding, for the HMOs, this is considered to be something that is very serious. If one of the hospitals in your area gets a commendation, HMOs and many people are not schooled as to what the deficiencies are—and when your deficiencies are silly, like 'You should have constructed this things about ten years ago to be two inches farther away from the nursing station,' or 'Your generator testing should run forty minutes instead of thirty'—try to translate this to consumers."

Despite the best preparation, unpredictability hovers like a bird of prey. A QA/I coordinator said,

What changed from '95 was, the standards were the same and technically the survey was the same, but the feeling of the surveyors was they were here to find something wrong. We were back to minutia this time, which was very discouraging. We did do drills and tried to emulate as much as possible based on first-hand accounts we had from other hospitals in the area. We had to emulate the style of the surveyor in doing our preparation. The Joint Commission gathered all our information well in advance but the Department of Health Services (DHS) was calling us with about a week to go, asking for information. This only adds to the last minute hysteria. The California Medical Association (CMA) also changed their wish list of documents they wanted and we didn't know this much outside of about six weeks ahead of time. They were asking us to fill out extensive pieces of information which was totally new to this survey. And then we were not only receiving information from the CMA main office, but we were receiving individual pull lists from the two CMA surveyors themselves. This certainly adds to the feeling of impending doom. So you're riding with it but then both the Joint Commission and the DHS let us know at the last minute that they were going to bring extra people with them. Technically, that should not be a big deal. You know, like set another plate. But there's the worry with hospitals that you should be assigning people to them because where are they going and what are they doing? You're kind of in a free fall.

After the lull provided by the Joint Commission's statements regarding *collaborative* surveys, other contingencies may have interceded. It is likely that the stricter surveillance many hospitals experienced in 1998 was a reaction to serious breaches in accredited hospitals. "The pendulum's swung the other way, the heat's being turned up. I think the pendulum just keeps swinging back and forth along with the times, and sometimes the planets are aligned and you're in the right spot and sometimes you're not." Contingencies can trip up the survey in other ways, such as when "the beautiful slide projector system that had worked so beautifully the day before didn't work for our opening presentation. So the CEO had to kind of talk it through. And I thought, 'there's this black cloud . . . '"

Finally, the heavy sigh of relief that marks the end of a survey may be premature. The commission conducts one-day, random, unannounced surveys at the midway point in the triennial accreditation cycle for a 5 percent random sample of accredited organizations. These typically focus on the performance areas that generated the highest percentage of Type I recommendations in the previous year.

Moreover, the Health Care Financing Administration (HCFA) is required to perform its own assessments of a percentage of Joint Commission surveys to validate that the commission is doing a good job. The surveyors use Medicare and Medicaid standards and are usually on the premises for three to five days of intense scrutiny. The general perception is that these surveys are even more to be dreaded, "more picky," than those of the Joint Commission. Furthermore, the HCFA provides only a short time to correct deficiencies.

RECONCEPTUALIZING THE PLOT

In an institution as complex and risky as a hospital, mechanisms must be in place to monitor a high standard of care.

> Hospitals are unsafe places where we're giving chemotherapy, we cut into people, we remove people's protective reflexes, and put them on tables where they have no control. That's part of our industry so there have to be some very strict standards. But how do you meld all the things that we really need to make sure we have the safety, the equipment, the high standards? How do we do that and yet somehow be able to let institutions absolutely live and breathe and be a quality institution and at the same time give them as much flexibility as possible?

The research that led to this book was not an attempt to do an in-depth study of Joint Commission procedures and methods. While the commission figures prominently in the drive for hospital accountability, it is but part of the larger picture. Nevertheless, the current state of affairs has a number of shortcomings, the most glaring of which are the variability of surveyors, structural flaws in the survey mechanism, and the all-too-human tendency in organizations to engage in "defensive work."

Surveyor Variability

After all of the angst in anticipation of the survey, one comes away from the experience sensing the enormous role that chance plays in the matching of surveyors and hospitals. Although some surveyors are prone to nit-pick and possibly enjoy the role of cop on the beat, many see themselves as educators, are serious and conscientious, and are driven by an ideal of hospital perfection. Otherwise, why would they repeatedly undertake the travel, stay in motels far from home, and subject themselves to published profiles that list their pet peeves and may characterize them unfavorably?

In a hospital I observed, the QA/I coordinator dismissed all the expensive graphs and storyboards as superficial. Using the analogy of a sailboat, she said the surveyors should have poked at the deck with a screwdriver, looking for dry rot—when it goes through, you've got a problem. Although she blamed a lack of time, the problem really is one of surveyor variability. Some surveyors do indeed follow up on claims of performance improvement made in the initial presentation; some do not. Some apparently run the "the nickel test" to check for gaps under doors; others do not.

Some are good teachers; others are not. Obviously, "fairness," "rigor," and even "nitpicking" are subjective terms, defined differently by hospital personnel and surveyors. Few QA/I coordinators quarrel with the commission's standards; it is the varying interpretations of the standards that is disconcerting. The commission has tried to deal with this problem by improving its surveyor training and by publishing in its manuals the intent of the standards and examples of how they can be met. They also provide continuing education (at a hefty fee) and a number of free publications, most of which are accessible from their website.

Notwithstanding all that training, consistency among surveyors is as elusive as it is in any other human endeavor. In one survey I observed, much time and money had been spent on coaching the medical staff and choosing representative physicians for the physician meeting. After the physician-surveyor spent the entire session lecturing on the history of the Joint Commission instead of interviewing the well-coached physicians as expected, a QA/I professional said to me, "Do you realize how many dollars were represented in that room, and for what?" Conversely, in another hospital I observed, the physicians were given a chance to describe their improvement projects and a number of them commented on how much they had learned from the process.

Structural Flaws in the Survey Mechanism

In 1994, when the Joint Commission was under attack (see Chapter Two), the Hospital Council of Southern California charged that "the current system allows for one organization to maintain a monopoly over the accreditation and regulation of health care facilities with little oversight of their activities." This was when the American Hospital Association claimed that a conflict of interest exists when the organization that oversees organization performance also provides Medicare deemed status (the right to operate). The council found another conflict of interest "when the organization that makes the rules also conducts the surveys and determines the conditions for compliance" (Hospital Council 1994, 1). In addition, council members called the concept of "voluntary" when it comes to hospital accreditation a misnomer, since the demand by payers, state licensing or other government agencies, malpractice insurers, and public-interest groups for Joint Commission–accredited providers dismisses the consideration of any alternative. Finally, they called for sweeping change in accreditation:

> The cost to comply with all of the current regulations and accreditation standards is too high. The JCAHO, with its monopoly on accreditation, can raise fees, change standards and arbitrarily enforce and interpret its own requirements. It can sell the results of its surveys as another method to raise income.

It can expand its customer-base to include the general public and payers—clients with different needs and motives than its provider-customers. There currently exists no oversight or competitor to the JCAHO. Without a recognized, real alternative, most providers feel no choice but to continue with the existing system. Our goal is to reassert the health care systems and networks as the primary customers of a surveying agency. This should lower fees and assure higher quality. (ibid. 3–4)

Soon after, the Public Citizen Health Research Group (HRG) put the issue in a completely different perspective: "In practice, the JCAHO is so dominated by the industry it regulates that it does not, indeed cannot, do an adequate job of protecting the public" (1996, 2). The HRG pointed out that despite an elaborate accreditation process, "the bottom line is that almost all hospitals seeking accreditation end up getting it. According to the JCAHO, it typically denies accreditation to only 1 percent of the hospitals it surveys every year" (ibid.). Furthermore, argued the HRG, "the JCAHO imposes meaningful penalties so infrequently that it fails to adequately deter violations of quality standards designed to safeguard the public's health" (ibid.). Making a more elaborate case in its full report for the failure of private hospital regulation, the HRG again raised the issue of conflict of interest due to the commission's governance, funding, and multiple roles as educational consultant and regulator (Dame and Wolfe 1996).

Not much had changed three years later, when the *Boston Globe* ran a series on hospital mistakes. The demographics of the organization's makeup underscored the accusation that it is a captive of the industry it oversees: "Seven of its 28 board members represent the American Hospital Association, and another 15 come from other parts of the medical industry, such as the American Medical Association." Moreover, the *Globe* reported, the average score of hospitals nationwide in 1998 was 92 out of a possible 100, fewer than one percent of hospitals were denied approval, and inspectors are called "surveyors" to reinforce the sense that they are not examining health care organizations as independent reviewers but as part of a process of self-regulation. Sidney Wolfe, who had coauthored the HRG report, again protested:

It's a joke, it really is. . . . They've been talking about reforms for 14 or 15 years. Their response to all criticism is, "We're changing it." It's just like a floating crap game: the changes that have been made are mainly ones favored by hospitals that they regulate. (Tye 1999, 6)

Once more, we are told that the pendulum is swinging back. "For the first time ever," the Joint Commission told surveyors that in 1999 they will have the full support of the central office for all Type Is they report that are "fair" (Opus Communications 1999, 2). In the past, appeals by hospitals had led to reversals of surveyors' judgments. Furthermore, hospitals would no longer be able to avoid a Type I by correcting a deficiency during the on-site survey. Also, to add more strength to its system-wide approach, the commission encouraged surveyors to give multiple Type Is for the same issue. "For instance, if surveyors give a hospital a Type I for a restraint issue, then they must also investigate the leader's role in why the problem occurred. If leaders didn't take the appropriate action, surveyors should hit the hospital with another Type I recommendation" (ibid. 4). Revealed in the discussion of a leaner and meaner Joint Commission was the reciprocal incentive underlying high scores, namely: "One possible reason for the higher-than-average scores, (a surveyor) said, is that until now the Joint Commission appeared to base a large portion of surveyors' annual evaluations on how individual hospitals rated them. Therefore, it was in the surveyors' best interest to give high scores and please hospitals" (ibid.). The big 1999 change, debatably "big," is that the hospitals' opinions were reduced to 15 percent of evaluations of surveyors' work.

Undoubtedly, this tightening up was prompted by a government report that criticized Joint Commission surveys as "unlikely to detect substandard patterns of care or individual practitioners with questionable skills" [Office of Inspector General (OIG) 1999, 2]. The agency recommended more unannounced surveys, more random selection of records, better instruction for surveyors regarding the hospitals they are about to survey, and more rigorous assessment of hospitals' internal quality improvement efforts. The OIG identified external hospital oversight in terms of a continuum, characterized by a collegial approach on one side and a regulatory approach on the other. External reviewers in the collegial mode, they explained, focus on education and improved performance; those in a regulatory mode focus on investigation and enforcement of minimum requirements. Given the attitude of hospital personnel toward the Joint Commission, it is ironic that the OIG concluded that the commission leans toward a collegial mode, suggesting that this "may undermine the existing system of patient protections afforded by accreditation and certification practices" (ibid. 18).

Defensive Work

The concept of "defensive work" emerged from a three-year study of nursing homes conducted in the 1980s, and designates the strategies staff employ to protect themselves and / or their institution (Wiener and Kayser-Jones 1989). As mentioned in Chapter Four, it has been useful in health research to distinguish between the course of an illness and its "trajectory," the latter used to embrace all work done over the course of a disease by health care workers and the patient (including the patient's "significant others"). Regulations in nursing homes are frequently criticized for focusing on the physical components of the building rather than on the resident's care. Moreover, there is a heavy emphasis in nursing homes on record keeping, staffing patterns, and the facility's capacity to provide services rather than on the quality of patient care or services provided (Institute on Medicine 1986; Johnson and Grant 1985; Vladeck 1980). Critics also charge that regulations are so vague and inadequate as to be unenforceable. And finally, public sanctions for noncompliance are ineffective (Harrington 1984). By making the trajectory framework central to our analysis, we found that "though well-meaning and absolutely necessary, regulations, as they are frequently interpreted and implemented, have created an *adversarial structure* under which nursing homes operate, resulting in *defensive work.*"

Although the defensive work so dominant in nursing homes is not quite so prevalent in hospitals, a pending accreditation survey brings it out. Molding and shaping performance improvement projects so that they will "fit into the Joint Commission keyhole," in the words of a QA/I professional, collecting surveyor profiles, drawing upon network sources for hot issues, scrambling at the last minute to polish the Policy and Procedures handbook, flagging "good" charts for medical review, coaching physicians on how to use the Joint Commission language, the preparation of story boards for instant impact—all of these are defensive strategies that consume precious resources. Ingenuity is the watchword. A QA/I professional recalled that a hospital stored large pieces of equipment illegally in a vast anteroom; just before the Joint Commission arrived, the room was cleared and the equipment loaded into moving trucks, which were driven around the city until the survey was finished.

It is simple human nature to try to evade regulations, no matter how well-meaning they are. In the rush to prepare for a survey, regulations that are supposed to ensure clinical safety are all too often subsumed in the drive to safeguard the institution. Critics may feel that the Joint Commission is too lenient since so few hospitals are denied accreditation, but there is no complacency among those whose job it is to strive for that score of 100—and to avoid any expense from being found deficient.

Finding a Workable Solution

New contingencies are always arising, triggering new batteries of regulations. The issue of conscious sedation is a case in point. One of the better oxymorons in health care, "conscious sedation" refers to administering medication to sedate a patient for an outpatient procedure such as a bronchoscopy or colonoscopy. Although less potent medications can be used for these procedures than would be used for surgery, patients with low tolerance could lose protective reflexes. This became a hot issue for the Joint Commission because of changed technological capability—improved drugs, skill in titration of anesthesia, and improved diagnostic tools such as flexible tubes and electronic imaging—that allow some procedures to be done on an out-patient basis. Since they were no longer confined to the operating room (OR), physicians would perform the procedure and leave. Being outside an OR meant, however, that a back-up system (emergency equipment, continual monitoring of patients by an anesthesiologist, trained emergency nurses, availability of reversal agents) was not always available.

Hospitals had slipped into this new way of doing things gradually, resulting in some laxity with safeguards. As out-patient procedures have became more and more routine, the commission has drawn attention to the need to tighten up conscious-sedation standards. There now must be clear parameters regarding who administers the drug, who monitors the patient, and stipulations for the administration of reversal agents and when to involve an anesthesiologist (for instance, age or health status of patient). Also, proof of education and certification of all providers involved in conscious sedation is required.

The use of restraints provides another example of how an outside monitoring agency can stop caregivers drifting into practices that make their lives easier but expose patients to potential harm. Because only the very sick are now in hospitals, and at the same time the staff-to-patient ratio has decreased, patient falls have increased. To avoid a poor showing when number of falls became an outcome measure, hospitals used restraints (devices such as a vest or velcro cuff) more routinely to keep patients from hurting themselves. A sense that restraints were being overused, coupled with increased awareness of patients' rights, led the Joint Commission to develop standards requiring that:

- Restraint orders must be rewritten every twenty-four hours.
- A verbal order may be taken to initiate restraint but must be co-signed promptly (no longer than twenty-four hours).
- A bedside assessment must be done every twenty-four hours and the reason for continued restraint documented.
- Alternatives to restraint must be considered and documented.
- When restraint is discontinued, the behavior that allows this must be documented.

With these two examples to fortify the need for oversight, it can also be said that the time has come to determine (preferably without years of deliberation by yet another committee) what is overkill on the part of surveyors, what is nonsense, and which standards truly protect the safety of patients. To the commission's credit, the number of standards—up to 2,900 in the late 1980s and early 1990s—has been reduced to 564 for the year 2000. Nevertheless, the range remains wide and their relative importance is not adequately taken into account. On the one hand, the commission, at some of its 1999 seminars, was still stressing that all hospital personnel, from the leadership down to the staff level, must be able to state exactly how his or her job relates to the mission of the hospital—not just to memorize or read the statement off their badge cards. Then, at the other extreme, hospitals were warned to expect questions about the statistics they are producing as part of the ORYX requirements described in Chapter Three: what are their strategic measurement priorities; why did they choose specific measures; how complete are their data; are they using standardized data element definitions; have improvement opportunities been identified based on the data analysis (Joint Commission on Accreditation of Healthcare Organizations 1999)?

As the scope of oversight mushrooms, a reassessment beyond that taken periodically by the commission itself is in order, in light of the adversarial relationship that has now become entrenched. Obviously, some aspects of regulation are crucial. For example, adequate backup of utilities must be maintained in a hospital. When utilities go down it is not just a matter of inconvenience; ventilators do not operate without electricity. But how should the fact that the bottom shelf of the nonsterile linen cart is made of wire rather than solid material rank with inadequate monitoring of conscious sedation? Is the fact that a postprocedure note contains a date but not the time of day of equal import to adverse drug administration? Or, to take another issue, there are now at least 33 regulations pertaining to the use of restraints. If this prompts hiring "sitters" from the registry, at exorbitant cost, for the six months preceding survey (as one Bay Area hospital did) in order to minimize restraint usage, one has to ask how this practice has fulfilled the intent of the standards—a genuine evaluation and reduction of a procedure that the layman may view as onerous and staff may view as essential. Were the sitters necessary because of reduction in staff? Are sitters a substitute for qualified nursing? Under what conditions are restraints called for? These seem like more pertinent questions.

Close examination of the existing standards and how they are dealt with in hospitals would be at least a small step in reprioritizing important considerations and delegating those that are unimportant, but cumbersome, to the dust heap. Hopefully, this reassessment would eliminate some instances of defensive work that are excessive and downright dishonest. Furthermore, attention must be directed to the conflict of interest issue that is raised from time to time only to subside again. To have the organization that is responsible for making the rules also serve as interpreter, enforcer, and educational consultant does not make sense especially when its board of directors is dominated by the medical and hospital establishment. An experienced surveyor admitted, "There is a major dissonance there. All you need is a call from the hospital CEO to a board member to 'set things straight.'" If the point of oversight is to assure hospital accountability, health policy experts who have clinical expertise with substantial input from those who do the work of QA/I should address this behemoth.

6

Reassessing Accountability

It is impossible to rock a boat resting at the bottom of an ocean.
The thing to do is to get it back to the top.

—*John V. Lindsay*

"**D**oes quality improvement make a difference?" Just before starting to write this chapter, I was suddenly asked this question by a QA/I coordinator who had been working in the arena for many years. While struck by the enormity of the query, I was tempted to give her the sociologist's typical answer: "Sometime it does and sometimes it doesn't." But the question deserves more than that. This chapter attempts to fill that need by addressing whether quality improvement can make a difference under *present conditions*, given the five deadly weaknesses that impede its success.

THE FIVE DEADLY WEAKNESSES

Underestimating the Unique Qualities of Contemporary Health Care

Efforts to achieve hospital accountability based on an industrial model do not deal with—in fact divert attention from—the problematic character of most of today's illnesses. Today, patients tend to be hospitalized for acute episodes of their chronic diseases. Such illnesses are uncertain; their phases are unpredictable as to intensity, duration, and degree of incapacity. They are episodic: acute flare-ups followed by remissions. Chronic diseases are often multiple: long-term breakdown of one organ or physical system leads to involvement of others. Accordingly, for the most part, patients are not being rolled off the assembly line "cured." Rather, their diseases are being "controlled." Moreover, the management of today's

187

diseases changes with medical discoveries and the sharp ideological differences about treatments among those doing the treating (Wiener et al. 1982; Groopman 2000). Chronically ill people live longer, but only by depending utterly on sophisticated technology (medical machinery and pharmacology). Today, for example, we treat patients with End Stage Renal disease; before the dialysis machine was developed, there was no end-stage to kidney failure, only protracted death (Plough 1981). Nor would anyone dispute that drugs for ulcers, high blood pressure, asthma, and a host of other conditions—notwithstanding their high cost and the profits of the pharmaceutical industry—contribute mightily to extended life.

Making it possible for people to live with chronic diseases from which they would previously have died, does not mean that the survivors are always physically comfortable or without grave symptomology. Statistics on the pain management industry are telling. Valued at $13.8 billion in 1996, the industry included 2,000 U.S. hospitals and centers in that year and generated more than $3 billion a year in revenues—in what was seen as a "growth market" ("Pain management" 1998). The usual pattern in chronic illness is that new developments in the illness, as well as new symptoms, appear. In time, clinicians learn to handle these new symptoms by using, for example, new drugs. Unfortunately, these drugs may produce additional symptoms—"side effects" that perhaps will require additional drugs or other technologies to manage, and so on. New phases of illness frequently call for multiple therapies (most evident in cancer treatment, but occurring with other diseases). Complications may occur years after treatment, as when patients who have had coronary bypass surgery develop problems with the veins in their legs, such as thrombosis, or the harvested veins become occluded. Hernia repair using a new procedure has been found to create scar tissue that interferes with subsequent surgery for prostate cancer. Prolongation of a chronic illness such as arthritis may increase the need for total knee or hip replacement (sometimes both!). And to complete this untidy picture, the chronically ill, their lives prolonged, often have multiple diseases—each illness moving into previously unknown phases.

Unexpected and often difficult-to-control contingencies inevitably arise in the hospital not only from the illness itself but also from a host of organizational and work sources. Scheduling tests and procedures in the right sequence may be the staff's intent but sometimes the insurer demands a different plan of attack. Equipment sometimes breaks down. The ratio of nurse to patient may have been worked out but then can change suddenly with the introduction of another patient who is critically ill or mentally impaired. All sorts of contingencies arise from the history and lifestyle of patients and their families—even staff members themselves. Furthermore, the "product" being worked on is not inert. Patients react and affect the work; health workers likewise.

A case in point from my prior research is that of an 83-year-old man, scheduled for cataract surgery—today considered a simple procedure. As is the practice with same-day surgery, he agreed to be at the hospital at dawn for a scheduled 6 A.M. implant. This entailed arising at 4 A.M. after a sleepless night, driving through heavy fog, and then waiting until 10 A.M. to be taken to the preoperative room—only to learn that in the anxiety of his protracted waiting his blood pressure had shot up to the point where surgery was too risky. The patient (who had no history of hypertension and whose blood pressure returned to normal before leaving the hospital) was sent home and told he would have to wait six weeks for rescheduling. The financial and emotional costs—the prehospital workup that had to be repeated on readmission because of the time interval, the surgeon's, nurses', and clerical staff's time, the stress on the patient and his family do not show up on cost-effectiveness balance sheets.

Chronic disease, medical specialization, technological innovation, skyrocketing costs—all are common to industrialized countries. Also global are the biotechnology companies that have formed conglomerates because of the expensive process of bringing new drugs to market and, in some cases, because medical-device makers can sell products more quickly if they conduct clinical trials and set up manufacturing in different markets (Hall 1996). Medical specialization leads to technological innovation, involving industrial development, production, and distribution. In turn, this process creates further sophisticated specialization and associated medical work, and organizational structures in which to perform that work. This is evident in the growth of intensive-care units (ICUs). When first developed, they were general ICUs, where a variety of very ill patients were cared for. With further refinement of cardiovascular monitors and respirators (aided by large research funds for cardiac disease), separate intensive-care cardiac units evolved. Then, specialized diagnostic cardiac units were differentiated by age—adult and pediatric. Over time, heart surgeons have invented more and more sophisticated cardiac surgical technology and cardiologists have more finely delineated cardiac pharmacology. Completing the loop, more and more patients are living longer.

Innovation in health care is vastly different from that in most industries, where gains are easier to assess and failures can be eliminated based on cost-effectiveness with little impact on human life. The costs and benefits of innovation in health care are harder to pinpoint and enmeshed in quality of life issues.

Reformers may regard technology as the cause rather than the cure of high costs. They often dwell, say, on the $1 million cost of a magnetic resonance machine while ignoring the diagnoses doctors can make with it and the expensive exploratory surgery it avoids. . . . New drugs to prevent postsurgical infections can reduce hospital stays as much as 10 days. Gene therapy for illnesses like cystic fibrosis and Parkinson's disease can eliminate years of chronic care costs, while also improving patients' quality of life. (Porter et al. 1994, F11)

Costs connected to innovation in biotechnology vary over time. Heart disease is a case in point. In 1995, more than 570,000 heart patients underwent surgery to bypass blocked coronary arteries at an average cost of $45,000. Heart specialists performed nearly 420,000 angioplasties—a procedure using tiny inflated balloons to push out plaques of fatty material that can narrow the inner lining of coronary arteries. Heart transplants were performed on 2,345 patients in 1996, at an average cost of more than $209,000 for each operation, plus the first year of follow-up care. Each additional year of follow-up costs another $15,000 (Perlman 1998). Such surgery had been impossible before the development of the heart-lung machine, which maintains life while the heart is stopped. Now a cardiac surgeon, working with a biotechnology corporation, has developed a plastic stabilizer that will "bypass the bypass machine" and is training other surgeons in its use (Groopman 1999, 45). Its developer, surgeon Billy Cohn, continues to improve it:

> Generation Two is being tooled in my basement, Generation Three is on the computer, and Generation Four is in the back of my head. . . . To stop the heart in order to sew on its outside—and that is where the coronary arteries are, right smack on the surface—is simply barbaric. . . . You'll see. Over the next decade, nearly all coronary surgery will be done on a beating heart. (ibid. 51)

If Cohn is correct, this will drastically reduce cost and improve the rate of recovery and the quality of patients' lives. It will also increase the number of candidates for heart bypass surgery.

There is a significant return on investment in specialized care. For instance, data abstracted from HCFA's Cooperative Cardiovascular Project (CCP) reveal that Medicare HMO heart attack survivors with regular cardiology care were more likely to take cholesterol-lowering drugs and beta-blockers than those without regular appointments with a cardiologist. Also, consistent with other studies of this nature—for example, on asthma (Vollmer et al. 1997; Legoretta et al. 1998)—this study concluded, "Specialist physicians, by virtue of their narrower focus, can more readily keep up with changes in clinical knowledge as they occur. . . . Moreover, cardiologists are generally quicker to put successful innovations into practice and to discontinue using therapies shown to be less effective" (United States General Accounting Office 1998, 4).

Prescient, but not recognized as such until recently, was the first comparative analysis of the direct costs of common chronic conditions among adults based exclusively on data from managed care. Data in this study were gleaned from the records of all adults who were continuously enrolled in a large staff-model HMO during 1992. More than one-third of these adults were diagnosed with at least one chronic condition and costs for this population were at least twice those of the population without such ailments. A diagnosis of a chronic condition resulted in an expected increase in costs of 80–300 percent, depending on age, sex, and chronic condition profile (Fishman et al. 1997).

Not to be overlooked, then, is the powerful element of patient demand. A comment by economist Robert Fogel captures the force of this influence. Upon receiving the Nobel Prize in 1993, he observed that as we get more and more control over chronic illness, costs will continue to grow no matter what we do: "Most people my age would rather have a new knee than a new VCR" ("Morning Edition," 1993). It is not that our appetite has increased and that we are demanding more and more from a fixed menu of technological possibilities. Nor is it that the insured are choosing the expensive entrees. What is happening, rather, is that the menu continues to expand. Furthermore, our collective experience of medical technology is shaped, in large part, by media and other public accounts in which "the successful patient is emphasized, . . . the image of mastery over death is prominent, and any problems with this technologically mediated life are only marginal concerns" (Plough 1986, 19). Not only has this type of health reporting accelerated but, increasingly, patients search for treatment options on the Internet and are encouraged by patient advocacy groups to take more control over their treatment.

Small wonder, then, that the cost of heath care continues to grow relentlessly. Small wonder that a commentator has called hospitals "giant ICUs" (Neighmond 1997), nor that patients' demand for treatment motivates them to petition their government representatives for a Patient's Bill of Rights that will provide better access, choice, and the assurance that the decisions that affect their lives will not be made by managed-care functionaries. Small wonder, also, that, given a choice, managed-care subscribers, when given the option, move from health plan to health plan in search of better coverage. In such an energetic structure, unintended consequences abound:

> Pressure on doctors also increases drug costs. HMOs evaluate physicians on how many patients they churn through their offices in a day, and patients grade them by how much time they spend in a waiting room; so a quick prescription can be handy. "To terminate a visit, you hand the patient a prescription," says Thomas Schmidt, associate medical director at HealthSystem Minnesota. "It's quicker than telling a patient about changing his lifestyle." (Winslow 1998, A14)

A host of technologies are bumping up costs for HMOs: a product that makes it easier to analyze Pap smears (a common test for signs of cervical cancer) and adds about $3 million a year to one HMO's costs; new brain surgery for Parkinson's disease; three different $10,000-a-year drugs approved in 1998 for multiple sclerosis; a near-tripling in price to $90 in just one year for improved inhalers for asthma patients. The shift to managed care may have produced significant short-term cost savings but it has "squeezed out most of the savings that can be derived from such a transition" ("Health costs expected to resume rising sharply" 1998). Rising demand and new technologies will accelerate spending, experts predict, and total national spending for health care will more than double, from $1 trillion in 1996 to $2.1 trillion in 2007 (Smith et al. 1998).

These are the dynamics that contribute to the complexity of medical care, that vary the work of caring for patients, that cause coordination problems, that defy simple solutions, and that confound the notion of outcome measures and treatment based on algorithms. Every day, patients are wading through this morass, often left to figure things out for themselves, dealing with technology that is sophisticated but care that is archaically coordinated. An added element, our multiethnic population, would be humorous if it were not so life-threatening. In radio coverage of Cook County Hospital in Chicago, the reporter revealed that since the hospital only employed Spanish and Polish translators full time, it was not uncommon for the hospital to call ethnic restaurants to translate for its patients. Needed that year were translators for Korean, Chinese, Russian, Albanian, Serbian, Latvian, Lithuanian, Assyrian, Bulgarian, Egyptian, Italian, and Iranian patients! ("Weekly Edition" 1995) This is to say nothing of the clash of belief systems within the conventional hospital organization and the effect on medical decision making as large segments of our diverse population vary the mix between conventional and folk medicine.

Overstating and Overselling
Accountability Proposals

In 1994, the Agency for Health Care Planning and Research (AHCPR) received a federal appropriation of $185 million, largely to support effectiveness research conducted by its Patient Outcomes Research Teams and for the development of practice guidelines under its Medical Treatment Effectiveness Program. Predictions of unrealistic expectations regarding the dramatic changes that would be achieved turned out to be justified. A contemporary critic assailed "the tendency to seize upon clever new theories as solutions to intricate problems." He proposed a lowering of expectations regarding the cost-saving potential of outcomes research, echoing the proposition delineated above that health care reform needs to deal directly with the growth of demand stemming from new technologies and the growth and aging of the population (Stano 1994).

Another veteran commentator tackled the serious problem of overstating and overselling:

> Although there are continuing sincere—even heroic—efforts to find better methodologies, measures, and evaluative techniques, it is also true that many claims about quality are overblown. Too often, what little we do know about quality, risk adjustment, and outcomes is ballooned into outlandish claims about quality measurement products—claims that can be invalid, or at least premature, in terms of how well the product has been tested and evaluated in real-world situations.
>
> This type of hucksterism is a long way from the stated goal: being able to measure quality of care received by diverse patients, with diverse diagnoses, who live in diverse locations, under diverse socio-economic conditions, and who belong to diverse health plans. A companion goal is to measure and enhance the health status of entire populations. Health services research is nowhere near attaining either goal—and, frankly, probably will never get there. It can only hope to come close and thus *should not oversell what it accomplishes. The stakes are too high* (emphasis added). (Friedman 1997, 177)

Similar charges have been leveled against Total Quality Management (TQM), or Continuous Quality Improvement (CQI), as it is more commonly called in health care. As explained in Chapter Three, CQI focuses on organizational systems rather than individuals and replaces inspection with continual improvement. In the classical CQI model, the use of specific techniques by interdisciplinary groups, will lead to consensus on improvement goals, which are implemented and monitored. The transfer of this manufacturing philosophy to hospitals has been called a "field of dreams," whose proponents take for granted that it is beneficial in every respect (Bigelow and Arndt 1994). Critics charge that two important assumptions implicit in CQI—hierarchical control of management over the technical core and the dominance of rational decision-making processes—do not translate directly to the hospital setting (Arndt and Bigelow 1995).

The CQI principle that "managers own the work processes" defies the reality of hospitals, where management does not have control over many aspects of physicians' work and where physicians themselves decide how involved they want to be in organizational decisions and practices. QA/I professionals acknowledge that the success of CQI projects depends on a supportive "physician champion" and often tailor their goals around that ingredient or around the satisfaction of physicians who admit a heavy volume of patients. Such a special role for physicians contradicts the rational CQI approach—identify, measure, and prioritize customers and their needs. Other CQI-related issues include: (1) the negative impact of physicians' limited participation on the commitment and effort of other employees; (2) the extent to which the selection of improvement projects and setting of priorities among them are influenced by negotiation, compromise, or personal values; and (3) the constraints presented by behavioral and political considerations. (such as resource limitations and legal or regulatory requirements) in the identification of solutions. CQI appears to be most effective in its application to administrative processes and support services—for example, improving admitting, laboratory, and patient transport problems.

Proponents of CQI continue to argue that hospitals are not that unique compared to other organizations.

> All organizations have important stake holders. All organizations could have powerful vendors or scarce resources. All organizations can have ambiguity about their purpose or about clear lines of authority and accountability. (Smith 1995, 26)

But Smith agrees that "fit" is a function of the internal and external conditions within which an organization is operating and that "CQI should not be undertaken by every hospital any more than it should be undertaken by every Dairy Queen" (ibid. 27). Tell *that* to the Joint Commission surveyors!

There was increasing agreement in the mid-1990s with the call for well-designed studies into whether CQI as a philosophy or process is capable of achieving its promise in hospitals (Gann and Restuccia 1995; Berwick 1994). Research conducted in sixty-one hospitals drew attention to the need for "a culture that supports quality improvement work and an approach that encourages flexible implementation" if CQI is going to work (Shortell et al. 1995, 377). Furthermore, this research highlighted the difficulty of implementing quality improvement projects in larger hospitals with more bureaucratic and hierarchical cultures. Greater insight has been gained from the first multisite, randomized, controlled trial of guideline implementation using CQI teams and academic detailing (AD) techniques. (AD is modeled on the methods of pharmaceutical sales representatives, where physicians or pharmacists offer providers brief, one-on-one education and feedback sessions.) Guidelines for two common chronic conditions—hypertension and depression—were chosen. From these guidelines, the study's steering committee developed five recommendations on which intervention activity would focus. Results were disappointing. Both the AD techniques and the CQI teams were evaluated as "generally ineffective in increasing compliance with hypertension and depression guidelines" (Goldberg et al. 1998, 140). The researchers felt that their experience with CQI teams was an adequate real-world test, one that involved a commitment of time, resources, and expertise in excess of what would typically be available. Most important, in regard to overpromising and overselling an accountability endeavor, the researchers report:

> even the improvement in blood pressure control observed at the best-case clinic was achieved at the expense of hundreds of hours of effort. . . . In conclusion, we found both AD techniques and CQI teams to be socially complex interventions whose implementation is sensitive to local differences in the organizations' cultures, particular personnel, and disease conditions involved. (ibid. 141)

For yet another example—indeed, a textbook case—of overstating and overselling, one need look no farther than the promise held out by re-engineering of the hospital structure and the attendant job distribution. A proponent argues that "most nonprofit managers, bred in a gentler age, don't have the stomach to cut costs and re-engineer health care delivery." He then gives examples of what he believes are sensible innovations:

> As Ed O'Neill, director of the Center for the Health Professions, explains, smart hospitals are also finding that half the work done by registered nurses can be handed off to lower-cost file clerks or janitors. New medical technologies, meanwhile, have combined with old-fashioned guild instincts to span a crop of narrowly licensed, underutilized technologists who've made themselves the only sanctioned operators of respiratory or radiology gizmos. Progressive hospitals are cross-training such folks so they're fully employed. (Miller 1996, 19, 22)

This attitude toward technologists and their gizmos was apparently shared by the consultants who advised one of the hospitals where I observed the re-engineering process. While the impact of redesign on nurses, as it was called in this particular hospital, was substantial (described in Chapter Three), its impact on the rest of the staff and on patients was disruptive and potentially fateful. Following the consultants' advice by making the charge nurse a team leader meant delegating new tasks to clinical partner I's (licensed vocational nurses) and clinical partner II's (nurse attendants). Reducing the clinical laboratory staff and training clinical partners to do blood draws were foreseen as benefits of redesign. Very soon, however, problems on the units with this transfer of responsibility became a recurring theme at meetings of the troubleshooting committee. The laboratory representative continued to report that she was getting frequent calls because staff were having difficulty with blood draws. She would tell them to call the doctor since, having let most of their phlebotomists go, "we have to get it through to them that the lab is not a resource." Furthermore, she reported that staff were using butterfly needles at a cost of $1 each, instead of a standard needle that costs two cents, because butterflies are easier to manipulate. Tales of numerous attempts to draw blood from a patient before calling for help became part of the hospital lore.

Similarly, respiratory-therapy staff were cut on the supposition that their work could be transferred to the unit staff. Problems with this were manifold. First cited was the difficulty in getting the morning treatment completed due to the competition of other tasks during this high-activity time. Second, treatment was continued inappropriately due to the lack of expertise and experience to evaluate whether the respiratory care plan was effective or if changes were required. Third, in some cases records were not started, in others procedures were not documented due to lack of time. Fourth, amid the pressure of learning new skills, more time was being taken with each patient than management deemed necessary. Compounding all these problems was a predictable, but not anticipated, condition: In their zeal to get started, administrators had not taken into account that the new system was being implemented during the winter months when there is a heightened incidence of at-risk pulmonary patients. Despite tales of nebulizers discovered on sleeping patients' foreheads and of patients' discomfort—"patients who have COPD (chronic obstructive pulmonary disease) watch the clock and get angry when no one comes back"—the hospital stuck stubbornly to its redesign plan.

More obstacles arose. One nurse told of the challenge of teaching clinical partners how to do electrocardiograms (EKGs):

> I had someone do one the other day and the leads were on the abdomen instead of the chest. One of the nurses saw it; she just happened to walk by. A doctor came to me the other day with an EKG and said the leads were on backwards. Where before there were maybe five people in the house doing EKGs, now we have fifty.

As the committee struggled with these problems month after month, at times it seemed that their belief in redesign—sold to them at great economic and emotional cost—resembled the belief of Soviet revolutionaries that forced grain levies would foster a cooperative relationship between the peasantry and the state. In reality, faith in the expertise of the consultants the hospital had hired kept them going. Weaknesses in the services they received from these consultants could be seen only in retrospect. One member of the redesign committee expressed her discomfort much later: "It may be how hospitals utilize consultants. They come in, do the work, but really most of the work needs to be done after they leave—the support and reassurance and getting systems in place." Asked if the consultants follow up on the successes and failures that flow from their recommendations, she answered: "No, but that should have been part of the fee, to come back at certain intervals and see what's working and what's not. We could call them but they would say, 'we're more than willing to come back at $2,500 a day per person.'"

The need for education over and above training was obvious. Overwhelming emphasis was placed on mandatory training which, out of frugality, was left to one nurse-educator and the instructor she hired. Although the latter put great effort into the sessions, trying to be creative to keep the less-than-enthusiastic participants engaged, in retrospect she was realistic about the obstacles:

> The six-week training course for clinical partners was a dangerous process. Throw them on the front lines with nurses who don't want them there . . . these are the people who, a month ago were working in the kitchen and the laundry. And I worried about language, I don't mean teaching them better English, but making sure that with their colleagues and with patients there is clarity enough so that important information gets passed on. If the patient support technician goes into a room and the patient says, "My head really hurts," can he or she really comprehend that that's something to take to a nurse versus, "Oh, yeah, I got a headache too, life isn't easy"—to give them permission to *not* understand things and to ask. Whereas the nurses, of course, they're still in that mode of criticizing them for not understanding. So they will always pretend that they understand.

Other significant problems arose in conjunction with the training. Alas, even the best educational session cannot impart common sense and pride in the job and, most important, the analytical skills that come with experience. A nurse manager told me:

> I've been a critical-care nurse my entire career. And with that comes sophisticated skills and critical thinking. That's another one of those things that not everybody has. So sometimes we have a clinical partner on the unit who puts a food tray in front of her restrained patient and leaves. And it's like, "What's wrong with this picture? Would you do this at home if your husband was restrained?"

Furthermore, team training does not necessarily a team make. The director of nursing lamented the fact that RNs were being asked to draw upon unfamiliar skills. She described the previous role of a charge nurse as being an "enabler, a resource, more or less the mom of the unit." She continued:

> Now we have nursing staff not calling the doctor because they're afraid to. . . . That's why nurses are in so much pain and misery right now. They're being forced to develop skill sets they have not been encouraged to develop. And some of them maybe are not even capable. And some of them are still

back in denial. And some of them just don't want to. You know, nurses tell me all the time, I don't want to be a leader. I like being a follower.

"Area managers," nurses who supervised a number of units, found themselves with what they felt were unreasonable demands on their already restricted time. Said one, "I now make housekeeping rounds. I have to inspect the venetian blinds to make sure there is no dust on them and look in the grates in the shower to see that they're clean." When area managers of equal authority were alternated for each shift, she protested, "There was good logic to it on paper but now the staff play mom against dad, creating animosity between the two of us."

All of this puts quite another face on "skill mix" and "cross-training." On more than one occasion, re-engineering has been used not very subtly to get rid of employees who have outlived their usefulness. In sum, re-engineering is easier to achieve on paper than in real life. "Like any radical change, re-engineering is more difficult to achieve than many leaders would like. They want to do it quickly and easily, and therefore they ignore or neglect the human dimensions of the process" (Jaffe and Scott 1997, 15).

Almost two years after implementing redesign, the hospital where I observed the process announced to its employees and professional staff, "Although a lot of our staff have worked hard to make 'Redesign' work, we have concluded that 'Redesign' has not delivered the desired impact on either improved quality of service or reduced cost." The quotation marks surrounding "redesign" spoke volumes. All the classifications that had been reclassified to clinical partners were changed back to their traditional roles of certified nurse attendant, licensed vocational nurse, and licensed psychiatric technician. Patient-support technicians returned to their previous roles as environmental services workers, food services workers, or transporters. In an understated epitaph to this protracted and disruptive experience, hospital administration informed all parties that, "Just as the decision to undertake the original 'Redesign' activities was difficult, this decision to change 'Redesign' is equally difficult and not being undertaken without a great deal of thought and planning."

Ignoring the Irrationality Intrinsic to Rationalization Ventures

One way to assess attempts to rationalize health-care delivery is to look at industrial production, where many elements are almost fully rationalized (experimentation, followed by trial, followed by elimination of "bugs") and the remainder are rationalized as far as possible (evaluating the market for the product, calculating the potential financing). All of that can be done because goals are clear, tested means for reaching them are available, and assessment of results throughout the course of work is both possible and feasible. But contrary to the notion that what works for General Motors works for health care, medical production is quite different—not only due to the complexity described above but also because the hospital does not have control over its services and practices:

> Hospitals cannot add or delete services with the same freedom as most firms in private industry. The community, medical staff, managed care organizations, and ethical consideration all play a role in these decisions. Similarly, changes in clinical practice often cannot be made at the discretion of an individual hospital. Clinical trials may be needed, approval from human studies committees or governmental agencies may be required, and even then refusal of third party payers to cover a new treatment may prevent implementation. As well, licensure requirements, insurance carriers, regulators, and other external bodies often place constraints on decisions concerning staffing levels, job design, cost accounting methods, billing and collection practices, internal controls, and even the hospital's organizational structure. (Arndt and Bigelow 1998, 62)

Another important element that is a fundamental stumbling-block to rationalizing medical work is the entrance of the patient to the hospital unit.

> We have in mind here not simply a patient's behavioral responses but his or her unanticipated and unlooked for entrance into the staff's self-circumscribed division of labor, for that entrance may immediately or eventually confound the staff's order of business as they conceive of it. . . . The staff readily recognizes that a monkey wrench can be thrown into the coordination of their work by a patient's becoming impatient or angry at the way a procedure is being carried out or depressed by the implications of the necessity for that procedure, or that a patient's discomfort might need to be handled quickly because it can directly affect physiological functioning, which in turn can limit the effectiveness of ongoing therapy. . . . Too many conditions mitigate against rationalization to permit more than some proportion of component segments of the arc of work to be standardized—and then they, too, are subject to potential disruption. (Strauss et al. 1997, 154–55)

In truth, there are plenty of irrationalities in rationalization. Just look at what has happened to some of the hospital mergers. These panaceas of the 1990s were expected to capture more of the market than has been the case. Here the interaction between organizational factors—an arena in flux, undergoing what has been called "the biggest industrial revolution it has ever experienced"[1]—and the behavioral response of its workers has created unexpected—read, irrational—consequences. Three mergers that were supposed to ease the money pressure and lessen the impact of managed

care—Beth Israel Deaconess Medical Center in Boston, New York Presby-
terian Hospital, and UCSF Stanford—have been disappointing:

> It hasn't worked out that way. Some hospitals that merged are losing more
> money than ever. The cost-cutting drives they promised have stalled, and
> their staffs are warring. Internal squabbling has felled more than one hospi-
> tal chief executive officer. Some mergers have fallen apart. Others have re-
> tained mediation specialists and turnaround experts to keep their unions
> viable. Meanwhile, recent reductions in Medicare reimbursement are taking
> their toll on weakened institutions. (Lagnado 1999, B1)

As in any organization, policies and procedures that look good on paper can be subverted when hospital staff do not behave according to plan.
One example is maintaining patient confidentiality (a potential Type I de-
merit from the Joint Commission). It is a mistake to assume that hospitals
can control confidentiality of patient or hospital information with the most
stringent system and rules governing documentation. No system can be
secured in such a way that a user can only access information needed to do
his or her job. There simply is no guarantee against a hospital worker viewing, accidentally or on purpose, information that s/he has no business ac-
cessing. One online discussion among QA/I professionals confirmed this
problem. A respondent, emphasizing the need for rules, nevertheless observed, "Even though a maintenance person is an employee and has signed
a confidentiality agreement, we don't have a clue about this person's motivation, agenda, financial need, marital relationships, etc." Said another,
"Please realize that education is only the first step. Often when asked, staff
will say they know it's wrong to discuss confidential patient or staff information with those who don't need to know, but they continue to do it any-
way because it's accepted in the hospital culture as part of doing daily
business." Yet a third reported on a conference she attended during which
the presenter highlighted a California case, where the hospitalization of a
well-known actor prompted 350 accesses to his medical record within a 24
hour period by many employees who did not require the information for
their jobs!

Similarly, a quintessential example of best-laid plans gone awry is the
issue of "legal consent," obtaining written approval from a patient before
commencing a diagnostic procedure or treatment. ("Informed consent" is
the discussion, which must be documented in the medical record, between
physician and patient on the risks, benefits, and alternatives of a proposed
procedure or treatment. "Legal consent" is the form the patient signs.)
Strict regulation regarding this practice stems from a long history of disre-
gard for patient's rights and is testimony to the sincere efforts of people involved in the field of bioethics. Unfortunately, they would be the first to
agree that a breech too often occurs between rules and practice in obtain-

ing consent. All situations may not be as coarse as mine when, minutes prior to orthoscopic surgery, a three-page consent form was thrust in front of me by the anesthesiologist, who said, "Don't bother to read this. Just sign it." Nevertheless, patients may find this description more familiar than would be expected from the prescriptive literature on the ethics of obtaining consent. Despite protracted discussions in policy-and-procedures development groups and documentation/forms design committees, too often the consent process has become a formality with little substance. In their zeal to conform to regulations with a written policy and explicit (often lengthy) forms, hospitals overlook the actual practice and attitudes that can make or break the intent of consent.

A number of researchers have provided observational data on the problems of implementing consent in clinical practice (Guillemin and Holmstrum 1996; Anspach 1993; Zussman 1992). In a particularly poignant rendition, Weitz (1999) writes as both a sociologist and a relative concerning a case that demonstrates how the intent of obtaining consent can be subverted when physicians withhold or selectively offer information—whether from inability or unwillingness to share decision-making. All of the evidence in these reports comes from intensive care units where often aggressive treatment is begun before the family has been consulted. And, it must be stated, as information on risks, benefits and alternatives has become more and more graphic, many patients either think or say, "Spare me the dismal possibilities." But the result is of note here: a decided gap between a rational approach, providing the patient with full information, and the irrational elements that govern behavior, or as Wietz's subtitle underscores, between rhetoric and reality.

Emphasizing the Superiority of Market Forces to the Neglect of Other Values

"You can't measure what goes into quality—you can't measure kindness and the emotional side of providing care. You can't measure feelings and you can't measure skill." This comment came from a nurse with thirty years of bedside experience. While undoubtedly considered hopelessly naive in the context of today's hard-edged business mentality, her position is not isolated. Couching their doubts in different language, distinguished scholars are raising questions about one of the sacred cows dear to health-care reformers—that market forces will ensure quality.

Uwe Reinhardt, an internationally respected expert in health-care economics and policy, says that the objective of health reform—to hold providers of health care more fully accountable for the resources they use and to force them into a continuous search for methods that will improve both the health status of the population and its health-care experience—is endorsed all over the world. He warns, however, that the purely clinical quality of health care should not be confused with the quality of the health-care experience. Addressing the perplexing question of why the technically sophisticated, expensive, and often very luxurious American health system frequently earns relatively low scores in satisfaction surveys, he suggests that quality is being judged in terms of dimensions quite apart from the quality improvement efforts described in this book. Among the criteria he isolates are the distributive ethic (for instance, the exclusion of prescription drugs and long-term care under Medicare, to which can be added the recent cutbacks in rehabilitative services); freedom of choice (both for insurance contracts and providers); the bureaucratic hassle factor (the monetary and nonmonetary costs American patients bear as they wrestle with the administrative facet of their health system); and trust in the integrity of the system. Regarding the last, he cites the payment system that rewards health professionals for withholding care from patients—the "gatekeeper model" that sets up a conflict of interest and contributes to the growing hostility toward managed care. "That hostility is a cost to be booked against any economics the gatekeeper model may achieve" (Reinhardt 1998, 390).

> But the awkward complexity of the financial and managerial systems that Americans have put in place to encourage continuous improvement in clinical quality may serve as a negative role model, examples of approaches that other nations might spare themselves. Even if it turned out eventually that with their administratively ever more complex systems of financial incentives Americans did purchase some additional life expectancy or superior clinical quality overall, that achievement may well drown in a chorus of hassled, bewildered and financially insecure citizens who judge their health system inequitable. For the ordinary American, "consumer driven" health care might lead to a rather mediocre health care experience overall. (ibid. 394)

Others are questioning the impact of the competitive market on health-care quality. In an editorial accompanying a special edition of the *International Journal of Quality in Health Care* devoted entirely to this topic, Andrew Thompson, a Scottish academic, points to the lack of evidence regarding either positive or negative effects of competition. He charges that "There is some evidence that the soaring cost of American health care has been brought under control, but not without some unacceptable effects on the public and without solving the problems of equity and universality" (Thompson 1998, 372).

Economist Thomas Rice has taken the debate a step farther, urging policy analysts to reconsider how well market mechanisms fit health care. In a thorough review of both market competition theory and the theory of demand, Rice demonstrates that conclusions about the desirability of competitive markets are based on a large set of assumptions "that are not and cannot be met in the health care sector" (Rice 1997, 384). He argues that health policy based on market theory will not enhance economic efficiency or increase social welfare. He cautions, "If analysts misinterpret economic theory as applied to health—by assuming that market forces are necessarily superior to alternative policies, and that other tools of the trade neatly translate to health care—then they will blind themselves to policy options that might actually be best at enhancing social welfare, many of which simply do not fall out of the conventional, demand-driven competitive model" (ibid. 426).

Somehow lost in the rush to a business approach to health care are the truisms that market decisions are money decisions, not value decisions, and that health care is a social good, not a commodity. Columnist Cynthia Tucker takes issue with the notion that the free market will cure what ails medicine. Referring to examples of the "unhealthy outcomes created when profit drives medical decisions," she asks, "Can you imagine the tyranny that would ensue if police departments had balance sheets that posted a rise on Wall Street every time a citizen was arrested?" (Tucker 1995, A20). At the height of the furor over Columbia/HCA, Bill Cox, Executive Vice President of the Catholic Health Association participated in a radio discussion in which he explained why his organization would not allow any of its members to be controlled by this behemoth: "We don't mind it when Walmart and other retailers go at it and drive down the price of video cassettes; we have found that they generally maintain the quality. But health care is different." Cox posed a larger issue: "There's nothing wrong with capitalism except when it gets into an area that is such a basic service. Our concern is that capitalism, just by its very nature, is not loyal to communities, is not loyal to the professionals who work in health care organizations, is not loyal to the long term needs of patients" ("All Things Considered" 1996).

> If medicine is a business, to be operated for profit under Commodore Vanderbilt's rules, then unquestionably Columbia/HCA is following the right formula. But if medicine has duties beyond those to stockholders—duties to care for those in need, to educate future generations of caregivers, to conduct lifesaving research and to expand the frontiers of knowledge, then it will have to play by another set of rules. And what rules, and laid down by whom? (Wolfe 1996, 3)

Now that the public has had a substantial taste of the health care that has replaced the Rockwellian medicine of yore, it is time for renewed dialogue regarding what our needs are and how much (through that ugly mechanism, taxation) *we* are willing to pay to satisfy them. Of course, such a discussion requires that the public be educated regarding reasonable expectations by legislators who can move beyond such simplistic solutions as posting the Ten Commandments in classrooms. If, as seems to be the case, we want the best care available, we must be willing to bear some of the financial burden—not to protest the minute a Medicare rate increase is proposed (as happened in the past when consumer groups stubbornly fought means-tested catastrophic care) but rather to understand the full implications of such proposals. Nor should this discussion be the political football and advertising blitz that Clinton's health plan became; instead it should be an honest appraisal of the who-is-going-to-pay issue. The fact that American politics have become even more polarized than they were when President Clinton introduced his plan does not deflect from the urgency—it is simply one more condition that must be dealt with.

> The only kind of market which can be made safe for democracy resides in a truly mixed economy where the public and private sectors maintain an equilibrium. . . . A strong public sector is absolutely necessary to balance the raw power of the private sector. The era of big government is most certainly not over. Only a big government can match the power of big business as an equal. (Lipson 1999, A19)

Downplaying Medical Accident and Error

To the imperatives driving contemporary health care—technology, chronic illness, cost, and accountability—must be added another, patient safety. In early 1998, the CEO of a large HMO appeared on national television and tried to justify the length-of-stay restrictions imposed by managed care by saying, "Hospitals have to be used very, very carefully. People get sick in hospitals, people die in hospitals from medication and treatment errors that occur there." It seems reasonable to ask, if hospitals are not safe, why not strive to make them safer?

Existing mechanisms for reporting accidents and errors are grossly inadequate. "Incident reports" often become punitive, with the emphasis on fingerpointing and finding a scapegoat, rather than analyzing the incident as a whole. Asked to explain the process after an incident report is turned in, a nurse laughed, "People feel like it goes into a black hole. The nurse may give it to the manager and the manager may say 'this isn't important' and throw it away; or she may pass it on to the Risk Management Department and it sits there." Also, physicians do not trouble themselves with incident reports. In the words of a QA / I coordinator, "They'll sometimes say, 'I told the nurse to fill one out.'" A study found that although RNs voluntarily filed incident reports when they discovered their own errors, doctors pursued the problem directly with the nurse. Moreover, although nurses often complained about physicians' inadequacies and errors, they did so informally with other staff members. They did not complain directly to doctors, nor were written complaints submitted to them (Brannon 1994,

153). Peer review, which physicians prefer, remains within the cloistered walls of the meeting room and is not set up to examine clinical error in relation to the entire system.

Although proportionately small in relation to the larger health care literature, the literature on medical accidents is revealing, its authors assiduous in the Sisyphean task of drawing attention to the extent of these occurrences (Leape et al. 1991; Brennan et al. 1991; Leape 1994). Furthermore, an indication that adverse events are even more prevalent than suggested by these studies can be found in research undertaken by Andrews et al. (1997), who exhibited originality by deriving their data from discussions at routine meetings rather than medical records. Of the 1,047 patients in the study, 185 (17.7 percent) were said to have had at least one serious adverse event. The likelihood of experiencing an adverse event increased about 6 percent for each day of hospital stay. In 37.8 percent of the cases, the adverse events were caused by an individual and 25.4 percent could be traced to interactive or administrative causes—all of these figures presumably an underestimate since "additional discussions, perhaps about other adverse events, doubtless occurred in more casual settings, such as the cafeteria, and at other times" (ibid. 312). Feldman and Roblin (1997, 568) underscore one historical locus of the problem: "Focus on clinician errors and the current mode of appraisal have created an environment that, all too often, begins with accusations and blame and often ends with discussion and rationalization of the injury as an event 'not likely to occur again.'" An important source of such a defensive attitude toward error is medical school and residency, which socialize physicians to strive for error-free practice. "In everyday hospital practice, the message is equally clear: mistakes are unacceptable. Physicians are expected to function without error, an expectation that physicians translate into the need to be infallible" (Leape 1997, 1851–52; *see also* Bosk 1979)—a sentiment shared by patients. The range of diagnostic and treatment options, the fact that results of each of these options might turn out better, worse, or identical to other options, the uncertainty about whether the right decision was made, and the potential for failure from physicians who are willing to take the greatest risks to help their patients—all of these increase the likelihood of medical accidents.

And then there is the extent to which hospitalized patients are already compromised by their chronic conditions. As a colleague has commented in disputing the tendency to use an industrial model, "The hospital is more like a garage. They're dealing with 'damaged goods' but the difference is that the carburetor is affected by the fenders."[1] To which it must be added, the patient does not come with a manual. Nor can he or she be recalled when discovered to be defective. The inescapable conclusion is that with a process so imbued with uncertain and highly contingent judgments, regulation cannot eliminate failures. "Even elimination of error through regulation is highly problematic. Error is inevitable and ubiquitous; everyone errs" (Jost 1995, 845).

Therefore, medical accidents and injuries must be examined from a *systemic* perspective:

> Preventing medical injury will require attention to the systemic causes and consequences of errors, an effort that goes well beyond identifying culpable persons. . . . In this context, our description of adverse events represents an agenda for research on quality of care. Adverse events result from the interaction of the patient, the patient's disease, and a complicated, highly technical system of medical care provided not only by a diverse group of doctors, other care givers, and support personnel, but also by a medical-industrial system that supplies drugs and equipment. *Reducing the risk of adverse events requires an examination of all these factors as well as of their relation with each other.* (Leape et al. 1991, 383–84, emphasis added)

Analysts suggest that hospitals look to other high-risk settings for guidelines. A growing body of literature on accidents—in aviation and other transportation as well as in the nuclear industry—is there to be drawn upon (Perrow 1984; Reason 1990; Rasmussen 1990; Eagle et al. 1992; Richetson et al. 1980; Turner and Pigeon 1997). These accidents are usually the result of the adverse confluence of active errors and latent system faults:

> Active errors are those erroneous decisions and actions which have an *immediate* impact on system state and function. They are often conspicuous and recognized as slips, mistakes, and violations of rules or accepted standards of practice. . . . Latent system faults are erroneous decisions and actions that have a *delayed* impact on system state and function. . . . Latent system faults—errors of design, maintenance, operation, or organization—exist long before the accident to which they are related, and can often be recognized only after an accident has occurred. System faults create the background conditions which make possible the occurrence of an accident from active error such as a slip, a mistake, or a deliberate unsafe act. (Feldman and Roblin 1997, 569)

A turning point occurred with the 1996 Annenberg Conference—which brought together such organizations as the Joint Commission, the American Medical Association, the American Academy for the Advancement of Science, and the Annenberg Center for Health Sciences. Among its key lessons were that although perfect performance is impossible, the goal of error reduction has not been given enough attention; the epidemiology of errors in health care is unknown; and reliance on self-reporting followed by a punitive response is ineffective.

Early in 1995, a series of highly publicized hospital errors—including the death of *Boston Globe* reporter Betsy Lehman from a drug overdose and the amputation of the wrong foot of another patient—had caused a breakdown in public trust and been an embarrassment to the Joint Commission. As a commission representative reported two years later, however, placing these organizations into a category of conditional accreditation or denying them accreditation "was a mistake—it didn't encourage them to find solutions."[3] In 1996, the commission came out with its "sentinel event" policy. Slightly revised from its original formulation, the commission's definition of a sentinel event is:

> an unexpected occurrence involving death or serious physical or psychological injury, or the risk thereof. Serious injury specifically includes loss of limb or function. The phrase "or the risk thereof" includes any process variation for which a recurrence would carry a significant chance of a serious adverse outcome. (Joint Commission on Accreditation of Healthcare Organizations, 1999b)

In addition to the wider definition, the commission specifies the following subset as falling within their sentinel event policy: suicide of a patient in a setting where the patient receives around-the-clock care; infant abduction or discharge to the wrong family; rape; hemolytic transfusion reaction involving administration of blood or blood products having major blood group incompatibilities; or surgery on the wrong patient or wrong body part. Any time a sentinel event occurs, the organization is expected to complete a "root cause analysis" (RCA), "to dig down to underlying organization systems and processes that can be altered to reduce likelihood of human fallibility in the future" (Joint Commission on Accreditation of Healthcare Organizations, 1999c).

> The event may have several direct causes (e.g., mistranscribed order, failure to check patient's ID band, etc.) However, these direct causes are merely symptoms of larger problems that "allowed" the direct causes to happen. . . . Root cause analysis is any methodology that identifies the foundation cause (s) that, if corrected, would prevent recurrence of the same or similar incident. Root cause analysis is not an exact science and therefore requires a certain amount of judgment. The Joint Commission has developed a root cause analysis model and in private industry there are several models.[4]

In 1997, the American Medical Association (AMA), apparently sensing a trend, reversed itself and set up a National Patient Safety Foundation; its fifty-person board of directors included two consumer-group representatives. Executive Director Martin Hatlie, addressing a session of the International Congress on Performance Measurement in 1997, proclaimed that the foundation's goal was to turn around "the culture of blame," to learn from such sectors as the airlines and nuclear power plants, and to model itself on entities such as the National Transportation Board. Physicians and nurses working double shifts and the storing of two drugs on the same shelf were "accidents waiting to happen," Hatlie said. Urging attention to common system failures, he cited findings that errors resulting in preventable adverse drug events occurred most often at the stages of ordering and administration and could be circumvented through computerized detection programs and a computerized information system led by a dedicated person or group (Bates et al. 1997).

Sentinel event reporting and root cause analysis illustrate once more the commission's vulnerability to pressure from state hospital associations on its industry-dominated board. Since first introducing the program, there has been considerable parsing of words and some back-tracking. Initially, reporting a sentinel event within 30 days of its occurrence was mandatory. By 1999, organizations were "encouraged but not required" to report the event. However, if the commission becomes aware of a sentinel event through communication from a patient, family member, employee of the organization, or the media, the hospital must prepare a root cause analysis and action plan and submit it within 45 days. Failure to do so in a manner acceptable to the commission puts the hospital at risk for being placed on Accreditation Watch, "a publicly disclosable" classification that signifies the "organization is under close monitoring by the Joint Commission" (Joint Commission on Accreditation of Healthcare Organizations 1999c). Initially also, the commission was to conduct on-site reviews in immediate response to learning about a sentinel event. Now, a "for cause" survey is conducted at the rate of $3,500 a day "if the commission determines that there is a potential ongoing threat to patient health or safety or potentially significant non-compliance with major Joint Commission standards" (ibid.). The latter wording is particularly important since beginning in 1999 standards relating to sentinel events were added to the Leadership and Improving Organization Performance chapters of the accreditation manual. The responsibility of hospital leaders to see that a process is established for the identification, reporting, analysis, and prevention of sentinel events is now specifically spelled out.

Hospitals continue to raise the issues of confidentiality and liability. A task force of lawyers from the AMA, the AHA, and other organizations such as the American Society of Health Risk Managers has been set up to develop legislative and regulatory remedies and to work with the states, where the law varies greatly. In the meantime, unease persists. QA / I professionals discuss not only the issues noted above but peer protection, public release of information, and the fine distinctions drawn in defining a sentinel event. For its part, the commission has set up a Sentinel Event Hotline, to answer questions, provide consultation, and review the hospital's root cause analysis. The commission assures hospitals that talking to hotline representatives is not reporting a sentinel event. Nevertheless, residual anxiety regarding Joint Commission surveys persists, calling to mind the hackneyed but reasonable suspicion, "Just because I'm paranoid doesn't mean that people aren't out to get me."

If the issue of error prevention becomes one more exercise in finding the easiest way to conform selectively to regulations, along the lines of the ORYX initiative discussed in Chapter Three, it will be a sad day for the drive to improve quality. And it could well happen. One need only look at the range of regulations QA/I professionals are dealing with to see how dispersed their attention is and how quickly root cause analysis will be viewed as one more "hot issue" for surveyors to search out. As one QA/I professional told me:

> I think people will see that root cause analysis absolutely is wonderful. I mean it's great that there is this awareness, but when the Joint Commission says, "You have to do it in x amount of time or we're going to do this and that to you" . . . they're now in a position where they feel they have to be an additional watch dog. If you have a bad incident, it's not enough for you to have a terrible event, be dealing with your lawyers and the local newspapers and everything else, they're adding to it by saying "and now you have to do an analysis for us within a time frame."

This is bound to lead to the defensive stance described in Chapter Five, reinforcing the tendency to direct energy toward protecting the institution and/or protecting oneself—to the detriment of the recommendations on patient safety and error reduction. The usual response to errors, to assume negligence and blame someone, has traditionally led to discipline and retraining. Hospitals really do not know how bad their error problem is because personnel have a strong incentive to underreport errors (Leape 1997, 3). The airline and space industry offers some useful experience in such situations. Both the Federal Aviation Administration (FAA) and the National Aeronautics and Space Administration (NASA) remove names from reports of near misses so that workers will feel protected from punishment.

Complicated illness trajectories are error-prone because so much work has to be coordinated. When they "go wrong," it would be instructive to apply a root cause analysis that breaks down the sources of disruption and examines the lack of articulation. This would do much to promote "coordination of care," for which personnel constantly strive but know they rarely attain (Strauss et al. 1997, 151–90). Health care professionals are not used to thinking of what they do as "work," or of breaking their work down into tasks, but much can be learned from those who have looked at safety in other settings.

The analysis of the Challenger disaster, for example, applies to the hospital. The explosion happened because people at NASA did exactly what they were supposed to do and a series of seemingly harmless decisions were made that incrementally moved the space agency toward a catastrophic outcome (Vaughan 1997). Applying to medicine the principle that it is the process, not the individuals in it, that requires closer examination, a physician affirms that "the real problem isn't how to stop bad doctors from harming, even killing, their patients. It's how to prevent good doctors from doing so" (Gawande 1999, 40). He cites the ground-breaking work of a small contingent of risk theorists (Pierce and Cooper 1984; Pierce 1998; Ellison and Pierce 1998) who were able to bring about significant changes in anesthesiology:

> Hours for anesthesiology residents were shortened. Manufacturers began redesigning their machines with fallible human beings in mind. Dials were standardized to turn in a uniform direction; locks were put in to prevent accidental administration of more than one anesthetic gas; controls were changed so that oxygen delivery could not be turned down to zero. (Gawande 1999, 53)

Root cause analysis, done without outside pressure, might reveal instances of "risk homeostasis," the idea that a reduction of risk in one area *sometimes* triggers a compensatory (and in some cases greater) increase in risky behavior in another (Evans 1991; Wilde 1994). Some examples are better brakes, which induce faster and less careful driving, and marked crosswalks, which make pedestrians less mindful than at unmarked crossings—suggest that applying this theory to patient care could provide useful insights.

Error theory has been applied productively to health care (Spath 2000). Moreover, there is considerable evidence that paying attention to risk issues and their origin within the organization leads to improved patient care (Weinberg and Stason 1998; Pronovost et al. 1999). In other words, what is needed is not more regulation but leadership from all of the hospital professions—medicine, nursing, administration, quality improvement, pharmacy.

> It is apparent that the most fundamental change that will be needed if hospitals are to make meaningful progress in error reduction is a cultural one. Physicians and nurses need to accept the notion that error is an inevitable accompaniment of the human condition, even among conscientious professionals with high standards. Errors must be accepted as evidence of systems

flaws not character flaws. Until and unless that happens, it is unlikely that any substantial progress will be made in reducing medical errors. (Leape 1994, 1857)

SUMMARY AND CONCLUSION

This book began with the question, Is the accountability enterprise directed toward making hospitals better or toward making them only look better? In 1998, when I gave a presentation before the QA/I professional group sketching the outline of this book, there was general consensus (or perhaps polite acceptance!) concerning my talk. One QA/I analyst in the group came up to me afterward, however, and said: "You can't take away their hope." Thus, the following must be said. I have found the people involved in improving the quality of patient care to be intelligent, highly motivated, well-intentioned, and sincere in their hope that improvement is possible. Despite the weaknesses discussed in this chapter—or for that matter the barriers and assumptions discussed in Chapter Four—these people represent the strength of the accountability movement. They exhibit integrity, the desire to do a good job and to fulfill their professional commitment. Paper exercises do not make them feel valued or valuable. For their work to have meaning, they need to feel satisfaction in what they are doing and comfortable with the conditions under which they are working. Upon his inauguration as Chancellor of the University of California San Francisco (UCSF), Michael Bishop vowed to do his best to make UCSF a place where people of all assignments believe that whatever they are doing is serving a higher purpose and is appreciated. He also vowed to change the ambiance of the work place to one that nourishes souls rather than assaults them. Such words resound especially throughout the health care arena, where service and healing are the underpinnings of that nourishing. That is the spirit in which this book was written.

Nurses are repeatedly told, "If it isn't documented, it isn't done." The need for documentation is obvious—for continuity of care, for communication among the many team players, and for legal protection. The flip side of this directive is to assume that something is done, or done well, because compliance with a regulation is documented in the chart.

Certainly, in the past, neither the medical profession nor hospitals have done a good job of policing themselves either in terms of quality of care or fiscal responsibility. Certainly also, there must be standards and accreditation. Who would want to go to a hospital that is not accredited? But to pile one regulation upon another and to mix the most important with the less important is to insure a distortion of the intent of these standards, out of their sheer weight. Furthermore, all too much legislation is for political, not clinical, reasons. In the words of a quality analyst interviewed in my research: "People who think up the rules in Congress have no clinical experience. They are replying to their constituents and so we get stuck with a certain rule because of some guy's mother's pacemaker." Surely there is a way to write regulations to allow for the kind of flexibility required by the conditions outlined in this book so that staff will want to comply out of good sense rather than out of fear of censure.

As to the information revolution stemming from electronic capability, computers do have myriad applications that promise greater efficiency and the ability to measure more and do it more quickly. But what good is that if a hospital is not investigating what kind of data it needs to enlighten its course—or to reduce errors—but rather is dancing as fast as it can to provide the data that managed care organizations and surveillance agencies insist upon. Hospitals are collecting so much data that there is seldom time or opportunity for it to be pulled together to be used to improve the overall institution. Worse still, the need to keep up with the demand creates a climate for fudging, or for settling for a 1 percent reduction in pneumonia admissions as at least something to show the surveyors.

Unquestionably, computerization—access to a reference source like Medline and the development of software that the physician can use to find relevant research findings in the published literature—can be an aid in the practice of "evidence-based medicine." This term has been defined as "integrating individual clinical expertise with the best available external clinical evidence from systematic research"—in other words, what we all would like to assume our doctors were doing even before this term became trendy. If, as proponents hope, evidence-based medicine can supplant medical myth—in pain management, for example (Carr 1996; Rosenberg and Donald 1995; Bauchner 1998)—more to the good. If a practice guideline is integrated with individual clinical expertise to decide whether and how it matches the patient's clinical state, predicament, and preferences (Sackett et al. 1996), few would quarrel with its use. But if, as some fear, managed care organizations apply practice guidelines rigidly to determine if a doctor's actions are worth paying for (Grahame-Smith 1995), then good intentions will have been subverted. Furthermore, from a physician who feels evidentiary medicine lacks humility, these words:

> There has always been a balanced tension between the science and the art of medicine. We currently threaten that balance by failing to understand the limitations of the science and the power of the art. To those physicians who write clinical guidelines, quote consensus panels, or produce clinician report cards, I recommend spending a little more time in the rich yet humble world of patient care. You cannot be a good physician if you ignore science, but you also cannot be a good physician if you believe in it too much. (Fischer 1999, 345–46)

Finally, a better-informed patient is a better patient. And a better-informed press is a better press. But, some information—for instance, the type of information that appears in report cards on hospitals—may not be useful and, in fact, may do harm to the extent that it does not capture the complexity of risk-adjustment and case mix. Report cards misrepresent what is being done by putting the emphasis on one place to the detriment of whatever else the hospital is doing and they push the system more in terms of actuarial insurance rather than social insurance (Fuchs 1997). Hospital marketing departments often throw figures into briefing sheets and give them to journalists who accept them without question. Disseminating such information does more harm than good.

Hospitals can learn a useful lesson from the *accountability excess* that has besieged the field of education. In 1997, to great fanfare, Governor Wilson of California signed the Statewide Testing and Reporting Program (under the suggestive acronym STAR), funded at $35.4 million. The governor pledged that "we must assure that every school meets the basic test of accountability" (Rojas 1997, A23). Within a few months, teachers at a San Francisco high school were protesting that they were being told to increase the number of As, Bs, and Cs by five percent, because, as one said, "I think the principal is under a lot of pressure to make our school look good." The report continued:

> Pressure to produce attractive "academic indicators" is especially intense in San Francisco. Schools are expected to improve each year according to a variety of measures that include test scores, dropout rates—and eligibility to attend UC (University of California) Berkeley. Those numbers are touted in an annual press conference and posted on the district's web site. (Asimov, 1998, A15)

By 1999, the comment of the director of research and evaluation for Oakland schools spoke volumes: "Everybody is very much aware that the state has upped the ante on accountability. It has become a high-stakes game" (Schevitz and Fernandez 1999). High-stakes is an understatement, with reports of months and tens to hundreds of thousands of dollars being spent to prepare students for the state-approved six-hour tests, to hold teachers and principals responsible for student achievement, and to tie funding to student improvement. Now a national phenomenon, motivating students for state-mandated tests reportedly includes rap songs, banners, and pep rallies, and preparations include feeding them sugary foods and nutrition-supplemented doughnuts on test days. With what results? A boom in the already booming private tutoring centers that teach students how to take tests, and the indictment of a top administrator in Austin, Texas, for altering records to exclude the scores of some low-performing students—no doubt the tip of the accountability iceberg. For now, the voices asking, "Is this *education*?" seem to be in the minority.

We are entering another period where all aspects of health care must be re-examined. Our usual approach—a remedy here, a band-aid there—means that as we direct attention to one problem we ignore another. Attention shifts to a Clinton proposal for a prescription drug benefit for seniors but a looming crisis in skilled-nursing facilities gets little attention. Under the 1997 Balanced Budget Act, such institutions, like hospitals before them, are no longer cost-based but receive per diem payments for Medicare patients. Within a year, a disturbing trend had becoming apparent: More and more skilled nursing facilities were refusing to admit high-cost patients (those who depend on ventilators or need intravenous drug therapy, kidney dialysis, or tracheotomy care). With nowhere else to go, these patients are staying in the hospital longer (McGinley 1999), placing yet another burden on the reduced staff of institutions already deeply involved in cost-cutting.

Surely courageous political leaders and policy analysts could find a way to present the full-health care picture for public examination. Ideally, such a examination should point out the eclipsing of public good by private gain and ask just how much the public is willing to assume through taxation some of the costs of health care. It should also present the reasons good care comes at such a high price, and should ask what we expect of Medicare and Medicaid. Other topics for discussion include the growing ranks of the uninsured, long-term and assisted home care, the problems and prospects of managed care, the bioethical considerations of prolonging life, if and how we want to finance medical education, and—most urgent—the high rate of medical accidents and error.

And, of course, this examination must also include the accountability endeavor—its underlying assumptions, the barriers to its implementation, and the weaknesses in its structure. Its inclusion is crucial because it is an invisible cost in an arena that is trying both to save money and seek quality. What are the benefits and costs of accountability? Do its accomplishments outweigh its weaknesses? Are we measuring what is important or only making important what we can measure? And ultimately, *Are we, at long last, ready to examine the value of a universal health insurance plan run by the federal government?*[5]

To be effective, such a public discourse would have to start with the lesson learned from President Clinton's aborted attempt at health reform. Nothing will be achieved without first taking into consideration the vested interests that will oppose any reform that does not benefit them, specifically the agencies (public and private) that rely on health care as a business, including the "ever expanding economic frontier for a huge and far-flung consulting industry that stands ready to accommodate ever more complicated arrangements" (Reinhardt 1998, 393).

Such an examination must also take into consideration America's conflicting values and governmental structure, subjects that have run like a leitmotif throughout this book as well as the insistence by Americans that public laws or private contracts be customized to their own individual circumstances. The examination must start with the premise that everything that counts is not necessarily countable, that there are intangibles that do not lend themselves to algorithms. Along with their treatment, patients need reassurance that their fate is in the hands of caregivers who are sensitive to their fears and responsive to what they are going through. They need the kind of attention that does not come from courses in communication as much as from a structure that supports the notion that time listening to and observing patients is time well spent—a notion that does not jibe with a business mentality.

The goal of this examination of the entire context of health care should be: (1) to serve patients by reordering priorities that tend to become skewed over time so that (2) health care can be provided by skilled professionals who feel satisfaction in their work and (3) are thereby motivated to treat patients with compassion, promptness, and effectiveness. If this sounds like a mission statement, so be it.

A comment made by a philosophy professor[6] during my undergraduate days has remained with me throughout my research in the health field. He described starting his studies as a medical student and earning extra income by assisting on autopsies. He recalled the day when he realized that, given the complexity of the human body, it is hardly surprising that a part or parts break down. Rather, he concluded, the miracle is that human physiology works at all. To some extent, the same can be said of health care. Given all the potential sources of breakdown in the interlocking systems, it is wondrous that the body of health care works at all. What is clear, however, is that it could work much better. While there are no quick-and-easy answers, it is possible for policy analysts, supported by political resolution and leadership, to prescribe the appropriate treatment for the symptoms outlined in this book.

NOTES

1. Jonathan Showstack on "Forum," National Public Radio, May 26, 1999.
2. With gratitude to Shizuko Fagerhaugh, who has brought her own unique nursing/sociological perspective to some of the issues discussed in this book and has been a trustworthy sounding board as I struggled with the emerging issues.
3. Richard Croteau, Vice President for Accreditation Operations, Joint Commission on Accreditation of Health Care Organizations, addressing the International Congress on Performance Measurement & Improvement in

Health Care, Chicago, November 12–15, 1997, session on "Errors in Health Care: Epidemiology, Taxonomy, and Root Cause."

4. P. Spath, May 24, 1998. This is taken from the online network for QA / I professionals. Spath has also written an article that is available through her website entitled "How to Conduct a Thorough Sentinel Event Investigation," in which she recommends that the inquiry answer questions regarding "what," "when," "where," "who," and "how." *See also* Spath (1998).

5. For a succinct and judicious discussion of this subject, see Light (1999).

6. Jacob Needleman, Professor of Philosophy, San Francisco State University. His numerous publications include *A Sense of the Cosmos: The Encounter of Modern Science and Ancient Truth* (New York: Doubleday, 1975); *The New Religions* (New York: Crossroad Publications, 1984); and *The Way of the Physician* (New York: Viking Penguin, 1993).

Glossary of Acronyms

AARP	American Association of Retired Persons
ACE	Angiotensin-Converting Enzyme
ACS	American College of Surgeons
AD	Academic Detailing
ADE	Adverse Drug Event
AHA	American Hospital Association
AHCPR	Agency for Health Care Policy and Research
AHRQ	Agency for Healthcare Research and Quality
AIDS	Acquired Immunodeficiency Syndrome
AMA	American Medical Association
AMAP	American Medical Accreditation Program
AMI	Acute Myocardial Infarction
ANA	American Nurses Association
CalPERS	California Public Employees Retirement System
CALS	California Accreditation and Licensure Survey
CCP	Cardiovascular Cooperative Project
CDACS	Clinical Data Abstraction Centers
CEO	Chief Executive Officer
CHA	California Healthcare Association
CHF	Congestive Heart Failure
CMRI	California Medical Review Incorporated
CMRR	Closed Medical Record Review
CNA	California Nurses Association
CON	Certificate of Need
COPD	Chronic Obstructive Pulmonary Disease
CPMC	California Pacific Medical Center
CPR	Computer-Based Patient Record
CQI	Continuous Quality Improvement
CT	Computed Tomography
DHHS	Department of Health and Human Services
DHS	Department of Health Services (California)
DNA	Deoxyribonucleic Acid
DRGs	Diagnosis Related Groups

EPR	Electronic Patient Record
ER	Emergency Room
FAA	Federal Aviation Administration
FACCT	Foundation for Accountability
GAO	Government Accounting Office
HCFA	Health Care Financing Administration
HCQII	Health Care Quality Improvement Initiative
HCQIP	Health Care Quality Improvement Program
HEDIS	Health Plan Employer Data and Information Set
HMO	Health Maintenance Organization
HRG	Health Research Group (of Public Citizen)
HSA	Health Systems Agency
ICU	Intensive Care Unit
IDS	Integrated Delivery System
IMSystem	Information Management System
IOM	Institute of Medicine
ISO	International Organization for Standardization
ISQua	International Society for Quality in Health Care
JCAHO	Joint Commission on Accreditation of Health Care Organizations
LPN	Licensed Practical Nurse
LVN	Licensed Vocational Nurse
M & A	Merger and Acquisition
M & M	Morbidity and Mortality
MBA	Masters in Business Administration
MCO	Managed Care Organization
MQIS	Medicare Quality Indicator System
NASA	National Aeronautics and Space Administration
NASS	North American Spine Society
NCH	National Claims History
NCHCT	National Center for Health Care Technology
NCI	National Cancer Institute
NCQA	National Committee for Quality Assurance
NIH	National Institutes of Health
NIST	National Institute of Standards and Technology
OIG	Office of Inspector General
OR	Operating Room
OTA	Office of Technology Assessment
P&P	Policy and Procedures
PCAC	Patient Care Assessment Council
PEP	Performance Evaluation Procedure for Auditing and Improving Patient Care
POS	Point of Service (Health Plan)

PPO	Preferred Provider Organization
PRO	Utilization and Quality Control Peer Review Organization
PSRO	Professional Standards Review Organization
QA/I	Quality Assessment/Improvement
QIO	Quality Improvement Organization
RCA	Root Cause Analysis
RN	Registered Nurse
SMH-LJ	Scripps Memorial Hospital-La Jolla
TEFRA	Tax Equity and Fiscal Responsibility Act
TQM	Total Quality Management
UCDS	Uniform Clinical Data Set
UCSF	University of California San Francisco
VRE	Vancomycin Resistant Enterococcus

REFERENCES

Abate, T. (1999). "This Week in Northern California," KQED-TV, February 12.
———. (1999). "Seniors scramble for health care," *San Francisco Chronicle* January 26, D1.
———. (1999). "Doctors' group in fee fight with Aetna," *San Francisco Chronicle* January 12, C1.
———. (1999a). "St. Luke's praying for victory," *San Francisco Chronicle* February 3, D1.
Abel-Smith, B. (1960). *A History of the Nursing Profession.* New York: W. Heineman.
Advisory Publications. Undated Letter sent with the sample issue of *Capitation Abstracts and Analysis.*
Agency for Health Care Policy and Research. (1995). *Using Clinical Practice Guidelines to Evaluate Quality of Care, Volumes I and II.* Washington, DC: U.S. Department of Health and Human Services.
Alford, R. (1975). *Health Care Politics: Ideological and Interest Group Barriers to Reform.* Chicago: University of Chicago Press.
All Patient Refined Diagnosis Related Groups. Definition Manual. (1993). Wallingford, CT: 3M Health Information Systems.
"All Things Considered," National Public Radio, December 30, 1996.
Allen, T., Brady, J., and Vonfrolio, L. (1995). *25 Stupid Things Nurses Do To Self Destruct.* New York: Power Publications.
Allison, M., and Toy, P. (1996). "Quality improvement team on autologous and directed-donor blood availability," *Joint Commission Journal on Quality Improvement, 22,* 801–10.
"AMAP, JCAHO, NCQA announce plans to merge performance measure development efforts," press release, January 26, 1999.
American Health Consultants. (1994). *Hospital Outcomes Management, 1* (August), 17.
American Health Information Management Association. (1993). "Position Statement. Issue: Roles of health information managers and coders in patient-focused care," *Journal of Ahima, 64,* suppl, 2.
American Hospital Association. (1994). "AHA calls for sweeping changes at JCAHO." Statement of the AHA Board of Trustees, December 8.
American Medical Association. (1994). "Resolution 816 of the AMA House of Delegates," December.
American Nurses Association. (1995). *Nursing Care Report Card for Acute Care.* Publication #NP-101, Washington, D.C.
American Nurses Association Press Release. (1995). "Nursing makes the grade in report cards," February 28.

American Nurses Association. (1994). "Survey finds loss of RNs jeopardizes patient safety," *The American Nurse, 27* (January/February), 1.

Anders, G. (1996). "Polling quirks give HMOs health ratings," *Wall Street Journal* (August 27), B1.

Anderson, C. (1994). "Measuring what works in health care," *Science, 263,* 1080–82.

Andrews, L., Stocking, C., Krizek, T., Gottlieb, L., Krizek, C. Vargish, T., and Siegler, M. (1997). "An alternative strategy for studying adverse events in medical care," *Lancet, 349,* 309–13.

Angell, M. (1996). Shattuck Lecture: "Evaluating the health risks of breast implants: The interplay of medical science, the law, and public opinion," *New England Journal of Medicine, 334,* 1513–18.

Angell, M., and Kassirer, J. (1996). "Quality and the medical marketplace—following the elephants," *New England Journal of Medicine, 335,* 883–85.

Annas, G. (1997). "Patients' rights in managed care—exit, voice, and choice," *New England Journal of Medicine, 337,* 210–15.

Anspach, R. (1993). *Deciding Who Lives: Fateful Choices in the Intensive-Care Nursery.* Berkeley, CA: University of California Press.

Arndt, M., and Bigelow, B. (1995). "The implementation of total quality management in hospitals: How good is the fit?" *Health Care Management Review, 20,* 7–14.

———. "Reengineering: Deja vu all over again," *Health Care Management Review, 23,* 58–66.

Aronovitz, L. (1997). "Medicare: Control Over Fraud and Abuse Remains Elusive," (Washington: Government Printing Office, June 26), GAO/T-HEHS-97-165.

Ashley, J. (1976). *Hospitals, Paternalism, and the Role of the Nurse.* New York: Teachers College Press.

Asimov, N. (1998). "Teachers told to pump up grades," *San Francisco Chronicle* (April 4), A1.

Baltalden, P., and Buchanan, E. (1989). "Industrial models of quality improvement." In N. Goldfield and D. Nash (eds.), *Providing Quality Care* (Philadelphia: American College of Physicians), 133–59.

Baltalden, P., and Stolz, P. (1993). "A framework for the continual improvement of health care: Building and applying professional and improvement knowledge to test changes in daily work," *Joint Commission Journal on Quality Improvement, 19,* 424–52.

Barnum, A. (1994). "Big firms flex health muscle," *San Francisco Chronicle* (June 21), D1.

Barron, H., Michaels, A., Maynard, C., and Every, N. (1998). "Use of Angiotensin-Converting Enzyme Inhibitors at discharge in patients with acute myocardial infarction in the United States: Data from the National Registry of Myocardial Infarction 2," *Journal of the American College of Cardiology, 32,* 360–67.

Bates, D., Cullen, D., Laird, N., Petersen, L., Small, S., Servi, M., Laffel, G., Sweitzer, B., Shea, B., Hallisey, M., Vander Vliet, M., Nemeskai, R., and Leape, L. (1995). "Incidence of adverse drug events and potential adverse drug events: Implications for prevention," *Journal of the American Medical Association, 274,* 19–34.

Bauchner, H. (1998). "Evidence-based medicine: A new science or an epidemiologic fad?" *Pediatrics, 103,* 1029–31.

Baumgartner, F., and Talbert, J. (1995). "From setting a national agenda on health care to making decisions in congress." *Journal of Health Politics, Policy and Law,* 20, 437–45.

Beatrice, D., Thomas, C. P., and Biles, Brian (1998). "Grant making with an impact: The Picker/Commonwealth Patient-Centered Care program," *Health Affairs,* 17, 236–44.

Belkin, L. (1996) "But what about quality?" *New York Times Magazine* (December 8), 68–71, 101–6.

Bendix, R. (1956) *Work and Authority in Industry: Ideology and Management in the Course of Industrialization.* New York: Wiley.

Benjamin, A. (1996). "Trends among younger persons with disability or chronic disease." In R. Binstock, L. Cluff, and O. Von Mering (eds.), *The Future of Long-Term Care: Social and Policy Issues* (Baltimore: Johns Hopkins University Press), 75–95.

Berger, P., and Luckmann, T. (1968). *The Social Construction of Reality.* New York: Doubleday Anchor.

Berwick, D. (1996). "Payment by capitation and the quality of care," *New England Journal of Medicine, 335,* 1227–31.

———. (1994). "Managing Quality: The Next Five Years." *Quality Letter for Healthcare Leaders, 6* (July–August), 1–7.

———. (1989)."Continuous improvement as an ideal in health care," *New England Journal of Medicine, 320,* 53–56.

Berwick, D., Godfrey, A., and Roessner, J. (1990). *Curing Health Care: New Strategies for Quality Improvement.* San Francisco: Jossey Bass.

Berwick, D., and Wald, D. (1990). "Hospital leaders' opinions of the HCFA mortality data," *Journal of the American Medical Association, 263,* 247–49.

Berwind, A. (1975). "The nurse in the coronary care unit." In B. Bullough (ed.), *The Law and the Expanding Nursing Role* (New York: Appleton-Century-Crofts), 82–94.

Bigelow, B., and Arndt, M. (1995). "Total quality management: Field of dreams," *Health Care Management Review, 20,* 15–25.

Blackwood, F. (1994). "Business gives high marks to health care 'report card,'" *San Francisco Business Times* (April 8–14), 6A–7A.

Blumenthal, D. (1996). "Quality of care—what is it?" *New England Journal of Medicine, 335,* 891–93.

———. (1996). "The origins of the quality-of-care debate," *New England Journal of Medicine, 335,* 1146–47.

———. (1994). "The variation phenomenon," *New England Journal of Medicine, 331,* 1017–18.

Blumenthal, D., and Epstein, A. (1996). "The role of physicians in the future of quality management," *New England Journal of Medicine, 335,* 1328–31.

Blumenthal, D., and Scheck, A., eds. (1995). *Improving Clinical Practice: Total Quality Management and the Physician.* San Francisco: Jossey-Bass.

Bohm, D. (1987). *Science, Order, and Creativity.* New York: Bantam.

Bosk, C. (1979). *Forgive and Remember: Managing Medical Failure.* Chicago: University of Chicago Press.

Bradley, B. (1995). Speech before the Commonwealth Club. San Francisco, California, March 10.

Brannon, R. (1994). *Intensifying Care: The Hospital Industry, Professionalization, and the Reorganization of the Nursing Labor Process.* New York: Baywood.

Brennan, T., Leape, L., Laird, N., Hebert, L., Localio, A., Lawthers, A., Newhouse, J., Wieler, P., and Hiatt, H. (1991). "Incidence of adverse events and negligence in hospitalized patients; Results of the Harvard Medical Practice Study I," *New England Journal of Medicine, 324,* 370–76.

Brook, R. (1997). "Managed care is not the problem, quality is," *Journal of the American Medical Association, 278,* 1612–14.

———. (1989). "Practice guidelines and practicing medicine." *Journal of the American Medical Association, 262,* 3027–30.

———. (1979). "Studies of process outcome correlations in medical care evaluation," *Medical Care, 17,* 869–73.

Brook, R., Davies-Avery, A., Greenfield, S., Harris, L., Lelah, T., Solomon, N., and Ware, J. (1977). "Assessing the quality of medical care using outcome measures: An overview of the method," *Medical Care, 15,* Suppl.

Brook, R., McGlynn. E., and Cleary, P. (1996). "Measuring quality of care," *New England Journal of Medicine, 335,* 966–70.

Brown, E. (1948). *Nursing for the Future: A Report Prepared for the National Nursing Council.* New York: Russell Sage Foundation.

Brown, M. (1995). "From the editor," *Health Care Management Review, 20,* 5.

Brown, R. (1979). *Rockefeller Medicine Men: Medicine and Capitalism in America.* Berkeley: University of California Press.

Buraway, M. (1991). "Introduction." In M. Buraway, A. Burton, A. Ferguson, K. Fox, J. Gamson, N. Gartrell, L. Hurst, C. Kurzman, L. Salzinger, J. Schiffman, and U. Shiori, *Ethnography Unbound* (Berkeley, CA: University of California Press), 1–7.

Burda, D. (1996). "JCAHO hit with 5 years' back taxes," *Modern Healthcare, 26,* 46.

———. (1995). "Joint Commission board ends ties with Margaret O'Leary," *Modern Healthcare, 25,* 13.

———. (1995). "Financial reasons lead quest for JCAHO approval," *Modern Healthcare, 25,* 28.

———. (1994). "JCAHO hits a wall with plan on indicators," *Modern Healthcare, 24* (March 14), 30–33, 36, 38–40.

———. (1994). "JCAHO still pulling in big profits," *Modern Healthcare, 24,* 18.

———. (1991). "Total quality management becomes big business," *Modern Healthcare, 21* (January 28), 25–29.

Burda, D., and Morrissey, J. (1994). "JCAHO hit with reform edicts," *Modern Healthcare, 24,* 2–3.

Burton, T. (1998). "Self-examination. An HMO checks up on its doctors' care and is disturbed itself," *Wall Street Journal* (July 8), A1.

Califano, J. (1986). *America's Healthcare Revolution: Who Lives? Who Dies? Who Pays?* New York: Random House.

California Work and Health Survey. (1999). San Francisco, CA: The California Wellness Foundation.

Campbell, J. (1999). Health Insurance Coverage: 1998. Washington, DC: Economics and Statistics Association, Bureau of the Census.

Caper, P. (1988). Letter to the editor. *New England Journal of Medicine, 319,* 800–1.

————. (1988). "Solving the medical care dilemma," *New England Journal of Medicine, 318,* 1535–36.

Carr, D. (1996). "Pain therapy," *Current Opinion in Anaesthesiology, 9,* 415–20.

Carr, D., and Johansson, H. (1995). *Best Practices in Reengineering.* New York: McGraw Hill.

Carr, E. (1964). *What Is History?* New York: Alfred Knopf.

Carr, M., and Jackson, F. (1997). *The Crosswalk: Joint Commission Standards and Baldrige Criteria.* Oakbrook Terrace, IL: Joint Commission on Accreditation of Hospitals.

Carr-Hill, R. (1995). "Welcome? To the brave new world of evidence based medicine," *Social Science and Medicine, 41,* 1467–68.

Cesarone, D. (1997). *Assess for Success: Achieving Excellence with Joint Commission Standards and Baldrige Criteria.* Oakbrook Terrace, IL: Joint Commission on Accreditation of Hospitals.

Champy, J. (1995). *Reengineering Management.* New York: Harper Business.

Chandler, A. (1980). *The Visible Hand: The Managerial Revolution in American Business.* Cambridge, MA: Belknap.

Chassin, M. (1996). "Improving the quality of care," *New England Journal of Medicine, 335,* 1060–63.

Chassin, M., Park, R., Lohr, K., Keesey, J., and Brook, R. (1989). "Differences among hospitals in Medicare patient mortality," *Health Services Research, 24,* 1–2.

Cherry, J., Carmichael, D., Shean, F. (1988). "Inaccurate data in 'solving the medical care dilemma,'" *New England Journal of Medicine, 319,* 800.

"Cincinnatus." (1981). *Self-Destruction: The disintegration of the United States Army During the Vietnam Era.* New York: Norton.

Clark, J. (1990). "Variation in Michigan hospital use rates: Do physician and hospital characteristics provide the explanation?" *Social Science and Medicine, 30,* 67–82.

Cleary, P. and Edgman-Levitan, S. (1997). "Health care quality: Incorporating consumer perspectives." *Journal of the American Medical Association, 278,* 1608–12.

Cleary, P., Edgman-Levitan, S., Walker, J., Gerteis, M., and Delbanco, T. (1993). "Using patient reports to improve medical care: A preliminary report from ten hospitals." *Quality Management in Health Care, 2,* 31–38.

Cleary, P., Edgman-Levitan, S., Robert, M., Moloney, T., McMullen, W., Walker, J., and Delbanco, T. (1991). "Patients evaluate their hospital care: a national survey," *Health Affairs, 10,* 254–67.

Cleary, P., Fahs, M., McMullen, W., Fulop, G., Strain, J., Sacks, H., Muller, C., Foley, M., and Stein, E. (1992). "Using patient reports to assess hospital treatment of persons with AIDS: A pilot study," *AIDS Care, 4,* 325–32.

Cleary, P. and McNeil, B. (1988). "Patient satisfaction as an indicator of quality of care," *Inquiry, 25,* 25–36.

Clymer, A., Pear, R., and Toner, R. (1994). "For health care, time was a killer." *The New York Times* (August 29), A1.

Coburn, R., and Harper, D. (1983). "Case-mix index: An alternative to cost-based hospital reimbursement," *Healthcare Financial Management, 37,* 40–44.

Cochrane, A. (1972). *Effectiveness and Efficiency: Random Reflections on Health Services.* London: Nuffield Provincial Hospitals Trust.

Codman, E. A. (1918). *A Study in Hospital Efficiency: As Demonstrated by the Case Report of the First Five Years of a Private Hospital*. Boston: Thomas Dodd.

———. (1915). *A Study in Hospital Efficiency: As Demonstrated by the Case Report of the Second Two Years of Private Hospital*. Boston: Thomas Dodd.

Collopy, B. (1993). "Do doctors need Deming?" *Quality Assurance in Health Care, 5,* 3–5.

"Columbia hospital chain posts $364 million profit," *San Francisco Chronicle* (August 8, 1996), D4.

Comarow, A. (1997). "Inside the rankings," *U.S. News and World Report* (July 28), 74.

———. (1998). "In search of the best: The rankings explained." *U.S. News and World Report* (July 27), 65.

Committee on the Function of Nursing (1948). Program for the Nursing Profession. New York: Macmillan.

Connors, A., Speroff, T., Dawson, N., Thomas, C., Harrell, F., Wagner, D., Desbiens, N., Goldman, L., Wu, A., Califf, R., Fulkerson, W., Vidaillet, H., Broste, S., Bellamy, P., Lynn, J., and Knaus, W. (1996). "The effectiveness of right heart catheterization in the initial care of critically ill patients." *Journal of the American Medical Association, 276,* 880–97.

Corbin, J., and Strauss, A. (1996). "Analytic ordering for theoretical purposes," *Qualitative Inquiry, 2,* 139–50.

———. (1988). *Unending Work: Managing Chronic Illness at Home*. San Francisco: Jossey Bass.

Court, J. (1999) "End rule by HMO empires," *San Francisco Chronicle* (January 4), A21.

Creps, L., Coffey, R., Warner, P., and McClatchey, K. (1992). "Integrating total quality management and quality assurance at the University of Michigan Medical Center," *Quality Review Bulletin, 18,* 250–58.

Crick, F. (1988). *What Mad Pursuit: A Personal View of Scientific Discovery*. New York: Basic Books.

Crosby, P. (1979). *Quality Is Free: The Art of Making Quality Certain*. New York: McGraw Hill.

Czarnecki, M. (1994). *Benchmarking Strategies*. Frederick, MD: Aspen.

Dalek, G. (1997). "Hospital care for profit." In C. Wiener and A. Strauss (eds.), *Where Medicine Fails*. Fifth edition. (New Brunswick, NJ: Transaction Publishers), 197–209.

Dalen, J., and Bone, R. (1996). "Is it time to pull the pulmonary artery catheter?" *Journal of the American Medical Association, 276,* 916–18.

Dame, L., and Wolfe, S. (1996). *The Failure of 'Private' Hospital Regulation: An Analysis of the Joint Commission on Accreditation of Healthcare Organizations' Inadequate Oversight of Hospitals*. Public Citizens Health Research Group, July.

Davidson, S., Restuccia, J., and the Boston University Health Care Management Program Group. (1998). "Competition and quality among managed care plans in the USA." *International Journal for Quality in Health Care, 10,* 411–19.

Davis, L. (1973). *Fellowship of Surgeons: A History of the American College of Surgeons*. Chicago: American College of Surgeons.

Deloitte and Touche. Announcement of the 1999 Conference on Healthcare. New York City, April 26–27, 1999.

Deming, W. E. (1986). *Out of the Crisis*. Cambridge, MA: MIT Press.

DeMoro, R. (1996). "It's the reality that's scary in current health care trends," *California Nurse, 92,* 3.

Denzin, N. and Lincoln, Y. (Eds.) (1994). *Handbook on Qualitative Research.* Thousand Oaks, CA: Sage.

Detsky, A. (1995). Regional variation in medical care, *New England Journal of Medicine, 333,* 589–90.

Deutscher, I. (1983). "Review of *Fatal Remedies,*" *Contemporary Sociology, 12,* 175–76.

Deyo, R., Cherkin, D., Loeser, J., Bigos, S., and Ciol, M. (1992). "Morbidity and mortality in association with operations on the lumbar spine: The influence of age, diagnosis, and procedure," *Journal of Bone and Joint Surgery American Volume, 74,* 536–43.

Deyo, R., Ciol, M., Cherkin, D., Loesser, J., and Bigos, S. (1993). "Lumbar spinal fusion: A cohort study of complications, reoperations, and resource use in the Medicare population," *Spine, 18,* 1463–70.

Deyo R., Psaty, B., Simon, G., Wagner, E., and Omenn, G. (1997). "The messenger under attack—intimidation of researchers by special-interest groups," *New England Journal of Medicine, 336,* 1176–80.

Dingwall, R., Murphy, E., Watson, P., Greatbatch, D., and Parker, S. (1998). "Catching goldfish: Quality in qualitative research," *Journal of Health Services Research Policy, 3,* 167–72.

Dobyns, L., and Crawford-Mason, C. (1994). *Thinking About Quality: Progress, Wisdom, and the Deming Philosophy.* New York: New York Times Books/Random House.

Donabedian, A. (1997). "Quality stewardship in Codman's life and work," *Joint Commission Journal on Quality Improvement, 24,* 52–55.

———. (1985). *The Methods and Findings of Quality Assessment and Monitoring.* Vol. 3. Ann Arbor, MI: Health Administration Press.

———. (1982). *The Criteria and Standards of Quality.* Vol. 2. Ann Arbor, MI: Health Administration Press.

———. (1980). *The Definition of Quality and Approaches to its Assessment.* Chicago: Health Administration Press.

Donaldson, M., and Capron, A., eds. (1991). *Patient Outcomes Research Teams: Managing Conflict of Interest.* Washington, DC: National Academy Press.

Draper, D., Kahn K., Reinisch, E., Sherwood, M., Carney, M., Kosecoff, J., Keeler, E., Rogers, W., Savitt, H., Allen, H., Wells, K., Reboussin, D., and Brook, R. (1990). "Studying the effects of the DRG-based prospective payment system on quality of care: Design, sampling, and fieldwork," *Journal of the American Medical Association, 264,* 1956–61.

Droppleman, P., and Thomas, S. (1996). "Anger in nurses: Don't lose it, use it," *American Journal of Nursing, 96,* 26–32.

Drucker, P. (1973). *Management: Tasks, Responsibilities, Practices.* New York: Harper and Row.

Eagle, C., Davies, J., and Reason, J. (1992). "Accident analysis of large-scale technological disasters applied to an anaesthetic complication," *Canadian Journal of Anaesthesia, 39,* 118–22.

Eddy, D. (1990). "Practice policies: Where do they come from?" *Journal of the American Medical Association, 263,* 1265–75.

Edgman-Levitan, S., and Cleary, P. (1996) "What information do consumers want and need?" *Health Affairs*, 15, 42–56.

"Editorial: Scandal exposes virtues, sins of for-profit hospitals," *USA Today* (August 13, 1997), 6A.

Ehrenreich, B., and Ehrenreich, I. (1971). *The American Health Empire: Power, Profits and Politics*. New York: Vintage.

Eichenwald, K. (1997). "U.S. examining Columbia's use of subsidiaries' cost reports." *New York Times* (August 27), D5.

Ellison, N., and Pierce, E., Jr. (1998). "Risk management in cardiac anesthesia: Analysis of critical. Introduction," *Journal of Cardiothoracic and Vascular Anesthesia*, (2 Suppl 1), 1–2.

Ellwood, P. (1988). "Outcomes management: A technology of patient experience," *New England Journal of Medicine, 319*, 865–67.

———. (1971). "Health maintenance strategy." *Medical Care, 9*, 291–98.

Ellwood, P., Enthoven, A., and Etheredge, L. (1992). "The Jackson Hole initiatives for a twentieth century American health system." *Health Economics, 1*, 149–68.

Enthoven, A. (1978). "Consumer-choice health plan," *New England Journal of Medicine, 298*, 650–58.

Enthoven, A., and Kronick, R. (1989). "A consumer-choice health plan for the 1990s," *New England Journal of Medicine, 320*, 94–101.

Escarce, J. J. (1993). "Would eliminating differences in physician practice style reduce geographic variations in cataract surgery rates?" *Medical Care, 31*, 1106–18.

Estes, C. (1990). "The Reagan legacy: Privatization, the welfare state and aging." In J. Quadagno and J. Myles, eds., *Aging and the Welfare State* (Philadelphia: Temple University Press), 59–83.

Estes, C., Gerard, L., Zones, I., and Swan, J. (1984). *Political Economy, Health and Aging*. Boston: Little, Brown.

Estes, C., Harrington, C., and Davis, S. (1994). "The medical-industrial complex." In C. Harrington and C. Estes, eds., *Health Policy and Nursing: Crisis and Reform in the U.S. Health Care Delivery System* (Boston: Jones and Bartlett), 54–69.

Etheredge, L., Jones, S., and Lewin, I. (1996). "What's driving health systems change?" *Health Affairs, 15*, 93–101.

Evans, L. (1991). *Safety and the Driver*. New York: John Wiley and Sons.

Fallows, J. (1981). *National Defense*. New York: Vintage Books.

Faulkner and Gray (1999). Disease Management CD-ROM.

Feder, J. (1977). *Medicare: The Politics of Hospital Insurance*. Lexington, MA: Lexington Books.

Feldman, S., and Roblin, D. (1997). "Medical accidents in hospital care; Applications of failure analysis to hospital quality appraisal," *Joint Commission Journal on Quality Improvement, 23*, 567–80.

———. (1992). "Standards for peer evaluation: The hospital quality assurance committee," *American Journal of Public Health, 82*, 525–27.

Feldman, S., and Rundall, T. (1993). "PROs and the Health Care Quality Improvement Initiative: Insights from 50 cases of serious medical mistakes," *Medical Care Review, 50*, 123–52.

Fetter, R., Mills, R., Riedel, D., and Thompson, J. (1977). "The application of diagnostic specific cost profiles to cost and reimbursement control in hospitals," *Journal of Medical Systems, 1,* 137–47.

Fetter, R., Shin, Y., Freeman, J., Averill, R., and Thompson, J. (1980). "Case mix definition by Diagnosis-Related Groups," *Medical Care, 18* (2 suppl.):iii, 1–53.

Field, M. J., and Lohr, K. N., eds. (1990). *Clinical Practice Guidelines: Directions for a Program.* Washington: National Academy Press.

Findlay, S. (1997). "Holding HMOs accountable," *USA Today* (August 7), 5A.

Finkelstein, K. (1997). "The sick business," *New Republic, 217,* 23–27.

Fischer, P. (1999). "Evidentiary medicine lacks humility," *Journal of Family Practice, 48,* 345–46.

Fishbein, M. (1946). "The public relations of American medicine," *Journal of the American Medical Association* (February 23), 509–13.

Fisher, B., and Strauss, A. (1978). "The Chicago tradition: Thomas Park and their successors," *Symbolic Interaction, 1,* 5–23.

Fishman, P., Von Korff, M., Lozano, P., and Hecht, J. (1997). "Chronic care costs in managed care," *Health Affairs, 16,* 239–47.

Fletcher, S. (1997). "Whither scientific deliberation in health policy recommendations? Alice in Wonderland of breast-cancer screening," *New England Journal of Medicine, 336,* 1180–83.

Folland, S., and Stano, M. (1990). "Small area variations: A critical review of claims, methods and evidence." *Medical Care Review, 47,* 419–65.

"Forum," National Public Radio, December 22, 1993; May 26, 1999.

Freeman, J., Fetter, R., Park, H., Schneider, K., Lichtenstein, J., Hughes, J., Bauman, W., Duncan, C., Freeman, D., and Palmer, G. (1995). "Diagnosis-related group refinement with diagnosis- and procedure-specific comorbidities and complications," *Medical Care, 33,* 806–27.

Friedman, E. (1997). "Managed care, rationing, and quality: A tangled relationship." *Health Affairs, 16,* 174–82.

———. (1996). "Capitation, integration, and managed care: Lessons from early experiments," *Journal of the American Medical Association, 275,* 957–62.

Friedson, E. (1970). *Professional Dominance: The Social Structure of Medical Care.* New York: Atherton.

Fuchs, V. (1997). "Economics and improving the quality of health care," Address before the International Congress on Performance Improvement in Health Care. Chicago, November 12–15.

"Future role of Joint Commission remains in doubt in Clinton bill," *Hospital Peer Review, 18* (December 1993), 189.

Gann, M., and Restuccia, J. (1995). "Total quality management in health care: A view of current and potential research," *Medical Care Review, 51,* 467–500.

Gaucher, E., Coffey, R. (1993). *Total Quality in Health Care: From Theory to Practice.* San Francisco: Jossey Bass.

Gawande, A. (1999). "When doctors make mistakes," *New Yorker, 74* (February 1), 40–55.

Geiger, H. (1983). "An overdose of power and money," *New York Times Book Review,* 1 January 9), 24.

Geist, P., and Hardesty, M. (1992). *Negotiating the Crisis: DRGs and the Transformation of Hospitals.* New Jersey: Lawrence Erlbaum.

Gerteis, M., Edgman-Levitan, S., Daley, J., and Delbanco, T. (1993). *Through the Patient's Eyes*. San Francisco, CA: Jossey-Bass.

Gerteis, M., Edman-Levitan, S., Walker, J., Stokes, D., Cleary, P., and Delbanco, T. (1993). "What patients really want," *Health Management Quality*. Third quarter: 2–6.

Gift, R., and Mosel, D. (1994). *Benchmarking in Health Care: A Collaborative Approach*. Chicago: American Hospital Publishing.

Ginzberg, E. (1988). "For-profit-medicine: A reassessment," *New England Journal of Medicine, 319*, 757–61.

Gladwell, M. (1994). "How safe are your breasts?" *New Republic, 211* (October 24), 22–28.

Glaser, B. (1978). *Theoretical Sensitivity*. Mill Valley, CA: Sociology Press.

Glaser, B., and Strauss, A. (1967). *The Discovery of Grounded Theory*. Chicago: Aldine.

Glasser, R. (1998). "The doctor is not in: On the managed failure of managed health care," *Harper's Magazine* (March), 35–41.

Goldberg, H., Wagner, E., Fihn, S., Martin, D., Horowitz, C., Christensen, D., Cheadle, A., Diehr, P., and Simon, G. (1998). "A randomized controlled trial of CQI teams and academic detailing: Can they alter compliance with guidelines?" *Joint Commission Journal on Quality Improvement, 24*, 130–41.

Goldman, R. (1992). "The reliability of peer assessments of quality of care," *Journal of the American Medical Association, 267*, 958–60.

Goldman, D. (1997). "Counterpoint: Sustaining CRI." *International Journal for Quality in Health Care, 9*, 7–9.

Goodman, E. (1997). "Beware when experts say . . ." *San Francisco Chronicle* (February 6), A23.

Gordon, S. (1997). "What nurses stand for," *Atlantic Monthly* (February), 80–88.

Gottlieb, M., and Eichenwald, K. (1997). "Health care's giant: The doctor as investor: A special report," *New York Times* (April 6), 1.

Grahame-Smith, D. (1995). "Evidence based medicine: Socratic dissent," *British Medical Journal, 310*, 1126–27.

Gray, B., ed. (1983). *The New Health Care For-Profit*. Washington: National Academy Press.

Green, J., and Winfeld, N. (1995). "Report cards on cardiac surgeons—assessing New York state's approach," *New England Journal of Medicine, 332*, 1229–32.

Green, J., Winfeld, N., Krasner, M., and Wells, C. (1997). "In search of America's best hospitals: The promise and reality of quality assessment," *Journal of the American Medical Association, 277*, 1152–55.

Greenberg, D. (1995). "Congress's 'think tank' struggles for survival." *Lancet, 346*, 171.

Greenberg, J. (1993). "Give 'em health, Harry," *New Republic, 209* (October 11), 20.

Greider, W. (1992). *Who Will Tell The People?* New York: Simon and Schuster.

Groopman, J. (1999). "Heart surgery, unplugged," *New Yorker, 74* (January 11), 43–51.

———. (2000). "Second opinion," *New Yorker, 75* (January 24), 40–49.

Guillemin, J., and Holmstrum, L. (1996). *Mixed Blessings: Intensive Care for Newborns*. New York: Oxford University Press.

Hacker, J. (1997). *The Road to Nowhere: The Genesis of President Clinton's Plan for Health Security*. Princeton: Princeton University Press.

Hall, C. (1996). "Finding the best HMO for you." *San Francisco Chronicle* (September 23), E1.

———. (1996). "HMO stocks fall as profits are pressured," *San Francisco Chronicle* (July 13), D1.

———. (1996). "Biotech going global," *San Francisco Chronicle* (July 5), E1.

———. (1996). "Highest marks for Bay hospitals," *San Francisco Chronicle* (May 20), A1.

Hall, P. (1976). "A symbolic interactionist analysis of politics." In A. Effrat, ed., *Perspectives in Political Sociology* (New York: Bobbs Merrill), 35–75.

Hall, P., and Spencer-Hall, D. (1982). "The social conditions of the negotiated order," *Urban Life, 11,* 328–49.

Hambleton, R. (1987). *The Branding of America: From Levi Strauss to Chrysler, from Westinghouse to Gilette, The Forgotten Fathers of America's Best-Known Brand Names.* Dublin, NH: Yankee Books.

Hammer, M., and Champy, J. (1993). Reengineering the Corporation. New York: Harper Business.

Hammer, M., and Stanton, S. (1995) *The Reengineering Revolution.* New York: Harper Business.

Harrington, C. (1984). "Public policy and the nursing home industry," *International Journal of Health Services, 14,* 481.

Harris, A., ed. (1994). *Best Practices in Hospital Quality.* Atlanta, GA: American Health Consultants.

Hart, R., and Musfeldt, C. (1992). "MD-directed critical pathways: It's time," *Hospitals, 66,* 56.

Hawking, S. (1988). *A Brief History of Time: From the Big Bang to Black Holes.* New York: Bantam.

Health Care Financing Administration. (June 30, 1997). "National summary of Medicaid managed care programs and enrollment," Obtained from web site: <www.hcfa.gov>.

Health Care Press. (1997). Letter sent with November issue of *The Digest of Managed Health Care.*

"Health Costs Expected to Resume Rising Sharply" (1998). *San Francisco Chronicle* (September 16), A5.

Hendren, J. (1998). "Bigger bills seen for health care," *San Francisco Chronicle* (January 20), B6.

Henig, R. (1992). "The unkindest cut of all: Unnecessary operations raise costs, risks to patients," *AARP Bulletin, 33* (September), 2.

Hershey, N. (1992). "Compensation and accountability: The way to improve peer review," *Quality Assurance and Utilization Review, 7,* 23–29.

Hibbard, J., and Jewett, J. (1997). "Will quality report cards help consumers?" *Health Affairs, 16,* 218–28.

Higgins, R., Elenteny, B., and Collins, B. (1996). "Three hospitals' survey experiences," *Journal for Healthcare Quality, 18,* 14–19.

Hilgartner, S., and Bosk, C. (1988). "The rise and fall of social problems: A public arena's model," *American Journal of Sociology, 94,* 53–78.

Hill, A., Tran, K., Akhurts, T., Yeung, H., Yeh, S., Rosen, P., Borgen, P., and Cody, H.

(1999). "Lessons learned from 500 cases of lymphatic mapping for breast cancer," *Annals of Surgery, 229,* 528–35.

Hirshfield, D. (1970). *The Lost Reform.* Cambridge: Harvard University Press.

"HMO lets patients rate their doctors," *San Francisco Chronicle* (March 25, 1997), A4.

"HMO's Medicare cuts jolt patients," *Wall Street Journal* (August 11, 1998), B1.

Hoffman, C., Rice, D., and Sung, H. (1996). "Persons with chronic conditions: Their prevalence and costs," *Journal of the American Medical Association, 276,* 1473–79.

Holding, R. (1995). "Health care lawyers do well," *San Francisco Chronicle* (December 4), B1.

Holohan, T. (1996). "The federal role in health technology assessment," *Lancet, 348,* 1006–7.

Hospital Council of Southern California. (1994). "Is there a role for voluntary accreditation in a reformed health care delivery system?" (August).

Hospital Research and Educational Trust (1981). "The case for case-mix: A new construct for hospital management," Working paper number 5 (September 11).

"Hospitals must decide how much data to release, and to whom" (1994). *Hospital Outcomes Management,* 21.

Huxley, E. (1975). *Florence Nightingale.* London: Weidenfeld and Nicolson.

"IDS survival strategies" (1997). *Medical Network Strategy Report, 6* (July), 3–8.

Iezzoni, L. (1997a). "The risks of risk adjustment," *Journal of the American Medical Association, 278,* 1600–7.

———. (1997b). "How much are we willing to pay for information about quality of care?" *Annals of Internal Medicine, 126,* 391–393.

Iezzoni, L., Ash, A., Shwartz, M., Daley, J., Hughes, J., and Mackiernan, Y. (1996). "Judging hospitals by severity-adjusted mortality rates: The influence of the severity-adjustment method," *American Journal of Public Health, 86,* 1379–87.

Iglehart, J. (1996). "The National Committee for Quality Assurance." *New England Journal of Medicine, 335,* 995–99.

"Industry insights," *Managed Care Outlook, 12* (March 26, 1999), 4.

Institute on Medicine, Committee on Nursing Home Regulation. (1986). *Improving the Quality of Care in Nursing Homes.* Washington: National Academy Press.

Ishikawa, D. (1985). *What Is Total Quality Control?* Englewood Cliffs, NJ: Prentice Hall.

Jaffe, D., and Scott, C. (1997). "The human side of re-engineering," *Healthcare Forum Journal, 40,* 14–21.

Jeffrey, N. (1998). "Who's on first?" *Wall Street Journal* (October 19), R16.

Jencks, S., and Wilensky, G. (1992). "The health care quality improvement initiative; a new approach to quality assurance in Medicare," *Journal of the American Medical Association, 268,* 900–3.

Jennings, B. (1991). "Patient outcomes research: Seizing the opportunity," *Advances in Nursing Science, 14,* 59–72.

Jensen, H. (1991). "The impact of managed care on physicians." *Quality Assurance and Utilization Review, 6,* 109–14.

Jewett, J., and Hibbard, J. (1996). "Comprehension of quality of care indicators: Differences among the privately insured, the publicly insured, and the uninsured," *Health Care Financing Review, 18,* 75–94.

Jirsch, D. (1993). "Patient-focused care: The systemic implications of change," *Healthcare Management Forum, 6,* 27–32.

Johannes, L. (1997). "On the ward: Primary nursing—a model for hospitals around the country—may not be able to survive the push for efficiency," *Wall Street Journal* (October 23), R12.

Johnson, H., and Broder, D. (1996). *The System: The American Way of Politics at the Breaking Point.* New York: Little, Brown & Co.

Johnson, C., and Grant, L. (1985). *The Nursing Home in American Society.* Baltimore: Johns Hopkins University Press.

Joint Commission on Accreditation of Healthcare Organizations. (1999a). *The Inside Perspective.* Oakbrook Terrace, IL (February).

———. (1998b). Sentinel event policy and procedures, revised June 15, JCAHO. ORG website.

———. (1998c). Facts about the sentinel event policy, JCAHO.ORG website.

———. (1998). "Joint Commission establishes initial focus areas for core performance measures for hospitals and long term care organizations." Press release (November 20), 2.

———. (1995). *An In-depth Review of the 1995 Functional Accreditation Process.* Oakbrook Terrace, IL (January 27).

———. (1993). *Process Improvement Models: Case Studies in Health Care.* Oakbrook Terrace, IL.

———. (1990). *Committed to Quality: An Introduction to the Joint Commission on Accreditation of Healthcare Organizations.* Oakbrook Terrace, IL.

Jost, T. (1995). "Oversight of the quality of medical care: Regulation, management, or the market?" *Arizona Law Review, 37,* 825–68.

———. (1989). "Administrative law issues involving the Medicare utilization and quality control peer review organization (PRO) program: Analysis and recommendations," *Ohio State Law Journal, 50,* 1, 8, 33.

Journal of Health Politics, Policy and Law, 16 (1991).

Judis, J. (1998). "Online Magaziner," *New Republic, 219,* 22–27.

———. (1995). "Abandoned surgery: Business and the failure of health care reform," *American Prospect, 21,* 65–73.

Juran, J. M. (1964). *Managerial Breakthrough.* New York: McGraw Hill.

Juran, J. M., Gryna, F. M., Jr., Bingham, R. S., Jr., eds. (1979). *Quality Control Handbook.* New York: McGraw Hill.

Kahn, K., Keeler, E., Sherwood, M., Rogers, W., Draper, D., Bentow, S., Reinisch, E., Rubenstein, L., Kosecoff, J., and Brook, R. (1990). "Comparing outcomes of care before and after implementation of the DRG-based prospective payment system," *Journal of the American Medical Association, 264,* 1984–88.

Kahn, K., Rogers, W., Rubenstein, L., Sherwood, M., Rubenstein, L, Reinisch, E., Kosecoff, J., and Brook, R. (1990). "Measuring quality of care with explicit process criteria before and after implementation of the DRG-based prospective payment system," *Journal of the American Medical Association, 264,* 1969–73.

Kahn, K., Rubenstein, L., Draper, D., Kosecoff, J., Rogers, W., Keeler, E., and Brook, R. (1990). "The effects of the DRG-based prospective payment system on quality of care for hospitalized Medicare patients: An introduction to the series," *Journal of the American Medical Association, 264*,1953–55.

Kaiser Family Foundation and The Commonwealth Fund. (1998). A survey of the public (June 11), 38.

Kanigel, R. (1998). *The One Best Way: Frederick Winslow Taylor and the Enigma of Efficiency.* New York: Viking.

Kaplan, Madge (1996). "Marketplace," WGBH Boston Bureau of National Public Radio (September 30).

Kassirer, J. (1994). "The use and abuse of practice profiles," *New England Journal of Medicine, 330,* 634–35.

Keeler, E., Kahn, K., Draper, D., Sherwood, M., Robenstein, L., Reinisch, E., Kosecoff, J., and Brook, R. (1990). "Changes in sickness at admission following the introduction of the prospective payment system," *Journal of the American Medical Association, 264,* 1969–73.

Kidder, Peabody and Co. (1994). "Health care industry dynamics." *Health Care Information Services Industry.* New York.

Kilborn, P. (1998) "End of HMO for the elderly brings dismay in rural Ohio," *New York Times* (July 31), A1.

———. (1997). "Health care plans are seen entering rocky new phase," *New York Times* (November 22), A1.

Kinzer, D. (1988). "Our realistic options in health regulation," *Frontiers of Health Services Management, 5,* 3–40.

Kleinke, J. (1997). "HMO's stocks lose big $," Dow Jones and Company, Inc. *Deja News* (December 22).

Kleinman, S., Stenross, B., and McMahon, M. (1994). "Privileging fieldwork over interviews: Consequences for identity and practice," *Symbolic Interaction, 17,* 37–50.

Knafl, K., and Burkett, G. (1975). "Professional socialization in surgical specialty: Acquiring medical judgment," *Social Science and Medicine, 9,* 397–404.

Kohn, L., Corrigan, I., and Donaldson, M., eds. (1999). *To Err Is Human.* Committee on Quality of Health Care in America, Institute of Medicine. Washington, DC: National Academy Press.

Kolata, G. (1997). "Stand on mammograms greeted by outrage," *New York Times* (January 20), C1.

Kosecoff, J., Kahn, K., Rogers, W., Reinisch, E., Sherwood, M., Rubenstein, L., Draper, D., Roth, C., Chew, C., and Brook, R. (1990). "Prospective payment system and impairment at discharge: The 'quicker-and-sicker' story revisited," *Journal of the American Medical Association, 264,* 1980–83.

Kosterlitz, J. (1991). "Cookbook medicine," *National Journal, 23* (March 9), 574–77.

KPMG Peat Marwick (1996). *The Impact of Managed Care on U.S. Markets.*

———. (1994). "Integrated delivery systems," *Market Issues*(Fall), 1.

Kramer, M. (1974). *Reality Shock: Why Nurses Leave Nursing.* New York: Mosby.

Kuttner, R. (1998). "Must good HMOs go bad? The search for checks and balances," *New England Journal of Medicine, 338,* 1635–39.

Laffel, G., and Blumenthal, D. (1989). "The case for using industrial quality management science in health care organizations," *Journal of the American Medical Association, 262,* 2869–73.

Lagnado, L. (1999). "Hospital mergers: Indications of severe trauma," *Wall Street Journal* (May 14), B1.

———. (1997) "Hospitals profit by 'upcoding' illnesses," *Wall Street Journal* (April 17), B1.

———. (1997). "Intensive care: Ex-manager describes the profit-driven life inside Columbia/HCA," *Wall Street Journal* (May 30), A1.

Lambert-Huber, D., Ellerback, E., Wallace, R., Radford, M., Krewowik, T., Gold, J., and Allison, J. (1994). "Quality of care indicators for patients with acute myocardial infarction: Pilot validation of the indicators," *Clinical Performance and Quality Health Care, 2,* 219–22.

Lambertsen, E. (1953). *Nursing Team Organization and Functioning.* New York: Teachers College Press, Columbia University.

Lang, D. (1991). *Medical Staff Peer Review: A Strategy for Motivation and Performance.* Chicago: American Hospital Publishing.

Langley, M. (1997). "Really operating: Nonprofit hospitals are sometimes that in little but name,"*Wall Street Journal* (July 14), A1.

Lansky, D. (1996). "Foundation for Accountability (FACCT): A consumer voice on health care quality," *Journal of Clinical Outcomes Management, 3,* 54–58.

Laouri, M., Kravitz, R., Bernstein, W., Leake, B., Borowsky, S., Haywood, J., and Brook, R. (1997). "Under use of coronary angiography: Application of a clinical method," *International Journal for Quality in Health Care, 9,* 15–22.

Larkin, H. (1998). "Market, legal pressures push health system accountability, but is it enough?" *Advances* (Robert Wood Johnson Foundation quarterly newsletter), *1*:1–2.

Lathrop, J. P. (1991). "The patient-focused hospital," *Healthcare Forum Journal, 34,* 17–21.

Lazarou, J., Pomeeranz, B., and Corey, P. (1998). "Incidence of adverse drug reactions in hospitalized patients: A meta-analysis of prospective studies," *Journal of the American Medical Association, 279,* 1200–5.

Leape, L. (1997). "Out of the darkness: Hospitals begin to take mistakes seriously," *Healthcare Leadership Review,* 16.

———. (1994). "Error in medicine," *Journal of the American Medical Association, 272,* 1851–57.

Leape, L., Bates, D., Cullen, D., Cooper, J., Demonaco, H., Gallivan, T., Hallisey, R., Ives, J., Laird, N., Laffel, G., Nemeskal, R., Petersen, L., Porter, K., Servi, D., Shea, B., Small, S., Sweitzer, B., Thompson, B., and Vander Vliet, M. (1995). "Systems analysis of adverse drug events," *Journal of the American Medical Association, 274,* 35–43.

Leape, L., Brennan, T., Laird, N., Lawthers, A., Localio, A., Barnes, B., Hebert, L., Newhouse, J., Weiler, P., and Hiatt, H. (1991). "The nature of adverse events in hospitalized patients: Results of the Harvard Medical Practice Study II," *New England Journal of Medicine. 324,* 377–84.

Lears, J. (1997). "Man the machine," *New Republic, 217* (September 1), 25–32.

Legoretta, A., Christian-Herman, J., O'Connor, R., Hasan, M., Evans, R., and Leung, K. (1998). "Compliance with national asthma management guidelines and specialty care," *Archives of Internal Medicine, 158,* 457–64.

Leibfried, K., and McNair, C. J. (1992). *Benchmarking: A Tool for Continuous Improvement.* New York: Harper.

Lembcke, P. (1967). "Evolution in medical audit," *Journal of the American Medical Association, 199,* 543–50.

———. (1959). "A scientific method for medical auditing," *Hospitals, 33,* 5–71.

———. (1956). "Medical auditing by scientific methods: Illustrated by major female pelvic surgery," *Journal of the American Medical Association, 162,* 646–55.

Leyerle, B. (1994). *The Private Regulation of American Health Care.* New York: M.E. Sharpe.

———. (1984). *Moving and Shaking American Medicine: The Structure of a Socioeconomic Transformation.* Westport, CT: Greenwood Press.

Light, D. (1999). "Good managed care needs universal health insurance," *Annals of Internal Medicine, 130,* 686–89.

———. (1986). "Corporate medicine for profit," *Scientific American, 155,* 38–45.

Lipson, L. (1999). "The free market versus democracy," *San Francisco Chronicle* (January 13), A19.

Lloyd, S., and Rising, J. (1985). "Physician and coding errors in patient records," *Journal of the American Medical Association, 254,* 1330–36.

Loeb, J., and O'Leary, D. (1995). "A call for collaboration in performance measurement," *Journal of the American Medical Association, 273,* 1405.

Lofland, J., and Lofland, L. (1984). *Analyzing Social Settings: A Guide to Qualitative Observation.* Belmont, CA: Wadsworth.

Lohr, K., ed. (1990). *Medicare: A Strategy for Quality Assurance.* Washington: National Academy Press.

Longo, D., Land, G., Schramm, W., Fraas, J., Hoskins, B., and Howell, V. (1997). "Consumer reports in health care; do they make a difference in patient care?" *Journal of the American Medical Association, 278,* 1579–84.

Longo, D., Ciccone, K., and Lord, J. (1989). *Integrated Quality Assessment.* Chicago: American Hospital Publishing.

Lord, J., and Ciccone, K. (1992). *IQA-2 Continuous Performance Improvement through Integrated Quality Assessment.* Chicago: American Hospital Publishing.

Louis Harris and Associates, Inc. (1990). "Trade-offs and choices: Health policy options for the 1990s," Survey conducted for Metropolitan Life Insurance Company.

Ludmerer, K. (1985). *Learning to Heal: The Development of American Medical Education.* New York: Basic Books.

Luft, H., and Romano, P. (1993). "Chance, continuity, and change in hospital mortality rates," *Journal of American Medical Association, 270,* 331–37.

Maas, M., Johnson, M., and Moorhead, S. (1996). "Classifying nursing-sensitive patient outcomes," *Image, 28,* 295–301.

Maines, D. (1982). "In search of a mesostructure: Studies in the negotiated order," *Urban Life, 11,* 2–3, 16.

Mallison, M. (1990). Editorial. "Access to invisible expressways." *American Journal of Nursing, 90,* 7.

Marek, K. (1989). "Outcome measurement in nursing," *Journal of Nursing Quality Assurance, 4,* 1–9.

Marmor, T. (1999). *The Politics of Medicare.* Hawthorne, NY: Aldine de Gruyter.

————. (1996). "The politics of universal health insurance: Lessons from the past?" *Journal of Interdisciplinary History, 26,* 671–79.

————. (1988). "Reflections on Medicare," *Journal of Medicine and Philosophy, 13,* 5–29.

Marmor, T., and Monrone, J. (1979). "HSAs and the representation of consumer interests: conceptual issues and litigation problems," *Health Law Project Library Bulletin, 4,* 117–28.

Marquerez, S. (1997). "integrating CGI in Health Organizations: Perspectives," *International Journal on Quality in Health Care, 9,* 5–6.

Martin, C. (1995). "Stuck in neutral: Big business and the politics of national health reform," *Journal of Health Politics, Policy and Law, 20,* 431–36.

May, K. (1994). "Abstract knowing: The case for magic in method." In J. Morse, ed. *Critical Issues in Qualitative Research Methods* (Thousand Oaks, CA: Sage), 10–21.

Mayer, T., and Mayer, G. (1985). "HMOs: Origins and development," *New England Journal of Medicine, 312,* 590–94.

McCall, T., Gordon, S., and Court, J. (1997) "Clinton's 'Bill of Rights' won't heal patients," *San Francisco Chronicle* (December 5), A29.

McGinley, L. (1999). "As nursing homes say 'no,' hospitals feel pain," *Wall Street Journal* (May 26), B1.

McLaughlin, C. G., Normalle, D. P., Wolfe, R. A., McMahon, L. F., and Griffith, J. R (1989). "Small-area variation in hospital discharge rates: Do socioeconomic variables matter?" *Medical Care, 27,* 507–21.

McMahan, E., Hoffman, K., and McGee, G. (1994). "Physician-nurse relationships in clinical settings: A review and critique of the literature, 1966–1992," *Medical Care Review, 51,* 82–112.

"McNeil Lehrer News Hour," Public Broadcasting System, September 13, 1984.

McPherson, K., Wennberg, J. E., Hovind, O. B., and Clifford, P. (1982). "Small-area variations in the use of common surgical procedures: An international comparison of New England, England, and Norway," *New England Journal of Medicine, 307,* 1310–13.

Medicare Payment Advisory Commission. (1998) *Health Care Spending and the Medicare Program: A Data Book* (July).

Meier, B. (1997). "For some patients, profit-minded psychiatric care was nightmare," *International Herald Tribune* (August 8), 1.

Melosh, B. (1982). *The Physician's Hand: Work Culture and Conflict in American Nursing.* Philadelphia: Temple University Press.

Melum, M., and Sinioris, M. (1992). *Total Quality Management: The Health Care Pioneers.* Chicago: American Hospital Publishing.

Menand, L. (1998). "After Elvis," *New Yorker, 73* (October 26 and November 2), 164–77.

Millenson, M. (1997). *Demanding Medical Excellence.* Chicago: University of Chicago Press.

Miller, I. (1997). *American Health Care Blues: Blue Cross, HMOs, and Pragmatic Reform Since 1960.* New Brunswick, NJ: Transaction Publishers.

Miller, M. (1999). "Premium idea," *New Republic, 220,* 24–27.

————. (1996). "Taking our medicine," *New Republic, 215,* 19–22.

Moloney, T., and Rogers, D. (1979). "Medical technology—a different view of the contentious debate over costs," *New England Journal of Medicine, 301,* 1413–19.

"Morning Edition," National Public Radio, October 12, 1993; June 4, 1998.

Morone, J. (1995). "Nativism, hollow corporations, and managed competition: Why the Clinton health care reform failed," *Journal of Health Care Politics, Policy and Law, 20,* 391–98.

National Institutes of Health Consensus Statement. (1997). "Breast cancer screening for women ages 40–49." Bethesda: National Cancer Institute (January 28).

Navarro, V. (1995). "Why Congress did not enact health care reform," *Journal of Health Politics, Policy and Law, 20,* 455–62.

Needleman, J. (1993). *The Way of the Physician.* New York: Viking Penguin.

———. (1984). *The New Religions.* New York: Crossroad Publications.

———. (1975). *A Sense of the Cosmos: The Encounter of Modern Science and Ancient Truth.* New York: Doubleday.

Neighmond, P. (1997). "Morning Edition," National Public Radio, November 25.

Nerenz, D. (1997). "Counterpoint: CQI in Health Care: Some Comments on 'Can It Really Work?'" *International Journal for Quality in Health Care, 9,* 3–4.

———. (1998). "Using outcomes data to compare plans, networks, and providers: What is the state of the art?" *International Journal for Quality in Health Care, 10,* 463–65.

Newman, L. (1999). "Medical management not possible with current flawed data," *Managed Care Outlook, 12* (April 16), 5.

"Nightly Business Report," Public Broadcasting System, July 25, 1997.

Noble, H. (1999). "Demand for new breast cancer test generates plea for proper training," *San Francisco Chronicle* (April 24), A9.

Nohria, N., and Berkley, J. (1994). "Whatever happened to the take-charge manager?" *Harvard Business Review, 72,* 128–37.

Nolin, C., and Clougherty, L. (1994). "Will critical paths keep you out of trouble?" *Inside Case Management, 1* (September), 4–5.

Normand, S., McNeil, B., Peterson, L., and Palmer, R. (1998). "Eliciting expert opinion using the Delphi technique: Identifying performance indicators for cardiovascular disease," *International Journal for Quality in Health Care, 10,* 247–60.

"Notebook," *New Republic* (November 30, 1998), 8.

Numbers, R. (1978). *Almost Persuaded: American Physicians and Compulsory Health Insurance.* Baltimore: Johns Hopkins University Press.

Office of Inspector General, Department of Health and Human Services (1999). *The External Review of Hospital Quality: A Call for Greater Accountability.*

Olesen, V., and Bone, D. (1998). "Emotions in rationalizing organizations: Conceptual notes from professional nursing in the USA," In G. Bendelow and S. Williams, eds., *Emotions in Social Life: Critical Themes and Contemporary Issues* (London: Routledge), 313–29.

Oliver, M. (1985). "Consensus or nonsensus conferences on coronary heart disease," *Lancet, 1,* 1087–89.

Opus Communications. "Up for a survey in 1999? Get ready for a leaner, meaner JCAHO," (1999). *Briefings on JCAHO, 10* (February), 2.

"Outliers: Asides and insides,"*Modern Healthcare, 28* (August 3, 1998), 4.

"Oxford Health Fined $3 million by New York State," *Reality Online Inc., a REUTERS Company*, December 23, 1997.

Paget, M. (1988). *The Unity of Mistakes; A Phenomenological Interpretation of Medical Work*. Philadelphia: Temple University Press.

"Pain management: Opportunities in an underserved growth market" (1998). *Healthcare Leadership Review, 17*, 6.

Paltrow, S. (1998). "Regulation of HMOs is far from perfect," *Wall Street Journal* (April 29), A14.

Park, R., Brook, R., Kosecoff, J., Keesey, J., Rubenstein, L., Keeler, E., Kahn, K., Rogers, W., and Chassin, M. (1990). "Explaining variations in hospital death rates: Randomness severity of illness, quality of care," *Journal of the American Medical Association, 264*, 484–94.

Parsons, T., and Shils, E. (1954). *Toward a General Theory of Action*. Third edition. Cambridge, MA: Harvard University Press.

Patel, K., and Rushefsky, M. (1998). "The health policy community and health-care reform in the U.S." *Health, 2*, 459–84.

Perlman, D. (1998). "Cost of cardiovascular ailments soaring." *San Francisco Chronicle* (January 1), A2.

Perrow, C. (1963). "Goals and power structures: A historical case study." In E. Freidson, ed., *The Hospital in Modern Society* (New York: Free Press), 112–46.

———. (1984). *Normal Accidents: Living With High-Risk Technologies*. New York: Basic Books.

Peters, T., and Austin, N. (1985). *A Passion for Excellence*. New York: Random House.

Peters, T., and Waterman, R. (1982). *In Search of Excellence*. New York: Harper and Row.

Peterson, P. (1998). "High on hedge funds," *San Francisco Chronicle* (November 17), A23

Picker Institute. (1999). *New visions for health care: ideas worth sharing*. Boston (January).

Pierce, E., Jr. (1998). "Promoting patient safety by preventing medical error" (letter), *Journal of the American Medical Association, 281*, 1174.

Pierce, E., Jr., and Cooper, J. (1984). *Analysis of Anesthetic Mishaps*. Boston: Little, Brown.

Plough, A. (1981). "Medical technology and the crisis of experience: The costs of clinical legitimation," *Social Science and Medicine, 15F*, 89–101.

———. (1986). *Borrowed Time: Artificial Organs and the Politics of Extending Lives*. Philadelphia: Temple University Press.

Poen, M. (1979). *Harry S. Truman Versus the Medical Lobby: The Genesis of Medicare*. Columbia: University of Missouri Press.

Poplin, C. (1997). "The piper's tune." In C. Wiener and A. Strauss, eds., *Where Medicine Fails*. Fifth edition (New Brunswick, NJ: Transaction Publishers), 317–32.

Porter, M., Teisberg, E., and Brown, G. (1994). "Innovation: Medicine's best cost-cutter," *New York Times* (February 27), F11.

Porterfield, J. (1970). Foreword to the Joint Commission publication, *Accreditation Manual for Hospitals*. Joint Commission on Accreditation of Hospitals, Oakbrook Terrace, IL.

Power, E. (1995). "From the Congressional Office of Technology Assessment," *Journal of the American Medical Association, 274*, 205.

"Preliminary CCP results are positive for Medicare AMI patients," *Medical Utilization Management* (February 6, 1997), 1–2.

"Proactive paradigms and the gullible execs," *San Francisco Examiner* (November 16, 1997), B4.

Pronovost, P., Jenckes, M., Dorman, T., Garrett, E., Breslow, M., Rosenfield, B., Lipsett, P., and Bass, E. (1999). "Organizational characteristics of intensive care units related to outcomes of abdominal aortic surgery," *Journal of the American Medical Association, 281*, 1310–17.

"Providers' global cap dissatisfaction leading to next-generation risk," *Managed Care Outlook*, 12 (April 2, 1999), 1.

Public Citizen Health Research Group. (1996). "The failure of 'private' regulation of hospitals," *Health Letter, 12* (August), 2.

Pugh, M. (1995). "Dissatisfaction with JCAHO widespread" (letter to the editor), *Modern Healthcare, 25*, 82.

Putnam, R. (1993). *Making Democracy Work*. Princeton: Princeton University Press.

QI/TQM. (1992, January). "Storyboards: TQM tools that save time for executives and QI teams," 4–8.

Ramsey, P. G., Carline, J. D., Blank, L. L., Wenrich, M. D. (1996). "Feasibility of hospital-based use of peer ratings to evaluate the performance of practicing physicians," *Academic Medicine, 71*, 364–70.

Rasmussen, J. (1990). "Human error and the problem of causality in the analysis of accidents." *Philosophical Transactions of the Royal Society of London, 327B*, 449–62.

Reason, J. (1990). "The contribution of latent human failures in the breakdown of complex systems," *Philosophical Transactions of the Royal Society of London, 327B*, 475–84.

———. (1990). *Human Error: Causes and Consequences*. New York: Cambridge University Press.

Reerink, E. (1992). "Quality assurance and health informatics," *Quality Assurance in Health Care, 4*, 1–2.

"Regular competency tests urged for doctors," *San Francisco Chronicle* (October 24, 1998), A3.

Reinhardt, U. (1998). "Quality in consumer-driven health systems," *International Journal for Quality in Health Care, 10*, 385–94.

Reinharz, S. (1979). *On Becoming A Social Scientist*. San Francisco: Jossey-Bass.

Relman, A. (1980). "The new medical-industrial complex," *New England Journal of Medicine, 303*, 963–70.

———. (1988). "Assessment and accountability," *New England Journal of Medicine, 319*, 1220–22.

Restuccia, J. (1995). "The Evolution of Hospital Review Methods in the United States," *International Journal for Quality in Health Care, 7*, 253–60.

Reverby, S. (1987). *Ordered to Care*. Cambridge: Cambridge University Press.

Rice, T. (1997). "Can markets give us the health system we want?" *Journal of Health Politics, Policy and Law, 22*, 383–426.

Richetson, D., Brown, W., and Graham, K. (1980). "3W approach to the investigation, analysis, and prevention of human-error aircraft accidents," *Aviation Space Environmental Medicine, 51,* 1036–42.

Roberts, J., Coale, J., and Redman, M. (1987). "A history of the Joint Commission on Accreditation of Hospitals," *Journal of the American Medical Association, 258,* 936–40.

Rockman, B. (1995). "The Clinton presidency and health care reform," *Journal of Health Politics, Policy and Law, 20,* 399–402.

Roemer, M., and Shain, M. (1959). "Hospital utilization under insurance," mimeographed. Ithaca, NY: Cornell University School of Business and Public Administration.

Rogers, W., Draper, D., Kahn, K., Rubenstein, L, Kosecoff, J., and Brook, R. (1990). "Quality of care before and after implementation of the DRG-based prospective payment system: A summary of effects," *Journal of the American Medical Association, 264,* 1989–94.

Rojas, W. (1997). "A poor test for schoolchildren." *San Francisco Chronicle* (November 19), A23.

Rorem, C. R. (1982). *The Quest for Certainty: Essays on Health Care Economics.* Ann Arbor, MI: Health Administration Press.

Rosen, G. (1963). "The hospital: Historical sociology of a community institution." In E. Freidson (ed.), *The Hospital in Modern Society* (New York: Free Press), 1–36.

Rosenberg, W., and Donald, A. (1995). "Evidence based medicine: An approach to clinical problem-solving," *British Medical Journal, 310,* 1122–26.

Rosenberg, C. (1987). *The Care of Strangers: The Rise of America's Hospital System.* New York: Basic Books.

Rosner, D. (1982). *A Once Charitable Enterprise.* Cambridge: Cambridge University Press.

Rothman, D. (1997). *Beginnings Count: The Technological Imperative in American Health Care.* New York: Oxford University Press.

Rubenstein, L., Kahn, K., Reinisch, E., Sherwood, M., Reinisch, E., Keeler, E., Draper, D., Kosecoff, J., and Brook, R. (1990). "Changes in quality of care for five diseases measured by implicit review, 1981–1986," *Journal of the American Medical Association, 264,* 1974–79.

Rubin, H., Rogers, W., Kahn, K., Rubenstein, L., and Brook, R. (1992). "Watching the doctor-watchers: How well do peer review organization methods detect hospital care quality problems?" *Journal of the American Medical Association, 267,* 2349–54.

Russell, S. (1997). "UC hospital merger deal near." *San Francisco Chronicle* (September 17), A15.

———. (1999). "Faculty to Weigh in on Hospital Merger," *San Francisco Chronicle* (October 1), A20.

Sackett, D., Rosenberg, W., Gray, J. M., Haynes, R. B., Richardson, W. S. (1996). "Evidence based medicine: What it is and what it isn't," *British Medical Journal, 312,* 71–73.

Sager, A. (1997). "Opiate of the managers." In C. Wiener and A. Strauss, eds., *Where Medicine Fails.* Fifth edition (New Brunswick, NJ: Transaction Publishers), 225–40.

Salmon, J. W. (1990). "Profit and health care," In J. W. Salmon, ed., *The Corporate Transformation of Health Care* (New York: Baywood), I, 55–77.

———. (1990). "The health maintenance organization strategy." In ibid., 83–96.

Salmon, J., White, W., and Feinglass, J. (1990). "The future of physicians: Agency and autonomy reconsidered," *Theoretical Medicine, 11,* 261–74.

Schatzman, L., and Strauss, A. (1973). *Field Research: Strategies For a Natural Sociology.* Englewood Cliffs, NJ: Prentice Hall.

Scherkenbach, W. (1986). *The Deming Route to Quality and Production.* Rockville, MD: Mercury.

Schevitz, T., and Fernandez, L. (1999). "Bay schools go all out to get children ready," *San Francisco Chronicle* (April 20) A1–A4.

Schlesinger, M., Marmor, I., and Smithey, R. (1987). "Nonprofit and for-profit medical care: Shifting roles and implications for health policy," *Journal of Health Politics and Law, 12,* 427–57.

Schneider, E., and Epstein, A. (1996). "Influence of cardiac-surgery performance reports on referral practices and access to care—A survey of cardiovascular specialists," *New England Journal of Medicine, 335,* 251–56.

Schoenbaum, S. (1998). "Improving the art and science of medical practice," *International Journal for Quality in Health Care, 10,* 81–82.

Schorr, L. (1997). *Common Purpose: Strengthening Families and Neighborhoods to Rebuild America.* New York: Doubleday.

Shactman, D., and Altman, S. (1995). *Market Consolidation, Antitrust, and Public Policy in the Health Care Industry.* Robert Wood Johnson Foundation (February 15).

Shaffer, F. (1983). "DRGs: History and overview," *Nursing and Health Care, 4,* 388–96.

Sharpe, A., and Lagnado, L. (1997). "Columbia says it plans to sell most of unit." *Wall Street Journal* (August 29), A3.

Sharpe, A., and Jaffe, G. (1997). "Cutting edge: Columbia/HCA plans for more big changes in health-care world," *Wall Street Journal* (May 28), A1–A8.

Shortell, S., O'Brien, J., Carman, J., Foster, R., Hughes, E., Boerstler, H., and O'Connor, E. (1995). "Assessing the impact of continuous quality improvement/total quality management: Concept versus implementation," *Health Services Research, 30,* 377–401.

Shortliffe, E., and Perrealt, L. (Eds.) (1990). *Medical Informatics.* Reading, MA: Addison-Wesley.

Shye, D., Freeborn, D., Romeo, J., and Eraker, S. (1998). "Understanding physicians' imaging test use in low back pain care: The role of focus groups," *International Journal for Quality in Health Care, 10,* 83–91.

Sieber, S. (1981). *Fatal Remedies: The Ironies of Social Intervention.* New York: Plenum Press.

Siegmann, K., and Eckhouse, J. (1993). "Computer game lets you reform health care." *San Francisco Chronicle* (November 16), B3.

Simborg, D. (1981). "DRG Creep: A new hospital-acquired disease," *New England Journal of Medicine, 304,* 1602–4.

"$60 million tab for health insurers' lobby," *San Francisco Chronicle* (November 28, 1998), A5.

Skillihorn, S. (1980). *Quality and Accountability: A New Era in American Hospitals.* San Francisco: Editorial Consultants, Inc.

Skocpol, T. (1996). *Boomerang: Clinton's Health Security Effort and the Turn Against Government in U.S. Politics*. New York: Norton.

Slee, V. (1966). "Information systems and measurement tools." *Journal of the American Medical Association, 196*, 1063–65.

Smelser, N. (1998). "The rational and the ambivalent in the social sciences: 1997 presidential address," *American Sociological Review, 63*, 1–15.

Smith, M. (1989). "Hospital discharge diagnoses: How accurate are they and their international classification of diseases (ICD) codes?" *New Zealand Medical Journal, 102*, 507–8.

Smith, S. D. (1995). Commentary: "The implementation of total quality management in hospitals: How good is the fit?" *Health Care Management Review, 20*, 26–27.

Smith, S. (1995). Commentary: "The role of institutions and ideas in health care policy," *Journal of Health Care Politics, Policy and Law, 20*, 385–89.

Smith, S., Freeland, M., Heffler, S., McKusick, D., and the Health Expenditures Projection Team. (1998). "The Next Ten Years of Health Spending: What Does the Future Hold?" *Health Affairs, 17*, 128–40.

Somers, H., and Somers, A. (1967). *Medicare and the Hospitals: Issues and Prospects*. Washington: Brookings Institution.

Sparrow, M. (1996). *License to Steal: Why Fraud Plagues America's Health Care System*. Boulder, CO: Westview Press.

Spath, P. (ed.) (2000). *Error Reduction in Health Care: A Systems Approach to Improving Patient Safety*. San Francisco, CA: Jossey-Bass.

———. (1998). *Investigating Sentinel Events: How to Find and Resolve Root Causes*. Forest Grove, Oregon: Brown-Spath and Associates.

———. (1993). "Critical paths: A tool for clinical process management," *Journal of the American Health Information Management Association, 64*, 48–58

Spragins, E. (1998) "Surviving the Medicare mess." *Newsweek* (November 16), 92.

Stano, M. (1994). "Outcomes research; High hopes, low yield?" *Journal of American Health Policy, 4*, 50–54.

———. (1993). "Evaluating the policy role of the small area variations and physician practice hypotheses," *Health Policy, 24*, 9–17.

———. (1991). "Further issues in small area variations analysis," *Journal of Health Politics, Policy and Law, 16*, 573–88.

Starr, P. (1982). *The Social Transformation of American Medicine*. New York: Basic Books.

Steinmo, S., and Watts, J. (1995). "It's the institution, stupid! Why comprehensive national health insurance always fails in America," *Journal of Health Care Politics, Policy and Law, 20*, 329–72.

Stern, Z. (1997). "Counterpoint: Can CQI Really Work in Health Care? For How Long?" *International Journal for Quality in Health Care, 9*, 1–2.

Stevens, R. (1989). *In Sickness and in Wealth*. New Haven: Basic Books.

———. (1997). "Past is prologue." In C. Wiener and A. Strauss, eds., *Where Medicine Fails*. Fifth edition. (New Brunswick, NJ: Transaction Publishers), 133–45.

Straus, R. (1988). "The 'deserving' and the 'undeserving' sick: A concept that will not go away," *Contemporary Sociology, 17*, 684–85.

Strauss, A. (1997). *Mirrors and Masks*. Second edition. New Brunswick, NJ: Transaction Publishers.

———. (1993). *Continual Permutations of Action*. Hawthorne, NY: Aldine de Gruyter.

———. (1989). *Qualitative Data Analysis for Social Scientists*. Chicago: University of Chicago Press.

———. (1978). "A social world perspective." In N. Denzin, ed., *Studies in Symbolic Interaction*. (San Francisco: JAI Press), I, 119–28.

———. (1978). *Negotiations*. San Francisco, CA: Jossey-Bass.

———, ed. (1956). *The Social Psychology of George Herbert Mead*. Chicago: University of Chicago Press.

Strauss, A., and Corbin, J. (1998). *Basics in Qualitative Research: Grounded Theory Procedures and Techniques*. Second edition. Newbury Park, CA: Sage.

Strauss, A., Fagerhaugh, S., Suczek, B., and Wiener, C. (1997). *Social Organization of Medical Work*. Second edition. New Brunswick, NJ: Transaction Publishers.

Strauss, A., Schatzman, L., Bucher, R., Ehrlich, D., and Sabshin, M. (1964). *Psychiatric Ideologies and Institutions*. New York: Free Press.

"Study says many Medicare patients not getting cancer tests," *San Francisco Chronicle* (April 19, 1999), A7.

Susman, E. (1996). "Spheres of influence," *Environmental Health Perspectives, 104*, 154–55.

Tague, N. (1995). *The Quality Toolbox*. Milwaukee, WI: ASQ Press.

Tannen, L. (1990). "Health planning as a regulatory strategy." In J. W. Salmon, ed., *The Corporate Transformation of Health Care: Issues and Directions* (New York: Baywood), 19–36.

Thomas, L. (1974). *The Lives of a Cell*. New York: Viking Press.

Thompson, A. (1998). "Competition and quality: Looking for evidence for health care reforms," *International Journal for Quality in Health Care, 10*, 371–73.

Thompson, J., Averill, R., and Fetter, R. (1979). "Planning, budgeting, and controlling—one look at the future: Case-mix cost accounting," *Health Services Research, 14*, 111–25.

Thompson, R. (1984). *Physicians and Hospitals: Easing Adversary Relationships*. Chicago: Pluribus Press.

"Traditional hospital medical staff structure may be doomed," *Hospital Peer Review*, 18 (1993), 185–89.

Traub, J. (1998). "Multiple intelligence disorder," *New Republic, 219*, 20–23.

Tucker, C. (1995). "The unprofitability of health care," *San Francisco Chronicle* (December 9), A20.

Turner, J., Ersek, M., Herron, L., Haselkorn, J., Kent, D., Ciol, M., and Deyo, R. (1992). "Patient outcomes after lumbar spinal fusions," *Journal of the American Medical Association, 268*, 907–11.

Turner, B., and Pidgeon, N. (1997). *Man-Made Disasters*. Second edition. Woburn: Butterworth-Heinemann.

Tye, L. (1999). "Review system for hospitals is ailing," *Boston Globe*, Online posting (March 16), 6.

United States Department of Health and Human Services, Agency for Health Care Planning and Research (1995). *Using Clinical Practice Guidelines to Evaluate Quality of Care* I, 35.

United States General Accounting Office (1998). "Not-for-profit hospitals: Conversion issues prompt increased state oversight," GAO/HEHS-98-24.

———. (1998). "Specialty care: Heart attack survivors treated by cardiologists more likely to take recommended drugs," (December). GAO-HEHS-99-6.

Vaughan, D. (1997). *The Challenger Launch Decision: Risky Technology, Culture and Deviance at NASA*. Chicago: University of Chicago Press.

Vayda, E. (1973). "A comparison of surgical rates in Canada and in England and Wales," *New England Journal of Medicine, 289,* 1224–29.

Vladeck, B. (1980). *Unloving Care: The Nursing Home Tragedy*. New York: Basic Books.

———. (1994). "From the Health Care Financing Administration," *Journal of the American Medical Association, 271,* 1896.

Vogel, D. (1993). "Patient-focused care," *American Journal of Hospital Pharmacology, 50,* 2321–29.

Vollmer, W., O'Hollaren, M., Ettinger, K., Stibolt, T., Wilkins, J., Buist, S., Linton, M., and Osborne, M. (1997). "Specialty differences in the management of asthma: A cross-sectional assessment of allergists' patients and generalists' patients in a large HMO," *Archives of Internal Medicine, 157,* 1201–8.

Wakefield, D., Hendrys, M., Uden-Holman, T., Couch, R., and Helms, C. (1994). "Comparing provider performance: Problems in making the 'report card' analogy fit" (abstract). *Association for Health Services Research and the Foundation for Health Services Research Annual Meeting Abstract Book,* 11:86 Joint meeting held June 27–29, 1993.

Wallace, C. (1983). "Managing along product lines is key to hospital profits under DRG system," *Modern Healthcare, 13,* 56.

Walston, S., and Kimberly, J. (1997). "Reengineering hospitals: Evidence from the field," *Hospital and Health Services Administration, 42,* 143–63.

Walton, M. (1990). *Deming Management at Work*. New York: Putnam Publishing Group.

———. (1986). *The Deming Management Method*. New York: Putnam Publishing Group.

"Wasted health care dollars," *Consumer Reports* (July 1992), 435–48.

Watson, J. (1980). *The Double Helix: A Personal Account of the Discovery of the Structure of DNA*. New York: Norton.

"Weekly Edition," National Public Radio, April 16, 1995.

Weinberg, N., and Stason, W. (1998). "Managing quality in hospital practice," *International Journal for Quality in Health Care, 10,* 295–302.

Weinstein, M. (1999). "Managed care's other problem: It's not what you think," *New York Times* (February 28), 1.

Weiser, J. (1996) "Denim downsize," *New Republic* (February 26), 10–11.

Weissman, C., Mossel, P., Haimet, S., and King, T. (1990). "Integration of quality assurance into a computerized patient data management system in an intensive care unit," *Quality Review Bulletin, 16,* 398–403.

Weitz, R. (1999). "Watching Brian die: The rhetoric and reality of informed consent," *Health, 3,* 209–27.

Wennberg, J. E. (1985). "On patient need, equity, supplier-induced demand, and the need to assess the outcome of common medical practices," *Medical Care, 23,* 512–20.

———. (1984). "Dealing with medical practice variations: A proposal for action," *Health Affairs, 3,* 6–32.

Wennberg, J. E., and Fowler, F. J. (1977). "A test of consumer contribution to small area variations in health care delivery," *Journal of the Maine Medical Association,* *68,* 275–79.

Wennberg, J. E., and Gittelsohn, A. M. (1982). "Variations in medical care among small areas," *Scientific American, 246,* 120–34.

———. (1973). "Small area variations in health care delivery," *Science, 182,* 1102–8.

White, J. (1995). "Commentary—The horses and jumps: Comments on the health care reform steeplechase." *Journal of Health Care Politics, Policy and Law, 20,* 373–83.

White, W. (1994). "The 'Corporatization' of U.S. Hospitals: What can we learn from the Nineteenth Century industrial experience?" In Salmon, J., ed., *The Corporate Transformation of Health Care: Perspectives and Implications* (New York: Baywood), I, 33–61.

Wiener, C. (1991). "Arenas and careers: The complex interweaving of personal and organizational destiny." In D. Maines, ed., *Social Organization and Social Process: Essays in Honor of Anselm Strauss* (Hawthorne, NY: Aldine de Gruyter), 175–88.

———. (1981). *The Politics of Alcoholism: Building an Arena Around a Social Problem.* New Brunswick, NJ: Transaction Books.

Wiener, C., and Kayser-Jones, J. (1989). "Defensive work in nursing homes: Accountability gone amok," *Social Science and Medicine, 28,* 37–44.

Wiener, C., Fagerhaugh, S., Strauss, A., and Suczek, B. (1982). "What price chronic illness?" *Society, 19,* 22–30.

Wiener, C., Strauss, A., Fagerhaugh, S., and Suczek, B. (1979). "Trajectories, biographies and the evolving medical technology scene: Labor and delivery and the intensive care nursery," *Sociology of Health and Illness, 1,* 261–82.

Wilde, G., Target Risk: *Dealing with the Danger of Death, Disease and Damage in Everyday Decisions.* Toronto: PDE Publications, 1994.

Will, G. (1997). "Capitalism may transform China," *San Francisco Chronicle* (July 3), A27.

Williamson, J. (1978). *Assessing and Improving Health Care Outcomes: The Health Accounting Approach to Quality Assurance.* Cambridge, MA: Ballinger.

Winslow, R. (1998). "Health-care inflation revives in Minnesota despite cost-cutting," *Wall Street Journal* (May 19), A1.

Winslow, R., and Paltrow, S. (1998). "Ill-managed care: At Oxford Health, financial 'controls' were out of control." *Wall Street Journal* (April 29), A1.

Wohl, S. (1984). *The Medical-Industrial Complex.* New York: Harmony.

Wolfe, S. (1996). "Merger mania: A second look," *Public Citizen Health Research Group, 12,* 1–3.

Yao, P., Wiggs, B., Gregor, C., Sigurnjzk, R., and Dodek, P. (1999). "Discordance between physicians and coders in assignment of diagnoses," *International Journal for Quality in Health Care, 11,* 147–53.

Ziegenfuss, J. (1991). "Organizational barriers to quality improvement in medical and health care organizations," *Quality Assurance and Utilization Review, 6,* 115–22.

Zussman, R. (1992). *Intensive Care: Medical Ethics and the Medical Profession.* Chicago, IL: University of Chicago Press.

Index